SHAKESPEARE'S MONEY TALKS

A Glossary of Coins and Economic Language in Renaissance Drama

Alexandra Mason

"*His purse is empty already, all's golden words are spent.*"

Revised and expanded second edition. Originally published as *Econolingua* (Newark: University of Delaware Press; London and Toronto: Associated University Presses, 1985) by Sandra K. Fischer. Coin photographs in the public domain. Coin illustrations not actual size.

Turnstone Books of Oregon, LLC
ISBN 978-1-7373958-0-5
Logo courtesy of Pepper Trail

Acknowledgments

I am grateful first of all to readers and scholars for their enthusiastic reception of the original volume. A career in academia has allowed me the stimulation, time, and resources to continue my research over the years; and I am perennially thankful for the opportunity to teach the works of Shakespeare and other dramatists and poets to an ever-replenished youthful appreciative audience. Second, I appreciate assistance from John Thomassen at the American Numismatic Society Museum in updating and refreshing coin illustrations for this study. All my teachers and colleagues may not realize their impact on my thinking, regardless of their areas of specialty. I have many role models, passionate thinkers, those who delve ever more deeply into the relation between language and meaning, language and form, language and culture. Without the inspiration of Lana Cable, Ellen M. Caldwell, Gretchen H. Gerzina, Warren Ginsberg, Richard M. Goldman, Thelma Greenfield, Gloria Johnson, Paul A. Jorgensen, Hugh Maclean, the dedicated readers at the Folger Shakespeare Library, and supportive friendships with Iliana Semmler, Diva Daims, and Ruth F. Harrison, I might have foundered. And this reissue would dwindle in personal significance without Donny King, who believes in the value of my scholarship and has been ever-eager to help me clarify concepts and historical circumstances as I apply the usage of econolingua to the plays.

Contents

Introduction

"La numismatique est une maitresse dangereuse pour l'amateur, et toujours adoree, bien que cruelle, pour ses fervents disciples."

Albert R. Frey, *Dictionary of Numismatic Names*[1]

Economics and Language

Two of the most illuminating glossaries for understanding language in Renaissance drama have been Eric Partridge's *Shakespeare's Bawdy* and Morris Palmer Tilley's *Dictionary of the Proverbs in England*. The aptness of these works seems clear to anyone studying the plays of Shakespeare and his contemporaries: sexual slang and truistic wisdom are indeed commonplace in the dialogue and rich in associative value. These glossaries, moreover, have helped critics to make thematic and linguistic connections. Not only have the dictionaries examined specific usages, but they have placed these discoveries in context, by juxtaposition and interrelation with similar occurrences of puns and proverbs.

A glossary of coin and economic terms may not seem as apparently helpful—that is, until one realizes that economic concerns permeate the drama of this period and indeed often define its characters, plots, and settings, as well as influence its language. Sex, love, and money share a nexus that appears even outside of its typical genre—comedy—and many proverbial expressions discuss wealth and its right use. Thus, economics may simply be the larger context of these other two glossaries; in many instances the insights offered by Partridge and Tilley gain extra significance when viewed with an economic eye.

The American scholar and the neophyte to Renaissance drama will readily understand the importance of the coin sections of the glossary. British coinage still stymies many today, especially when references are to the old pound rather than the metric new

[1] Albert R. Frey, *Dictionary of Numismatic Names,* glossary by Mark M. Salton (New York: Barnes and Noble, 1947), vi, quoting "a French author."

pound system. Slang words abound for seemingly esoteric amounts and coins, and the typical reader or playgoer has little inkling of the sums and puns involved in these catalogues of monetary exchange. Many Renaissance plays have foreign settings and attempt to employ the appropriate coinage of those settings—an additional bafflement even to the numismatist.

However, the serious scholar will find more here than simple identification of coins. The glossary attempts to illustrate the prominence of economic language and metaphor in Renaissance English drama and to demonstrate the extent to which economics began to define relationships, language, and individual motivation. Donald L. Mull, in describing the way in which money appears as a symbolic center in the fiction of Henry James, offers a valid beginning for the investigation of economic metaphor in Renaissance plays:

> One can say less that money symbolizes a given particular than that the emotive terms associated with money—ranging from highly favorable ("rich," "golden") to extremely pejorative ("sordid gain")—are brought into significant relation with a complex of varying attitudes (possibly, but not necessarily, attitudes toward the fact of money itself). The image becomes a nexus of meanings, significant in the totality of its relations, rather than a thing determinately meaningful in itself. . . . [M]oney is primarily an organic center rather than a thing of fixed aspects.[2]

In Renaissance drama money is anything but "fixed": its bywords are transition and confusion. A new emphasis on the power and possibilities of money—and its extended effect on language—stems primarily from historical reality.

To define economics in the Renaissance is difficult. As a science it was not yet born, operating almost exclusively in Aristotle's sense of household management.[3] The Church fathers and the Schoolmen had modified Aristotle's legacy only slightly, in turn bequeathing to the Renaissance a system of economic ethics

---

[2] *Henry James's "Sublime Economy": Money as Symbolic Center in the Fiction* (Middletown: Wesleyan Univ. Press, 1973), 5.

[3] *Politics,* bk. 1, 1256 b 27-1256 a 3, in *Politics and Economics,* translated by. Edward Walford, Bohn's Classical Library (London: Henry G. Bohn, 1853). See ***Appendix A*** for a brief discussion of the sources and concepts of usury in the Renaissance.

that worked handily under feudalism, when most economies were linked to the land, to subsistence production, and to personal and traditionally-sanctioned exchanges of goods. In fact, economy was a branch of religious morality, based on Biblical texts and classical teaching and indoctrinated into the public through standard sermons, morality plays, and econo-religious tracts warning of the spiritual consequences of the abuse and misuse of money.

However, personal microeconomics (as the theory of individual choices) began to change in the middle years of the sixteenth century. The old barriers started to fall with the demise of feudalism, as most economic exchanges became more impersonal, were transacted on a larger stage, and were done not for charity or commonweal, but for individual gain. This impersonality of economics was compounded by many unprecedented events beyond a layman's contemporary economic understanding: the great price rise, dearth, debasement of the currency, an influx of American precious metals, the development of negotiable instruments and representative currency, an evolving concept of human value, and, primarily, the daily necessity of violating basic medieval precepts against usury and for poor relief.[4]

Economic life was changing, but the causes and consequences of these changes were not understood. As the necessity of lending money at interest became clear, and as the "poor" were often impostors and rogues, not truly needy, government assumed the doctrinal role of the medieval church, prohibiting interest above a certain rate and enforcing the poor laws. This response was anachronistic and inadequate, and the populace and dramatists knew it. Elaborate methods for circumventing both civil and religious laws were devised, assisted by the rapidly-developing arena of new forms of wealth and a more fluid concept of money.

For instance, early banks were simply depositories, from which one could expect to withdraw on demand exactly the same coins left there for safekeeping. The idea of the transferability of value, even as embodied in different coins, was disallowed. In the

---

[4]See, *e.g.*, M. Beer, *Early British Economics from the XIIIth to the middle of the XVIIIth Century,* Reprints of Economic Classics (1938; reprint, New York: Augustus M. Kelley, 1967), 19-24; and Joyce Oldham Appleby, *Economic Thought and Ideology in Seventeenth-Century England* (Princeton: Princeton Univ. Press, 1978), 20-53.

Renaissance, in contrast, the need grew for widescale changing of coins of different denominations in foreign trade. To meet the demands of growing international trade, efficient ways of making payment were essential. Factors found it risky to carry large sums of money to market—in spite of the Truce of God, enacted in 1095, which forbade the use of violence toward merchants—and foreign trade involved divergent currencies that were difficult to reckon. Payment of large sums required endless counting and weighing out: in 1571, for example, it took two and a half hours to count and exchange £500, much of it in shillings, for a purchase made by Sir Nicholas Bacon.

Thus were instigated from necessity bills of exchange. These were a type of representative currency, allowing for large transfers of wealth without any coins actually changing hands, a radical transmutation of the concept of the intrinsic value and inviolable individual ownership of certain coins rather than the wealth that they would eventually simply represent. Moreover, bills of exchange and other negotiable instruments included an inscrutable system of commissions in which interest charges could be masked: dry exchange, absolute exchange, and real exchange; promissory or bailee notes, debentures, and Privy Seal demand notes; rent-charges, commenda, *damnus emergens,* and *lucrum cessans.*[5]

The preceding example follows a fundamental upheaval in the concept of the value of money, a change that, aided by other socio-scientific theories disrupting traditional hierarchy and social status, modified the appraisal of human value and the function of individual relation. [6] Perhaps the most important economic developments of the Renaissance, the concepts of exchange value, maximization of personal utility, and an extension of usury to the

---

[5] Described by Nissim da Pisa in *Banking and Finance among Jews in Renaissance Italy,* ed. Gilbert S. Rosenthal (1559; reprint, New York: Bloch, 1962), 117-28. See also Abbot Payson Usher, "The Origin of the Bill of Exchange," *Journal of Political Economy* 22 (1914): 567-76; Edward Jenks, "On the Early History of Negotiable Instruments," *Law Quarterly Review* 9 (1893): 70-83; R. D. Richards, *The Early History of Banking in England* (London: Frank Cass, 1958), 8-19; Dorothy Johnson Orchard and Geoffrey May, *Moneylending in Great Britain* (New York: Russell Sage, 1933), 29-44; and Lawrence Stone, *The Crisis of the Aristocracy 1558-1641* (Oxford: Clarendon, 1965), 511. See ***Appendix A*** for greater detail about devices used to circumvent usury.

[6] See Marian Bowley, *Studies in the History of Economic Theory before 1870* (London: Macmillan, 1973) for writers on value like Rice Vaughan and Nicholas Barbon.

"use" or exploitation of humans, were such fundamental and radical changes that they were of necessity explored in the drama. As dramatists acknowledged the inadequacy of the old economic theories, they also sought replacement values. Indeed, the drama for a time became a forum for the investigation of new economics, what Aristotle had termed "chrematistics" (pure acquisition for its own sake), as it conquered and usurped the old economy of household management and efficient allocation of resources.

Tragedy, chronicle, comedy, domestic drama—all to some extent draw from an economic understanding of society and become affected by this fundamental change in moral-economic values and behavior. Shakespeare perhaps best illustrates the conflict between Aristotle's two economies in what he portrays as "natural" and "unnatural" economy.[7] In Iago and Shylock, for instance, or even Edmund and Bolingbroke, he embodies the morality of chrematistics, characterized as violating nature's order of hierarchical relation and productivity.

Although not all of the plays examined here use the same distinction as Shakespeare and Aristotle to body forth the metamorphosed economy, they do share certain characteristics expressing their economic interests. Economy begins to penetrate all human relations: money becomes the only way of assessing value, profit the only impetus for human action. Comedy shows characters defined by economic status: usurers, misers, prodigals, younger brothers, heirs, merchants, shopkeepers, tradesmen, scriveners, new men, charitable gentlemen, impecunious rogues; widows, wives, virgins, marriageable daughters and sisters, prostitutes. Other genres, moreover, often rely on similar economic characterizations, like Timon, or the Lear family of Act I, or Charles of *A Woman Killed with Kindness.* Not always typical economic stereotypes, these characters are nonetheless economic creatures, as givers, takers, users, and used.[8]

Plots often treat the growing connection between money and love; courtship and marriage become economic games, legal contracts, exchange transactions. The transference of wealth begins

---

[7] This theory is clearly set out by Edward Hubler, in *The Sense of Shakespeare's Sonnets* (Princeton: Princeton Univ. Press, 1952).

[8] For elaboration of a genre of economic drama see Sandra K. Fischer, "Drama in a Mercantilist World," *Mid-Hudson Language Studies* (MLA) 6 (1983): 29-39.

to represent love, the possession of wealth to define social value and status, and human relations to offer themselves primarily as means to profit through exploitation of exchange value rather than appreciation of intrinsic worth. Sex and wooing become commercial transactions, often instigated in a market or shop setting. In some plays women are actually auctioned off to the highest bidder.[9] Invariably, amounts are minutely calculated and coins are catalogued, mentioned in almost any breath as the measure of human activity. For instance, in *The Blind Beggar of Alexandria* Leon tells Samathis how much he loves her: "I hold thee dearer than the pomegranate of my eye, and that's better by threepence than the apple of mine eye" (1.6.43-44).

In this context it is no surprise to see coins and economic terms insinuating their way into metaphor as well. Indeed, as economics defined behavior and value, it also fostered a new language, econolingua.[10] As characters test values, they also test words, finding in language as well an infinitely variable exchange medium with which they can reap profits (through wit and *bon mots)* and with which they can commit semantic usury (through puns). Dante foresaw the connection between economic and linguistic abuse, in Canto 30 of the *Inferno* tellingly juxtaposing Master Adam, counterfeiter *par excellence*, with Sinon, infamous counterfeiter of words. As they converse, we learn of the typical attitude toward alteration of value, as both have perverted the purpose of God. The first Adam's language truly revealed reality, as coins are to embody natural, intrinsic value: *'"S'io dissifalso, e tu falsasti il coinol / disse Sinon; 'e son qui per un fallo, I e tu per piu ch' alcun altro demonioT*" ("'If I spoke false, you falsified the coin,' / said Sinon; 'I am here for just one crime— / but you've committed more than any demon.'")[11] Roland Barthes pinpoints such a metaphorical event as a movement from index to sign that

---

[9]Most notably in *Women Beware Women, The City Madam,* and A *New Wonder, A Woman never Vext.* In the first, the suitor asks for a scrutinizing session during which he can evaluate the scent, eyes, nose, teeth, posture, feet, gait, and bodily charms of Isabella; in the last, one widow suggests that a market for wealthy widows be established at Smithfield, replacing the horse-market, in order to expedite economic matches with impecunious lords.

[10]For a suggestion of the language of merchandising, see Caroline Lockett Cherry, *The Most Unvaluedst Purchase: Women in the Plays of Thomas Middleton,* Salzburg Studies in English Literature, Jacobean Drama Studies, no. 34 (Salzburg: Universitat Salzburg, 1973), 48.

[11]Trans. Allen Mandelbaum (New York: Bantam, 1982), 11. 115-17.

epitomizes the fall of the medieval order:

> In the past . . . money "revealed". . .it was an index, it furnished a fact, a cause, it had a nature; today it "represents" everything: it is an equivalent, an exchange, a representation: a sign. . . .Shifting from a monarchy based on land to an industrial monarchy, society changed the Book, it passed from the Letter (of nobility) to the Figure (of fortune), from title deeds to ledgers. . . . The difference between feudal society and bourgeois society, index and sign, is this: the index has an origin, the sign does not: to shift from index to sign is to abolish . . . the origin, the basis, the prop, to enter into the limitless process of equivalences, representations that nothing will ever stop, orient, fix, sanction. [T]he two elements *interchange*, signified and signifier revolving in an endless process: what is bought can be sold. . . .[12]

Thus language succumbs to the power of exchange value: it is a measure of individual worth, a commodity, as Rossi-Landi suggests, economic by its nature as an exchange medium.[13]

Use of the new economic language and its application to all human interaction help to replace lost or transmuted values. Many economic figures of speech jokingly expand social understanding and awareness of economic motives. As such, they either juxtapose traditional and new economic values or draw the participants together in a novel economic pact, an acceptance or acknowledgment of their profit-motivated community of interest.[14] The first of these is illustrated in the following economic misunderstanding of "will" in *The Merry Wives of Windsor* (3.4.55-59), when Mistress Anne Page and Slender are considering

---

[12]Roland Barthes, *S/Z,* translated by Richard Miller (New York: Hill and Wang, 1974), 40.

[13] Ferruccio Rossi-Landi, *Linguistics and Economics* (The Hague: Mouton, 1975), 5-7, 134, 138-53.

[14]For this function of metaphor in a general context, see Ted Cohen, "Metaphor and the Cultivation of Intimacy," in *On Metaphor,* edited by Sheldon Sacks (Chicago: Univ. of Chicago Press, 1979), 6-8. Cf. Jacob Marschak, "Economics of Language," *Behavioral Science* 10 (1965): 139: "if greater complexity of language means its ability to express a greater variety of situations, and the environment tends to fluctuate strongly and frequently, a complex (or shall we say *flexible?)* language will have a higher chance of survival," and Malcolm Bradbury, *Rates of Exchange* (New York: Alfred A. Knopf, 1983): "What, after all, is our life but a great dance in which we are all trying to fix the best going rate of exchange . . . ?"

marriage:

> *Slen.* Now, good Mistress Anne—
> *Anne.* What is your will?
> *Slen.* My will? 'Od's heartlings, that's a pretty jest indeed! I ne'er made my will yet, I thank heaven. I am not such a sickly creature. . . .

She aims out of duty to please; he supposes that she is shrewdly calculating his marital value. After she learns of the jointure, he assumes it logical for her also to inquire about his will. The second type occurs typically in the bantering of those who understand the world of chrematistics, as in the following witty exchange between Hal and Falstaff in *1 Henry IV* (1.2.47-58):

> *Prince.* Why, what a pox have I to do with my hostess of the tavern?
> *Fal.* Well, thou hast call'd her to a reckoning many a time and oft.
> *Prince.* Did I ever call for thee to pay thy part?
> *Fal.* No, I'll give thee thy due, thou hast paid all there.
> *Prince.* Yea, and elsewhere, so far as my coin would stretch, and where it would not, I have us'd my credit.
> *Fal.* Yea, and so us'd it that, were it not here apparent that thou art heir apparent—

Clearly, the double meaning of the economic complex reckoning/pay/due/coin/stretch/credit and the wonderful paronomasia that ends this exchange bind the two in a pact of mutual understanding of the reciprocal exploitation of their relationship and their inverted values in society and in language. In the economic world, Falstaff, sans money, is richer, more valuable, than the Prince. His currency is words. The Prince, however, embodies value. As future king, he turns his countenance (which will later appear on coins) into money.[15]

With these examples in mind, one can further distinguish patterns of economic language in Renaissance drama in a system of recurring metaphor clusters that illuminate the transition from medieval economy to mercantilist ethics. The metaphors do not

---

[15]The idea that the king embodies value is evidenced in the concept of the ruler's *"character angelicus,"* a representation of "the Immutable within Time." This other body was often depicted emblematically on coins and medallions. See Ernst H. Kantorowicz, *The King's Two Bodies: A Study in Mediaeval Political Theology* (Princeton: Princeton Univ. Press, 1957), 3-23.

appear haphazardly; instead, they indicate first a resistance to the exchange ethic, then a grappling with its operation, and finally an acceptance of its metamorphosed system of economy as the dominant force in society. Terms in boldface type appear in the glossary proper, with detailed definitions and examples of their use in the drama.

1. Marriage as an Economic Contract

Love becomes less important than money in the metaphorical complex surrounding marriage. Although traditionally marriage was also an economic transaction in that it established the basic domestic unit for allocation of resources, in the new economics marriage operates as a means to financial profit or an opportunity for interpersonal exploitation. A **vendible** maid is marriageable; one may **purchase** and **possess** a love. To **contract** is to **seal** a sexual or nuptial agreement that becomes an enforceable **obligation** or **note,** complete with **specialties. Impost** and **custom** are metaphorical taxes paid for the **profit** of marriage or extra-marital sex, as commercial transactions. A **jointure** secures the bride's financial future; a **dowry** changes hands at the fulfillment of the marriage contract.

2. Women as Merchandise

This metaphor cluster indicates the transition from intrinsic to exchange value. Beauty becomes **booty;** a woman is **cattel** or **chattel,** a **commodity,** a **common-wealth,** a **creditress,** a **customer.** To seek her sexual or nuptial favor is to **broke,** to **cheapen,** to **cope,** to **rifle,** to **exchange,** to **use.** Her femininity is viewed as her **treasure,** her **business,** her **coffer.** Profit through sexual activities produces some scandalous puns: **comings-in, whole-sale;** to **employ,** to **work.**

3. The Economics of Sex

Similar to the metaphor of marriage as an economic contract, this cluster focuses on sexual contracts and sexual **usury,** as the **increase** or production of heirs. To **close,** to **compound,** to **put to** use, is to **buy** a sexual favor and enact the increase that it brings. **Assurance** is promise of such a sexual bond; to **cancel** the **bond** is to perform the promise, to **discharge** the payment (sexually). What ensues is, as in an economic transaction, **advantage** (the **interest** of sex), **increase, profit, golden fruit** (as heirs). **Custom** is the habit of such a transaction as well as the tax (payment) imposed on it.

4. Life as the (Representative) Currency (of God or Nature) Lent in a Bond

The following speeches can best introduce the logic and pervasiveness of this metaphor cluster:

> [T]his world is like a **Mynt,** we are no sooner cast into the fire, taken out agen, hamerd, **stampt,** and made **Currant,** but presently we are **changde. . ..**
>
> (*Westward Ho,* 2.1.174-77)

> **Siluer** is the Kings stampe, man Gods stampe, and a woman is mans stampe, wee are not currant till wee passe from one man to another.
>
> (*Northward Ho,* 1.2.81-83)

> Come, sir, are you ready for death? ... A heavy **reckoning** for you, sir. But the comfort is, you shall be call'd to no more payments, fear no more tavern-bills. . . . sorry that you have **paid** too much, and sorry that you are paid too much; **purse** and brain both empty; the brain the heavier for being too **light,** the purse too light, being drawn of heaviness. O, of this contradiction you shall now be **quit.** O, the charity of a **penny** cord! it **sums** up thousands in a trice. You have no true **debitor and creditor** but it: of what's past, is, and to come, the **discharge.** Your neck, sir, is pen, book, and **counters;** so the **acquittance** follows.
>
> (*Cymbeline,* 5.5.151, 157-71)

God (or Nature) is the **coiner** who **presses** or **stamps** the **figure** of value onto mankind. He is also the **bondman** who **seals** the contract of life. This metaphor is well-illustrated in the works of John Donne, who was fascinated by the relationship between metal and imprint and its implications for the bond between man and his maker: "The bullion represents the body; the stamp, the soul." Carrying the analogy a step further, Donne solidified the economy of Christianity in the currency of Christ: "To redeem man . . . God had to make Christ able to pay man's debt."[16] Life is

---

[16] John Carey, "Donne and Coins," in *English Renaissance Studies* (Oxford: Clarendon, 1980), 154-63.

current and interaction (including sex) the **changing** of value. Life lasts for the duration of the **bill** or **bond (band);** the Last Judgment is the final **audit, compt,** or **reckoning** that **cancels** the bond and discovers whether one has quitted the debt or been a **bankrout.** The equation of people to coins allows sexual intercourse to be expressed as a natural exchange transaction: money *will* change hands.

5. Human Worth: Intrinsic and Exchange Value

In men and women, value is expressed typically in terms of exchange or coinage. Individual worth is an **estimate,** a **jewel;** value becomes **price.** Men are **royal** or **noble** according to their possession of the coin of the same name. A true friend, like **true gold,** has been **tested, tried.** All people are **current** and can be **coined** into profit; a **cracked** maid has lost her virginity and, like a cracked coin, is worthless. However, her **chinks** remain valuable to the man who can obtain them.

6. Medieval Ethics and Proverbial Expressions

Proverbial expressions and truisms often derived from medieval religious economic ethics appear in the drama in three ways. First, standard sayings like "Endlesse follies follow endlesse wealth" *(Old Fortunatus,* 2.2.239) may be used as *ex post* instruction to someone who has "abused" wealth, that is, who has treated it as the measure of all value and the only means to human happiness. Second, they may be slightly transformed into sayings that support new economic ethics: "A heavy purse makes a light heart." Third, old truisms may be used in an entirely wrong-headed way to justify new economic ethics, as in the following exchange between Thomas Gresham and his roguish nephew John:

Gresh. Antonio reports you loue his wife.

John. Loue? why, alas, vncle, I hold it parcell of my duty to loue my neighbors. . . .

Gresh. He told me you bestow'd a gowne of a strumpet.

John. Why alas Vncle, the poore whore went naked, and you know the text commands vs to cloath the naked. . . .

Gresh. Well, if your prodigall expences be aim'd
At any virtuous and religious end
Tis the more tolerable, and I am proud
You can so probably excuse yourself.
Well, cousin, hoping you'll proue a new man.

John. A new man, what else Vncle? Ile be a new man from the top to the toe, or Ile want of my will.

(*2 If you know not me,* I, 255)

Proverbs about money and its use are pervasive and share a strong dramatic link with theme and metaphor.

7. Rogues' Cant

In addition to a new emphasis upon written economic contracts to define social relationships—complete with **scriveners** to write them up and sergeants to enforce them—the plays adapt the language of coins and commerce to other illuminating purposes. Many terms that describe the corruption or devaluing of coins, such as **clip, blanch, cut, pinch,** and **trim,** are also metaphorically extended to indicate roguish cheating for profit and specifically, when applied to women, tricking them out of sexual favors. A subset of this metaphor cluster includes to **finger,** to **firk,** and to **geld,** all of which are applied to stealing money but also carry specific sexual applications.

8. Coins as Animate Objects; Personification of Money

To justify usury in the context of Aristotle's argument that barren metal cannot breed, *dramatis personae* often refer to the **lechery** of coins if left together and to their ability to **engender** and **increase.** This metaphor further cements the link between sex and money. Coins sometimes metaphorically assume a religious significance, as representatives of God, especially **angels.** This God, in consequence, seems to resemble **Pluto** or **Plutus** more than a heavenly father. One's **purse** becomes a **temple.**

Seemingly neutral words referring to health or to moral qualities also become adapted to economic metaphor. One's fortunes may suffer from **pursiness,** an illness, and thus need to be **restored, mended, healed.** One's purse may be **hot** or cold, depending upon its contents and the tendency of its owner to spend. Ill fortunes beyond repair are said to **perish,** to **bate,** to be **disabled, defeated,** and **sunk.** A benefactor who grants wealth is said to **create** a new man.

9. The Value of Wit; Coins as Words

In "White Mythology" Jacques Derrida establishes an intricate connection between coins and metaphor. Whereas the inscription and exergue do not figure prominently in Renaissance drama, Derrida in another context pinpoints the function of coin metaphors in these plays, as "a theory of *value,* and not merely ... a theory of *meaning."*[17] The equation between words and coins not only rests on their similar function in the act of exchange—words as the tokens of intellectual exchange—but also encapsulates the transition from intrinsic to exchange value. Words, like individual worth, begin to be valuable not so much for what they represent (intrinsic worth), but for what profit or esteem their utterance can engender (exchange value). [18] As *dramatis personae* seek replacement values for the old economic hierarchy, they discover the status and profitability of wit, with words as their currency. The dramatic demonstration of wit functions similarly to the tacit bonds formed by economic pun and metaphor. Witty words or *bon mots* are **coined** in the **mint** of the brain and stored in the **budget** or **exchequer;** they are **sterling, golden,** and bring profit when used, exchanged. One without the currency of wit is **bankrout,** having spent his words prodigally.

10. Numismatic Slang

Coin names abound in Renaissance drama. Standard and well-known coins such as **royal, noble,** and **angel** assume logical metaphorical significance as indicators of value and the worship of money. However, many foreign coins and slang terms for standard coins confuse the reader, who may also overlook puns or metaphorical extensions because of this numismatic ignorance. Coin words that editors have commonly overlooked include **bit, black dog, bonnet, bullet, chink (chunk), circle, copper nose, cue, drop, gridiron, monkey, moy, offering, pax, picture, piece, pig, plow, portcullis, rag, ruddock, salute, shell, spangle, silverling, spur, stamp,** and **swine.**[19] Many of these slang terms

---

[17]Jacques Derrida, "White Mythology: Metaphor in the Text of Philosophy," *New Literary History* 6 (1974): 5-21.

[18]For a similar suggestion in a different context, see Fredric Jameson, *The Prison-House of Language* (Princeton: Princeton Univ. Press, 1972), 15. See also Marc Shell, *The Economy of Literature* (Baltimore: Johns Hopkins Univ. Press, 1978), 3-8; and Joseph Hall's sermon "Righteous Mammon" in *In God's Name,* edited by John Chandos (Indianapolis: Bobbs-Merrill, 1971), 218: "Wealth is like vnto words. . . .."

[19]From, *passim,* Frey; *Dictionary of Political Economy,* edited by Sir Robert Harry Inglis Palgrave, 3 vols. (1910; rpt. Detroit: Gale Research Co., 1976); J. Eric Engstrom, *Coins in Shakespeare: A Numismatic Guide* (Hanover: Dartmouth College, 1964); *Oxford English Dictionary,* 2 vols. (Oxford: Oxford Univ. Press, 1971); John Porteous, *Coins in History* (New York: G. P. Putnam's Sons, 1969); C.

for money appear in puns, that is, a speech with a tenable surface meaning and an extra significance submerged in its application to economics.

Two examples from Shakespeare illustrate the extra richness of these passages when one is aware of the underlying coin meaning. A **salute** was a coin issued for France, current in England in the sixteenth century, according to Stowe, for 22s. 8d. In *The Comedy of Errors* Antipholus of Syracuse reveals his economic confusion as he is mistaken for his twin, further revealing in his use of a coin word the link between money and kinship or community that is central to the action and denouement of this play: "There's not a man I meet but doth **salute** me / . . . Some **tender money** to me" (4.3.1, 4). Similarly, Philip the Bastard in *King John* rails against and then accepts a commercial mentality in his **"commodity"** speech, noting that "his fair **angels** would **salute** my palm" (2.1.590). The coin puns in each of these instances simply bolster the economic tone and import of the play.

A **bonnet** was also a coin familiar in the Renaissance, issued in Scotland. Shakespeare puns on this extended meaning in several places, illuminating the economic condition or intent of his characters in a subtle and humorous, even ironic, way. Othello boasts, "my demerits / May speak, unbonneted" (1.2.22-23), meaning, perhaps, that even if his value is unrewarded, it is apparent in the commercial world of Venice. This coin pun underscores the motivation of profit-seeking Iago and emphasizes Othello as an economic outsider, one who believes in intrinsic worth rather than exchange value. Lear, after giving all money, land, and power to his daughters, is forced impecunious into the storm: "unbonneted he runs, / And bids what will take all" (3.1.14-15). The double stripping of the king implied in this coin pun—bareheaded and penniless—illuminates the economic foundation of Lear's initial decision and his fundamental misunderstanding of natural and chrematistic economies. Finally, in *Coriolanus,* Volumnia instructs her son in how to seek and obtain favor. One must use both grace and money to the utmost: "Go to them, with this bonnet in thy hand, / And thus far having stretch'd it . . ." (3.2.73-74).

T. Onions, A *Shakespeare Glossary,* 2d ed. (Oxford: Clarendon, 1919); Alexander Schmidt, *Shakespeare-Lexicon,* 4th ed., 2 vols. (New York: G. E. Stechert, 1902); and Richard John Cunliffe, A *New Shakespearean Dictionary* (London: Blackie and Son, 1910); and notes to lines in the editions used and information gleaned from general historical reading.

Shakespeare is not meticulous in ascribing these coins to appropriate times and places. Indeed, in Renaissance England, a motley array of coins from many countries and ages were current (*e.g.*, King Harry **groats,** Edward **shovel-boards, galley halfpence, pistoles, doits, stivers,** French **crowns,** *etc.*). He is, however, like his colleagues, familiar with money and its terminology and uses this economic knowledge in a winking pact with his audience, purposely to hint at mercenary motives and undercurrents.

Numismatic History

The great price rise in England and its associated dearth can be traced to a myriad of interrelated causes, including population growth, imports of American metals, and governmental debasements of the currency in 1465, 1526, and 1542-1551. Attitudes toward the inviolable intrinsic value of money were shattered as any coin became only as good as the king's changeable word, an exchange value rather than a **store** of wealth. In the English monetary system alone, a general confusion that developed early in the sixteenth century contributed to a fluctuating economy and uncertainty in accepted standards of value. Besides the well-known English coins of **nobles, groats, farthings,** and so forth, also circulating during the Renaissance were numerous foreign coins brought back by traders and coins educed from ancient hoards or left by the Romans, in addition to **counterfeits.** Even though many of these coins eventually, for convenience, were proclaimed legal tender and assigned specific values, such a large number of discontinued English coins also circulated that some of the coins handled daily were entirely unfamiliar to the representative citizen.[20]

Despite such abundance in the circulating medium, merchants and tradesmen felt a dearth of coins small enough for daily transactions. Christopher Bumstead, a Renaissance London

---

[20] George Unwin, "Commerce and Coinage," in *Shakespeare's England* (1916; reprint, Oxford: Clarendon, 1970), 1:340. See also C. E. Challis, *The Tudor Coinage* (New York: Barnes and Noble, 1978), 214-17; Sir Albert Feavearyear, *The Pound Sterling: A History of English Money,* 2d ed. revised. by E. Victor Morgan (Oxford: Clarendon, 1963), 48; and *Tudor Royal Proclamations (TRP),* edited by Paul L. Hughes and James F. Larkin (New Haven: Yale Univ. Press, 1969), 2: nos. 406, 408, 412, 427, 473, 487, 533, and 538, especially, for royal concern about the coin problem.

mercer, argued that small money was as vital to the economy as "water is for the Thames" but conceded that if trifling coins were made of **silver**, they would be too small to handle. Moreover, confusion already was rife concerning silver coins of small value: their similarity provided cozeners and unscrupulous shopkeepers ample opportunity for short-changing or other fraud. For example, Beaumont and Fletcher allude in *The Scornful Lady* to the resemblance between the **penny** and **three-farthing** piece. By *"***washing***"* out the **rose** shown on the latter, one could easily pass it for the larger value. Two remedies for the shortage of small coins offered themselves. Out of necessity people broke pennies in halves and quarters, not a new practice, since the **shilling** had received its name from the Anglo-Saxon "scilling," a piece cut off. Before 1280, when the penny was the only coin in circulation, people regularly cut it into small fragments for petty transactions. The second remedy was for shopkeepers to issue **tokens** made of **brass,** tin, lead, and even leather for small *change,* their value stooping to the one-twelfth pence or one-sixth halfpenny witnessed by Thomas Platter in 1599. Eventually the city of Bristol was granted crown sanction to stamp tokens, but because these and the less formal tokens were easy to counterfeit, the very merchants who issued them became wary of receiving them back.[21]

The stalwart concept of the inviolable **pound sterling** certainly suffered under this confused currency system, some of it with only token worth, insinuating questions of enduring intrinsic value into the smallest daily transactions. Between 1556 and 1562, four proclamations appeared either "Prohibiting" or "Suppressing" rumors on currency devaluation: the populace feared that their money would lose value or instantly be proclaimed no longer current (*Tudor Royal Proclamations [TRP],* 2: nos. 431, 475, 488, and 492). Even though the pound was an intangible money of account, its reliability had been unquestioned. In 1819 a Mr. Smith was able to remark before the House of Commons, referring to the pound, "I find it difficult to explain it, but every gentleman in England knows it" (Feavearyear, 1). During the Renaissance this knowledge was not certain. Further chaos was wreaked by currency opportunists, those who deliberately violated coins in a number of ways in order to profit. Several Tudor proclamations

---

[21]C. R. Josset, *Money in Britain: A History of the Currencies of the British Isles* (London: Frederick Warne, 1962), 58; Unwin, 1:342-43; Challis, 200-209; Feavearyear, 9.

condemned counterfeiters, those "divers naughty and evil-disposed persons," and offered instruction on how to distinguish good coin from bad (*TRP*, 2: nos. 420, 427, 428, 472, 473, and 538).

Feavearyear comments on the extent and variety of counterfeiting practices: "The efforts of the official debasers and falsifiers, however, were far outshone by those of the unofficial practitioners of all classes, who clipped, filed, washed, and sweated the good money, and filled up every gap made by the exporters of coin with newly manufactured and imported base money of every conceivable sort. Their activities were continuous from Norman times until the eighteenth century" (5).

Clipping, that is, filing or **shaving** off the edges of coins, seems to have been the prominent fraudulent numismatic activity, for at times every coin in circulation had only slightly over half of its proper weight. Many private debasing activities were almost invited, however, by English coining methods. Until the seventeenth century coins were produced by hand, made "approximately circular with a hammer upon an anvil." Workmanship in coins was not something money-makers took pride in: the **stamp** itself was often not centered or even partially off the coin, leaving some of it blank. These carelessnesses in coin production resulted in inevitable divergences in size, shape, and weight of ostensibly equal coins, and until 1603 no standard was fixed for each coin as long as a certain number was forged from a pound of raw silver or gold.

Between 1108 and 1299 a pattern of "solving" the devalued coinage problem evolved: when fraud deprived enough coins of their full intrinsic value to the extent that they were no longer current for exchange at their intended rate, the ruler would order a recoinage. All bad coins would then be declared worthless and called in to the mint, where they would be reminted into brand new coins of correct weight, albeit a smaller number of them. Slowly, through this repeated process, the quantity of English money was continually reduced. Eventually the influx of foreign coins and American metals helped at least partially to restore the diminishing English currency. In 1553, for example, £17,592 of silver coins were produced from Spanish *reals* called in, melted down, and reminted.[22]

Official debasement of the coinage in Renaissance England began in the 1540s, when it became clear to what extent the realm was losing its wealth. To maintain an equilibrium in total currency value despite methods proliferating to eat away its substance, three measures were possible: *la mutation du poids,* in which the weight of a coin is reduced while it still nominally retains the same value as before; *la mutation de l'appellation,* sometimes called enhancement, in which the same coin is simply assigned a higher value; and *la mutation de la matière*, in which more base metal is included in a coin of the same valuation. Tudor rulers employed all three of these measures in their attempts to maintain a modicum of currency equilibrium (see **Appendix E**).

The government, too, however, manipulated the currency to its own best advantage, in ways which at times bordered on fraud, or at least trickery. For example, some of the first debased coins issued were used to pay the troops in Scotland. The total effect of mint policies from 1542 to 1547 was to substitute £526,000 of bad coin for £400,000 of good. The mint eventually became so blatant in its debasing activities that coins were merely **blanched** before issuance. This meant that **copper** coins were lightly covered with silver in order to make their appearance deceptively richer; however, with very little wear the base metal showed through and created an appropriate image for the basically fraudulent governmental antics with accepted and long-standing canons of value. Blanching was the common practice with silver **testoons** or testers of Henry VIII, for example, which quickly came to be called "**copper noses.**" With only a small amount of handling, the prominent nose on the portrait of these coins wore away, showing the base metals lying beneath the silver veneer.[23] Logically, people began to question intrinsic values in all areas of exchange; they had learned how easy it was to deceive with a simple appearance of richness.

Confronted with the growth of credit instruments and representative currency, a changing social hierarchy in which the

---

[22]J. D. Gould, *The Great Debasement: Currency and the Economy in Mid-Tudor England* (Oxford: Clarendon, 1970), 54.

[23]Gould, 9; Feavearyear, 61; Josset, 47; and Elgin Groseclose, *Money and Man: A Survey of Monetary Experience,* 2d ed. (New York: Ungar, 1967), 67.

rich did not always have liquid assets and the adventurous could make instant fortunes, and a market that continually charged more than before for the same foodstuffs while the government deigned not to mint coins small enough for change from these ever-more-expensive purchases, people of all classes were forced to countenance even more basic and confusing changes in their inherited system of values when the currency was tampered with. This upheaval cannot be overestimated; although no single cause for it exists, each is ample for creating social confusion. Macaulay's comment on the currency situation certainly is valid—"It may well be doubted whether all the misery which had been inflicted on the English nation in a quarter century by bad kings, bad ministers, bad Parliaments, and bad judges was equal to the misery caused by bad crowns and bad shillings" (Groseclose, 5)—but augmented as it was by other factors, this economic misery was to create a substantial rift between the individual and society.

Such governmental tampering with what appeared to be inviolable stores of value served only to offer sanction to the private tradesman for cheating at every opportunity. Proclamations promising no devaluation were often shortly followed by proclamations of devaluation (*TRP,* 2: no.475, 12/23/60 and no.478, 2/19/61; no.488, 1/30/62 and no. 491, 3/13/62). If the true value of coinage no longer held, neither, one supposed, did just price or commutative justice, or, by extension, temperance and alms-obligations. By 1612 mercantile violations of expected rules of operation were so blatant and widespread that William Perkins felt moved to summarize and condemn them in his *Treatise of Vocations:*

> In the calling of the Merchant and trades-man, there is false weights, and false measures, divers weights and divers measures, **engrossing,** mingling, **changing,** setting a glosse on wares by powdering, startching, blowing, darke shops, glozing, smoothing, lying, swearing, and all manner of bad dealing. In the patrone, there is presentation given, but with secret condition of having his owne tythes, or some other fleece out of the **living.** In the landlord, there is racking of rents, taking immoderate fines, **inclosing** of grounds that have laien common time out of mind: and the cause is, want of sobriety and temperance in diet and apparel. In the husbandman and cornemonger, there is exceeding injustice, in hording up graine till the time of further **advantage:** and

> in taking whatsoever they can get for their own, though it be to the shedding of the blood of the poore.[24]

Obviously the inherited medieval standards of behavior had already been replaced by out-and-out profit-seeking without regard for neighborly obligation. By 1632, when the unscrupulous practices were sophisticated and commonplace, D. Lupton in *London and the Countrey carbonadoed* had developed enough perspective to relegate the old precepts to their true position: "The merchants are men generally of good habit," he begins, but "their words are usually better than their consciences; their discourse ordinarily begins in water, but ends in wine. . . . Conscience is sold here for nought, because it is as old sermons, a dead **commodity.**"[25]

The transmutation of value witnessed in numismatic tampering combined with several parallel social changes to alter irrevocably the role and operation of microeconomics. The Renaissance witnessed the advent of Protestant economic individualism and the work ethic; the growth of cities and an accompanying impersonality of daily economics; the displacement of agricultural workers to service vocations or idle roguery; exploration and discovery of metals and lucrative trade routes, with an opportunity for unconscionable profits on joint-stock investments; increased social mobility and a status determined by wealth in possession rather than by tradition, land, nobility, or spiritual value; and the replacement of hierarchy and traditional social obligation with empiricism and the scientific method as determinants of behavior. In tandem with these changes, coins and their pervasiveness in the drama are indicative of a new focus on the tangibility of wealth: its power, its animate nature, and its metaphorical appropriateness to all social interaction.

Value and Metaphor

The two most important phenomena working in concord to define economic metaphor in Renaissance drama are the application of economic value to the appraisal of individual human worth and the

---

[24]In Helen C. White, *Social Criticism in Popular Religious Literature of the Sixteenth Century* (1944; rpt. New York: Octagon, 1965), 192.

[25]*The Harleian Miscellany,* edited by Thomas Park (London: White and Cochrane, 1812), 9:315.

equation of words to coins. The former initially takes a harmless and lighthearted form: Prince Hal, when pestered by the arrival of a **noble-man** with a message from his father, says, "Give him as much as will make him a **royal** man, and send him back again" *(1 Henry IV,* 2.4.290-91). However, soon dramatists begin to test the font of value, pitting intrinsic worth against exchange to see which is most profitable and best defines contemporary economic practice. Iago, for instance, can facilely argue for both systems, focusing on the intangible quality of "reputation." He teaches Cassio its artificiality (*Othello,* 2.3.262- 76) and conversely appeals to Roderigo to obtain the **jewel** of Desdemona by asserting new value: his "put **money** in thy **purse"** speech is nothing less than a paean to commercialism and materialism, to the ease of obtaining wealth and the value or power of **purchase** that it lends the possessor (1.3.319-72). Later, however, he convinces Othello that reputation is true intrinsic value and that material wealth is incidental to one's worth:

> **Good** name in man and woman, dear my lord,
> Is the immediate **jewel** of their souls.
> Who steals my **purse** steals **trash;** 'tis something, nothing;
> 'Twas mine, 'tis his, and has been slave to thousands;
> But he that filches from me my good name Robs
> me of that which not **enriches** him,
> And makes me poor indeed.

(3.3.155-61)

Lear, similarly, tests human bonds against economic bonds and finds the former more valuable but the latter more prominent. Eventually the language of coins, commerce, and economics attaches itself to the system of human appraisal. In *A Chaste Maid in Cheapside,* for instance, Sir Walter Whorehound contemplates his marriage with Moll as if looking at a price tag:

> ere to morrow noone,
> I shall receive two thousand **pound** in **Gold,**
> And a sweet Mayden-head
> Worth fourtie.

(4.4.60-63)

Brewen and Foster, two merchants in *A New Wonder, A Woman never Vext,* connect the exchange of commodities and emotions, finding the same language expressive of both:

> *O.Fos.* As evenly we will **lay** our bosoms
> As our **bottoms,** with love as merchandise,

And may they both **increase** t' infinities.
Brew. Especially at home; that **golden**
traffic, love,
Is scantier far than **gold;** and one **mine** of
that
More worth than twenty **argosies**
Of the world's richest **treasure.** (p. 100)

Here all social activity falls under the aegis of economic exchange. Appraising the uncertain value of coins as exchange media is similar to calculating the profitability of human relation: indeed, the understanding, appraisal, and use of human value are at the core of much Renaissance drama and logically assume an economic context—as well as adopting economic language. Coins and commercial expressions as the vehicle of metaphor indicate a tenor of pervasive economics. Love, courtship, friendship, marriage, sex, propagation, child-rearing, inheritance, celebration, and stewardship all become economic relationships expressed in the vocabulary of econolingua.

Words themselves as the coining of wit into profit extend the coin/value trope. In a certain sense coins become the metaphor for human value as well as a self-conscious commentary on the metaphor. Conversations that rely on economic wit tacitly acknowledge acceptance of a new mode of value. Stretching the value of coins/words becomes an economic game that asserts the value of the participants and cements a new form of linguistic community. Shylock's economic puns are misunderstood by the Christian community **(assurance, good, sufficient);** Pandarus instructs Troilus and Cressida in the crass economics of the exchange of love **(fee-farm, deed);** and Falstaff wins the admiration of all for his value as economic raconteur and thus is bound in a pact of exchange roguery with Pistol:

Fal. I **charge** you with a cup of sack, do you **discharge** upon my hostess.
Pist. I will discharge upon her, Sir John, with two **bullets.**
Fal. She is pistol-proof, sir; you shall not hardly offend her.
(*2 Henry IV*, 2.4.111-17)

Falstaff's economic-linguistic manipulation here is masterly, effectively **retorted** by soldier Pistol: a **charge** is a cost and a responsibility; to **discharge** is to shoot, to pay, and to ejaculate; **bullets** are **shot, coins,** semen, and, in paronomasia, billets, or IOUs; Pistol not only metaphorically shoots and sexually assails the Hostess, but he is to **pay** the **bill** perhaps with **pistoles** (coins), an embodiment of his name.

Four-level economic puns are not common in Renaissance drama, but this exchange perhaps best demonstrates the complexity of econolingua and its larger thematic implications. Other common rhetorical figures typical to economic metaphor are the following:

paronomasia or "punning, . . . playing on the sounds and meanings of words":[26]
booty/beauty; bullet/billet; expense/expanse; guilt/gild; indite/indict/invite; pistol/pistole; purse/person; purse/ purchase
aphaeresis or "omitting a syllable from the beginning of a word":
(a)bate; (ab)use; (ac)count; (ac)quit; (ar)rear; (be)get; (be)rate; (de)base; (dis)charge; (di)scourse; (e)state; (en)gage; (ex)change; (im)press; (re)count
adnominatio or "two words of different meaning but similar sound brought together":
brass/bras; dear/deer; guilt/gilt; peace/piece; ware/where; waste/waist
aphaeretic adnominatio or omitting an initial syllable and bringing the remaining two similar-sounding words together:
(de)mesnes/means; (de)features/features

Other common economic figures are adianoeta or a word or expression with an obvious meaning but a secret embedded one as well (**audit, bit, commodity, figure, score**), cacemphaton or a harsh-sounding or lewd allusion (**carract, chink, common-wealth, farthing, tally, trim**), and synecdoche or a part representing the whole (**bag, bottom, figure, golden waves, jewel, nose, parchment**) as well as simple pun and equivocation. An examination of these rhetorical figures further underscores the complex linguistic nexus between speech act/coin/value and the ethical transition to mercantilist morality.

---

[26]For this and the subsequent term definitions I rely on Richard A. Lanham, *A Handlist of Rhetorical Terms* (Berkeley: Univ. of California Press, 1968.

Shakespeare et al.

The tendency of Renaissance dramatic criticism is to treat Shakespeare separately, out of the context of lesser known or anonymous plays, and with only passing comparison to his more famous contemporaries. This method is tempting here as well, for Shakespeare's use of econolingua differs in both kind and degree from other playwrights'. However, it seems of greater value initially to show the scope and variety of economic metaphor in a large and diverse set of plays, using this grand set to establish ethical and linguistic patterns. Shakespeare easily fits into the pattern, but his use of economic foundations differs slightly.

Seldom in Shakespeare is an economic plot the sole or major focus, as it is in *Wily Beguiled, The Staple of News*, and *A New Way to Pay Old Debts*, for example. His most "economic" plays are *The Comedy of Errors, The Merchant of Venice*, and *Timon of Athens*, with *Othello, King Lear*, and *Troilus and Cressida* using economics as a secondary or supporting matrix addressing the role of money in society and the proper "valuing" of human relations. However, most of his plays as well as the sonnets use the language of economics in a manner that constitutes a subtext of meaning. His use of economic metaphor illuminates the fluctuating system of appraisal of human value and the determinants of individual action, crucial elements for all of Shakespearean drama. Bolingbroke's steely opportunism, for instance, usurps Richard's reliance upon medieval ethics, whose economic foundations he has blithely violated by bad management of the resources of the kingdom. Prince Hal, similarly, includes commercial economics as part of his education and justifies his deceptive behavior in econolingua (*1 Henry IV*, 1.2.195-217). Lear expects a "usury" of affection and nurturance for having raised and rewarded his daughters; Timon erroneously believes that materialism represents community; Cressida and Helen discover that they are appraised as valuable exchange objects.

While Shakespeare depicts a dramatic world in which values are changing from medieval to mercantilist economic ethics, his sympathetic characters do not find the new system satisfying. His plays reaffirm the operation of "natural" economics established in the sonnets: bounty, reciprocal obligations defined by service and tradition, and benevolent social use of material increase. While a character like Timon finds the old system in which he believes anachronistic, his servant and steward Flavius stands in example as a representative of the type of bond that Shakespeare values.

Other playwrights, in contrast, tend to exult in the new ethic, valuing characters like witty prodigals or tricksters who can coin profit from non-monetary sources, or prostitutes who by trickery can become "honest" and affluent wives. The commodity nature of human relations is affirmed over the intrinsic values—goodness, loyalty, honesty, nobility—that Shakespeare esteems. Valentine in *Wit Without Money* literally survives by the value of his witty companionship: others pay to be with him. Similarly, Wellborn in *A New Way to Pay Old Debts* depends confidently and successfully upon his wit to mend his fortunes and regain his estate. Activities that previously would have seemed economically immoral are exuberantly pursued by these characters, with impunity and a clear conscience.

Even though all of these plays employ the metaphorical potential of econolingua, Shakespeare uses the most complex and thematically telling figures. His are the only metaphors and puns with multiple levels beyond two, as in the discharge/bullet/pistol complex noted above. While all these playwrights pun on coin and economic terms at nearly every opportunity, the others are content with simple, entertaining word play. Jonson, for instance, enjoys allegorical correspondences and the easy lessons that they teach: in *The Staple of News*, for example, all sue for the sexual and financial favors of Lady Pecunia, her full name meaning "Golden Bright Money."

Slang or esoteric coin names appear more often in non-Shakespearean plays, Shakespeare focusing usually but not exclusively on the English coinage. Working or middle-class characters mention specific coins and sums of money more often than noble characters, perhaps as a function of their handling money daily, and the coins they exchange are of lower nominal value, sometimes even minuscule worth. Jonson, Marlowe, Dekker, and Beaumont and Fletcher seem to know more about foreign coinages than Shakespeare, including in their plays such terms as **bagatine, cecchine, gazet, kentall, livre, moccinigo, pistole, pistolet, plate, portague, silverling, sol,** and **stiver**. Shakespeare mentions **crusado, doit, dollar, drachma, ducat, ecu, guilder, obulus, shekel,** and **talent,** but these are larger and more international or well-known coins, and some have speculated that in *Timon of Athens* Shakespeare actually had no idea how much a talent was worth.[27] Theme rather than numismatic accuracy is Shakespeare's economic intent.

---

[27]Prominently Terence Spencer, "Shakespeare Learns the Value of Money: The Dramatist at Work on *Timon of Athens*." *Shakespeare Survey* 6 (1953): 75-78.

Methodology and Justification

Such a glossary at first seemed important merely because of the myriad coin names mentioned in the plays, which might prove confusing even to one familiar with English coinage because many of the plays have foreign or ancient settings and draw from the appropriate money system. However, in the course of assembling the list, I discovered that numismatics in fact reflects a larger thesis. On the one hand, the simple exuberance of coin-naming, along with an insistence on precise mention of exact amounts, shows the captivation of society with the new money economy. As the characters test what money can buy—and which coin or sum they must spend—they explore the limits of the money ethic. But some money terms also continue the medieval tradition of contempt for money, terming it **dung-hill-muck, lucre,** and **pelf.** At the same time that the drama celebrates or condemns wealth in the form of money, it also exhibits a confusion in values that stems partially from a debased and heterogeneous coinage. Foreign coins in circulation, along with counterfeit, token, clipped, and debased moneys, resulted in a questioning of the basis of value and its role in exchange. New forms of money challenged traditional precepts of social hierarchy, human behavior, relations, and standards. Problems brought to light by the coinage eventually were transferred to the social and individual realms of human worth.

Coin puns and metaphors particularly point out the search for the basis of human value in a world of exchange. Prince Hal's puns on **royal-man** and **noble-man,** social ranks dependent upon the value of their correspondent coins, are typical, as is reference to £30 knights. The devotion of misers to their money is revealed in puns on the **angels** (coins) that they enshrine in a **temple (purse)** and worship. Similarly, a **cracked crown** is a worthless coin and a shaky kingship, as well as a broken pate received while defending this dubious **sovereign.** Coin metaphors also indicate that the drama moves toward a **wholesale** acceptance of the merchandising ethic in human relations. In this context women especially are referred to as **current ware, light gold,** or merchants who will give a French **crown** (venereal disease) as change, and love is the highest form of merchandising, **golden traffic.**

Incidentally, some small coin details also can help to illuminate character in these plays. Barabas in *The Jew of Malta* disdains "paltry

silverlings" and prefers "wedge of **gold.**" This seems a logical enough preference, but it assumes added significance when we discover that a silverling was a **shekel,** the standard money of the Jews. Barabas thus, by rejecting the Jewish coins, demonstrates at least his ambivalence toward his race and religion, if not a complete abandonment of it. Similarly, when Shylock loses "Christian **ducats,**" most believe that he refers to money obtained by a system antithetical to his own moneylending trade. However, some ducats carried a device of Christ on the reverse, and Shylock probably refers only to these ducats as symbolic of the society that oppresses him. While the playwrights themselves were sometimes confused about the coinage, many references seem deliberately chosen to reflect the themes, characters, and preoccupations of a society moving toward a money morality. I hope the glossary will help to illuminate these changes.

Economic concerns manifest themselves in Renaissance drama in such great variety that an exhaustive glossary is nearly beyond the limits of human possibility. In this index it is inevitable that I have omitted someone's favorite economic play while including others that may seem less important or even less economic. While this list perhaps only opens access to the subject, the methodology of my selection of primary sources was rational and deliberate.

My first concern was to include those plays that could best demonstrate the development of an economic attitude toward morality over time. This necessity generally set the limits of my study, from 1582 to 1632. While several extremely good and famous plays with obvious economic emphases had helped to suggest the selection—plays like *Volpone* and *The Jew of Malta*—I also felt it important to include less well-known attempts at understanding economic behavior. This was to show that patterns of economic language, theme, character, and ethics exist in both the best and worst plays, and also to demonstrate the prevalence of economic unease in most dramatists of that time, from the anonymous playwright to the nearly anonymous Thomas May to the Bard himself. While economics has a natural affinity for comedy, I also wanted to show that economic concerns were so pressing and prevalent that they transcended standard generic separations, appearing as well in tragedy and domestic plays among others.

Second, I tried to choose works in which an economic action dominates or at least carries a large portion of the plot. This was sometimes difficult to ascertain, for economic motives are to a great degree present in most Renaissance plays. I devoted substantial energies to plays that include an economic abuser, like a miser or usurer or prodigal. Moreover, I attempted to avoid plays that have economically-allied actions but in which the primary emphasis is on an associated realm. Inclusion of plays like *The Alchemist,* I felt, would steer the glossary away from simple economics and give it too dispersed a focus. Finally, in dealing with Shakespeare I found the economic language to be pervasive and the apparatus for checking specific usages readily available, so that all plays in the standard corpus with economic references are included.

Because microeconomics stems from a consideration of relative values, it seems crucial to define these whenever they are mentioned in the plays, as coins, prices, and wages. Although these values are extremely difficult to pin down over a period of fifty years, I have drawn from contemporary descriptions whenever possible to give a feeling for what a certain amount of money would buy. See especially **crown, dolor, ducat, farthing, groat, mark, pence, penny, pound, price, shilling,** and **tester** and **Appendices B** and **C.** I have also included proverbial attitudes whenever appropriate, to indicate the common lore.

The glossary ***is not meant*** to be a concordance. I have omitted words that retain the same denotation in today's economic language, but I have included words that are recognizable yet have changed in meaning, like **outcry, unvalued,** and **undervalued,** in addition to words that require specific contextual definition. The examples that follow the definitions are meant only as illustrations, to show the range of meaning and usage and to allow the reader to re-experience the puns and other rhetorical figures firsthand, with the many possible definitions firmly in mind. Examples of the standard, literal, primary definition, if no pun, metaphor, or other rhetorical figure is employed, are also omitted. Words from the newly-developing science of extensive trade and economic contracts are also defined in their Renaissance usage under the assumption that they constitute a specialized lexicon. Antiquated economic machinery seems as murky in the minds of modern scholars as numismatics—and needs similarly to be clarified. Thus the glossary is composed of three general categories of words: coin and money names; the lexicon of economic machinery; and true econolingua, economic metaphor.

The glossary is meant to illuminate the entire complex of econolingua and the change in ethical thought that it represents. I hope that scholars, teachers, and students will find the Introduction and entries valuable enough to be read as an entity; I also hope that the book will be retained as a desk reference, to answer questions about specific economic terms as they arise, and to be consulted for new editions of plays. This index is not meant to be the last word on econolingua; instead, my intent was to open a new arena of inquiry and observation, to stimulate a close textual examination of economic language and theme as they illuminate the larger meanings of the plays. Critics must begin to realize, as did John Wheeler in 1601, that "There is nothing in the world so ordinarie, and naturall vnto men, as to **contract, truck,** merchandise, and trafficke one with another. ... In a word, all the world choppeth and changeth, runneth & raueth after **Marts** ... so that all thinges come into Commerce, and passe into **traffique."**[28]

[28] *A Treatise of Commerce,* Facsimile Text Society (1601; rpt. New York: Columbia Univ. Press, 1931).

Citation System and Plays Indexed

In the following glossary, each entry defines the term in its economic context and offers additional possible definitions and pun functions or rhetorical figures, if any. After the square bracket in each entry is a list of abbreviations of the plays in which the term occurs. This list, especially in the case of more common terms in non-Shakespearean plays, *is representative rather than exhaustive and is not meant to be a concordance.* If a particular combination use of the term is interesting, it is included after the line or page citation. The numbers following the play abbreviations refer to act, scene, and line, in Arabic numerals, or to the page on which the term appears in the edition used (see bibliography) when the lines were not numbered. Following is a master list of the play abbreviations. The approximate date of composition, first performance or printing, and the key word for locating the edition in the bibliography follow in parentheses. If no author or edition is included, the play is anonymous and listed under the title.

A&C = *Antony and Cleopatra* (*Riverside,* 1607)

Ado = *Much Ado About Nothing* (*Riverside,* 1598)

Ass = *The Devil is an Ass* (Jonson, 1616)

AYLI = *As You Like It* (*Riverside,* 1599)

BBofA = *The Blind Beggar of Alexandria* (Chapman, 1596)

BBush = *The Beggars' Bush* (Beaumont, 1622)

Beware = *Women Beware Women* (Middleton, 1621)

BFair = *Bartholomew Fair* (Jonson, 1614)

Bond. = *The Bond-Man* (Massinger, 1623)

Case = *The Case is Altered* (Jonson, 1597)

CofE = *The Comedy of Errors* (*Riverside,* 1592)

Corio. = *Coriolanus* (*Riverside,* 1608)

Cym. = *Cymbeline* (*Riverside,* 1609)

DCourt. = *The Dutch Courtesan* (Marston, 1604)

Debts = *A New Way to Pay Old Debts* (Massinger, 1621)

Dido = *Dido, Queen of Carthage* (Marlowe, 1587)

Drum = *John Drums Entertainment* (Marston, 1600)

Ed.2 = *Edward II* (Marlowe, 1592)

EHo = *Eastward Ho* (Chapman, 1605)

EMen = *English-Men for My Mone*y (Haughton, 1598)

EMOH = *Every Man Out of His Humour* (Jonson, 1599)

Fatal = *The Fatal Dowry* (Massinger, 1619)

Faust. = *Dr. Faustus* (Marlowe, 1592)

Gall. = *The Cittie Gallant* (Cook, 1611)

Ham. = *Hamlet* (*Riverside,* 1601)

Hater = *The Woman-Hater* (Beaumont, 1606)

Heir = *The Heir* (May, 1620)

1Hen.4 = *1 Henry IV* (*Riverside,* 1597)

2Hen.4 = *2 Henry IV (Riverside,* 1597)

Hen.5 = *Henry V* (*Riverside,* 1595)

1Hen.6 = *1 Henry VI* (*Riverside,* 1592)

2Hen.6 = *2 Henry VI* (*Riverside,* 1591)

3Hen.6 = *3 Henry VI* (*Riverside,* 1591)

Hen.8 = *Henry VIII* (*Riverside,* 1613)

HWhorel — *1 The Honest Whore* (Dekker, 1604)

HWhore2 = *2 The Honest Whore* (Dekker, 1605)

JC = *Julius Caesar* (*Riverside,* 1599)

JofM = *The Jew of Malta* (Marlowe, 1589)

John = *King John* (*Riverside,* 1596)

Killed = *A Woman Killed with Kindness* (Heywood, 1603)

Lear = *King Lear* (*Riverside,* 1605)

LLL = *Love's Labour's Lost* (*Riverside,* 1595)

Mac. = *Macbeth* (*Riverside,* 1606)

Madam = *The City Madam* (Massinger, 1632)

MadW. = *A Mad World, My Masters* (Middleton, 1606)

Magn.. = *The Magnetick Lady* (Jonson, 1632)

Maid = *A Chaste Maid in Cheapside* (Middleton, 1611)

Mass.atP. = *Massacre at Paris* (Marlowe, 1593)

MND = *A Midsummer Night's Dream* (*Riverside*, 1595)

MforM = *Measure for Measure* (*Riverside,* 1604)

MofV = *The Merchant of Venice* (*Riverside,* 1596)

MTerm = *Michaelmas Term* (Middleton, 1606)

MWives = *The Merry Wives of Windsor* (*Riverside,* 1600)

NHo = *North-ward Hoe* (Dekker, 1605)

OldF. = *Old Fortunatus* (Dekker, 1599)

Oth. = *Othello* (*Riverside,* 1604)

Per. = *Pericles* (*Riverside,* 1608)

Prod. = *The London Prodigall* (1604)

R&J = *Romeo and Juliet* (*Riverside,* 1595)

Ram. = *Ram-Alley (*Barry, 1608)

Rich.2 = *Richard II* (*Riverside,* 1595)

Rich.3= *Richard III* (*Riverside,* 1593)

Scorn.= *The Scornful Lady* (Beaumont, 1613)

Shrew = *The Taming of the Shrew* (*Riverside,* 1594)

Staple = *The Staple of News* (Jonson, 1626)

T&C = *Troilus and Cressida* (*Riverside,* 1602)

1Tamb. = *1 Tamburlaine (*Marlowe, 1587)

TAnd. = *Titus Andronicus* (*Riverside,* 1594)

Temp. = *The Tempest* (*Riverside,* 1611)

TofA = *Timon of Athens* (*Riverside,* 1607)

3Lad. = *Three Ladies of London* (Wilson, 1581)

Trick = *A Trick to Catch the Old One* (Middleton, 1605)

12N. = *Twelfth Night* (*Riverside,* 1600)

2Gents. = *Two Gentlemen of Verona* (*Riverside,* 1593)

Vex. = *A New Wonder, A Woman never Vext* (Rowley, 1625)

Volp. = *Volpone* (Jonson, 1606)

Well = *All's Well that Ends Well* (*Riverside,* 1602)

WHo = *West-ward Hoe* (Dekker, 1604)

Wily= *Wily Beguiled* (1602)

Wit = *Wit without Money* (Beaumont, 1614)

WTale = *The Winter's Tale* (*Riverside,* 1610)

Glossary

A

ABASE. See ***Debase.***

ABATE. See ***Debase.***

ABY, v. Archaic form of to buy: to pay for, to make amends for, as in suffering a penalty. *[**MND*** 3.2.175, 335.

ACCOMPT. See ***Account.***

ACCOUNT, n. and v. Also accompt. A reckoning or explanation made of any action or transaction. A judgment or estimation of value by means of a personal standard (esteem). The ability to tally up a total, to do arithmetic; "Commercial totting up" (Le Comte). A debt. The Last Judgment. Proverbially, "He that gains well and spends well, needs no account book" (Herbert). Appears in aphaeresis with (ac)count. *He has his account* means to be cheated (Postlethwayt). *[**1Hen.4*** 3.2.149: call ... to account; 5.1.37-38: in place and in account / Nothing so strong and fortunate as I; 5.1.95; ***TofA*** 2.2.133-34: I brought in my accompts, / Laid them before you; ***Lear*** 1.1.20-21: no dearer in my account; ***R&J*** 1.5.118: O dear account! my life is my foe's debt; 5.1.45: a beggarly account; ***Ado*** 2.1.62: make an account of her life; 4.1.333: Claudio shall render me a dear account; ***2Hen.6*** 4.2.85-86: he can write and read and cast accompt; ***Rich.2*** 1.1.130: remainder of a dear account; ***MTerm*** 3.4.107: two Cittizens of good account; ***1Hen.6*** 2.3.8: achievements of no less account; ***Mac.*** 1.7.39: Such I account thy love; ***Rich.3*** 3.2.69-70: The princes both make high account of you— / —For they account his head upon the bridge; ***Hen.5*** Pro.16: ciphers to this great accompt: ***2Gents.*** 2.1.61-62: How esteem'st thou me? I account of her beauty; ***MofV*** 3.2.155-57: only to stand high in your account, / I might in virtues ... / Exceed account; 4.1.416-17: am satisfied, / And therein do account myself well paid; ***John*** 4.2.216: the last accompt 'twixt heaven and earth; ***Hen.8*** 3.2.210-11: This paper has undone me. 'Tis th' accompt / Of all that world of wealth; ***Corio.*** 2.3.94: account me the more virtuous; 4.7.18, 26; ***TAnd.*** 3.1.197-98: I account of them / As jewels purchas'd at an easy price; ***Ham.*** 1.5.78-79: No reck'ning made, but sent to my account / With all my imperfections on my head; ***Oth.*** 1.3.5.

ACQUITTANCE, n. and v. A final accounting, in both an economic and moral sense. A written document recognizing full payment of a debt; a settlement; a discharge of obligation or duty. According to Postlethwayt, "a kind of discharge upon stamped paper," consisting of four categories: "those of payment; those of caution, or precaution ['a security that all shall be delivered as promised']; those for security of passing, or those of personal security, or bail; and those of certificates of franchise." Acquittances made without a notary are "not equally safe with regard to what may happen afterwards, . . . being sometimes liable to very great inconveniences." In the moral sphere, a release from guilt. See ***Quit, Quittance, Seal.*** ***[Cym.*** 5.4.170; ***LLL*** 2.1.160-61: you can produce acquittances / For such a sum from special officers; ***Ham.*** 4.7.1: Now must your conscience my acquittance seal; ***Rich.3*** 3.7.233: Your mere enforcement shall acquittance me.

ACTION, n. A lawsuit. "The taking of legal steps to establish a claim to obtain judicial remedy" *(OED)*. ***[12N.*** 5.1.275: upon some action; ***2Hen.4*** 2.1.1: have you ent'red the action?; ***Magn.*** 5.10.44: not for such a summe, as is this Action; ***Killed*** 4.4.38; ***Lear*** 2.2.17-18: lily-liver'd, action-taking, whoreson.

ADVANTAGE, n. and v. In an economic sense, lending with interest, or any profit, benefit, or augmentation from one's investment. Metaphorically applied to love. Proverbially, "In spending lies the advantage" (Herbert; Tilley, S745). See ***Interest, Use.*** ***[1Hen.4*** 2.4.548; ***MofV*** 1.3.70: upon advantage; 2.7.19: hope of fair advantages; ***John*** 3.3.22: with advantage means to pay; ***2Gents.*** 2.4.68: use and fair advantage; ***Rich.3*** 4.4.323-24: Advantaging their love with interest / Of ten times double gain; ***12N.*** 4.2.111: It shall advantage thee.

AGENT, n. One hired to act on the behalf of another; from merchandising, but when applied to love, a pander or one who woos. With unscrupulous or self-serving connotations. According to Postlethwayt, "To be well qualified for such kind of business requires a faculty and expertness. Such an one should not only have the expeditious mechanical use of his pen, but should be master of a plain, strong, and intelligible stile, in order to communicate his intentions with perspicuity. He should, in public business too, be as ready with his tongue as his pen. . . . [He] ought to be one of a good general education, a genteel, affable, and communicative disposition, and have nothing of the pedant about him." See ***Broker, Factor.*** *[**T&C*** 5.10.36; ***Cym.*** 1.5.76: the agent for his master; ***Ado*** 2.1.178-79: negotiate for itself, / And trust no agent; ***2Gents.*** 1.3.46: Here is her hand, the agent of her heart.

ALMS, n. and adj. Charity; economic duty to the poor. Metaphorically extended to poverty of language and to acts that consist more of duty than of charity. Also sexual favors. Proverbially, "Great Alms-giving lessens no man's living" (Herbert). Stow[e] reports that in 1533 a great dole was given at which there was "so great preace of pore people" that seven were smothered in the mob, "starke deade" (7). See ***Superfluity.*** *[**LLL*** 5.1.38- 39: they have liv'd long on the alms-basket of words; ***Cym.*** 2.3.114: bred of alms and foster'd with cold dishes; ***Gall.*** 186: always bought his victuals out of the alms-basket; ***T&C*** 3.3.145-46: Time hath ... a wallet at his back, / Wherein he puts alms for oblivion; ***3Hen.6*** 5.5.79: murther is thy alms-deed; ***A&C*** 2.7.5: They have made him drink alms-drink; ***Hen.5*** 1.1.17: almshouses; ***Corio.*** 5.6.10-11: by his own alms empoison'd / And with his charity slain; ***Ado*** 2.3.158; ***Rich.2*** 3.3.149: an almsman's gown [mean apparel]; ***Lear*** 1.1.278: at fortune's alms; ***Oth.*** 3.4.122; ***BBush*** 5.2.236: women's favours are a leading alms.

AMERCE, v. From *estre amercie,* to be fined at the mercy of another; to penalize or punish by assessing a fine. Also *remerce,* to ransom (Skeat). *[**R&J*** 3.1.190: I'll amerce you with so strong a fine.

Elizabethan angel.

ANGEL, n. An English gold coin worth 6s. 8d. when first issued in 1465. Later it was valued up, to 7s. 6d. in 1526, 10s. in 1551, and 11s. in 1610. The obverse gives the coin its name, from the archangel Michael pictured there. The reverse shows a ship with the Yorkist shield. The inscription is "PER CRUCEM TUAM SALVA NOS CHRISTE REDEMPTOR" ("By thy cross save us, O Christ, our Redeemer"). Generally about twenty-nine millimeters in diameter. Many puns and econolinguistic extensions of this term occur in the drama. The name of the coin along with the religious implications of the device and inscription prompts reference to the psychomachia. Its value is compared in a punning manner to other coins with allusive names, *e.g.,* the noble. A wealthy and beautiful or virtuous woman is assuredly an angel in a double sense. Reference to the coin often lurks beneath ostensible reference to a heavenly angel. Henry Smith, in his sermon "The Poor Man's Tears," refers to "coffers full of golden gods and glittering angels." Lust that is linked to "a radiant angel" refers simultaneously to the woman inspiring lust and the angel she will receive in payment for satisfying a man's lust. This double-level of meaning is typical in angel passages, especially in Shakespeare. See ***Noble, Royal, Salute. [MTerm*** 1.1.149-50: blacke Angels [of debased gold]; ***Bond.*** 5.2.4: my better angel; ***MWives*** 1.3.53, 56-57; 2.2.71-73: I had myself twenty angels given me this morning, but I defy all angels; ***CofE*** 4.3.40; ***Ado*** 2.3.33: noble, or not I for an angel; ***MofV*** 2.7.56: a coin that bears the figure of an angel; 2.7.58: an angel in a golden bed [Portia]; ***John*** 2.1.590: angels salute my palm; 3.3.8: bags of hoarding abbots, imprisoned angels; 5.2.61-64: Into the purse of rich prosperity / ... so, nobles, shall you all, / . . . methinks an angel spake; ***1Hen.4*** 4.2.6: this bottle makes an angel; ***2Hen.4*** 1.2.165: your ill angel is light; ***Ham.*** 1.5.55: [lust] to a radiant angel link'd; ***Beware*** 4.2.127: a hogshead of angels; ***Ass*** 2.1.138; ***OldF.*** 1.2.33—35: The famine of Gold gnawes his couetous stomacke. . . . Thou hast lookt very deuilishly euer since the good Angel left thee; 1.2.89: Kissing the ruddie lippes of Angels; 1.2.176-77: there's not one angell more wagging in this sacred Temple; 3.1.227: Twentie faire English Angels; ***EHo*** 1.2.24-25: to eat cherries only at an angel a pound; ***Rich.2*** 3.2.60-61: God for his Richard hath in heavenly pay / A glorious angel; ***Madam*** 4.1.43-44: he shall not / Sit long on penniless-bench.—There spoke an angel; ***MadW.*** 3.2.80; ***Killed*** 4.2.2: To try two seeming angels; ***EMen*** *477.*

ANGEL-GOLD. See ***Gold.***

ANGLE, n. and v., **ANGLER**, n. Metaphorically extended from fishing: to entice, to flirt, to attract sexually. Also from rogues' cant, to steal (from windows) by means of a pole or hook. *[**A&C*** 2.5.16; ***WTale*** 1.2.180-81: I am angling now, / Though you perceive me not how I give line; 4.2.46; ***Well*** 5.3.212: She ... did angle for me; ***Ado*** 3.1.29: So angle we for Beatrice; ***1Hen.4*** 4.3.83-84: did he win / The hearts of all that he did angle for; ***3Lad.*** 271: We are cunning anglers.

ANSWER, n. and v. Economically, to pay, to remit, to be responsible for certain charges. Also to render an accounting, both financially and spiritually. Generally, to meet with an offer, to contract, to come to an agreement, to redress an offense. Proverbially, "Money answers all things" (Tilley, M1052). *[**1Hen.4*** 1.3.185: to answer all the debt he owes to you; 4.2.8: I'll answer the coinage; ***CofE*** 4.1.81-82: You shall buy this sport as dear / As all the metal in your shop will answer; 4.3.30-31; ***MofV*** *4.*1.103:1 stand for judgement: answer; shall I have it? [say and pay]; ***Rich.2*** 4.1.159: Procure your sureties for your days of answer; 5.2.83: my poor life must answer; ***Well*** 1.1.155: answer the time of request; ***Shrew*** 2.1.359: all things answerable to this portion [according to the same scale and payable for this dowry]; ***Madam*** 5.2.45-47: Your bonds lie / For your sons' truth, and they shall answer all / They have run out; ***MWives*** 1.1.114.

ARGENT-LE-ROY. See ***Argentine.***

ARGENTINE, adj. Pertaining to the moon: silvery. *Argent-le-roy* was the standard for fine silver in France and the Low Countries in the early sixteenth century. It consisted of twelve deniers of 95.833 percent purity (Munro). ***Argent vive*** is quicksilver, mercury (Skeat). *[**Per.*** 5.1.250: Dian, goddess argentine.

ARGENT VIVE. See ***Argentine.***

ARGOSY, n. ***Una ragusca,*** a carract from Ragusa; any large merchant ship and its cargo. *[**3Hen.6*** 2.6.36; ***MofV*** 1.1.9; 1.3.18; 3.1.100; ***JofM*** 1.1.71; ***Vex.*** 100\ ***Faust.*** 1.1.131; ***Shrew*** 2.1.374-76.

ARREARAGES, n. Payments that are overdue. Perhaps extended to mean the remaining sum of the entire account. See ***Rear.*** *[**Cym.*** 2.4.13: send the arrearages.

ARSEDINE, n. Also called ***Dutch gold,*** an alloy of copper and zinc used to gild inexpensive items. *[**BFair*** 2.2.25.

ARTICLES, n. Separate portions, clauses, or provisions in any legal document or contract, *e.g.,* a bond; originally, that which joins. See ***Specialty. [Faust.*** 2.1.89-90: thou perform / All covenants and articles between us; ***Cym.*** 1.4.156: I embrace these conditions; let us have articles betwixt us; ***BFair*** Ind. 78, 84; ***2Hen.6*** 1.1.40: Here are the articles of contracted peace; ***Temp.*** 1.2.194-95: Perform'd . . . / To every article; ***3Hen.6*** 1.1.180.

ASPER. See ***White Money.***

ASSURANCE, n., **ASSURE,** v. In contracts and economic affairs, to make safe, to secure from risk, to guarantee, to ensure or pledge, to insure against loss. Also to become betrothed, assure a marital promise. An assurance is a surety against risk, a formal agreement or promise, or a conveyance of property by means of deed or promissory document. Often the betrothal (assurance) is predicated upon an assurance (promise, conveyance, insurance) of wealth, thus reducing the marriage contract to a basic economic transaction. Proverbially, "A good paymaster starts not at assurances" (Herbert). See ***Jointure, Surety. [Prod.*** 2.4.7-9: first get your ashurance made, touching my daughters ioynter; ***Shrew*** 2.1.387: let your father make her the assurance [promise plus conveyance of wealth]; 2.1.123-24: I'll assure her of / Her widowhood [insure her against]; 2.1.345: What can you assure her? [promise as a marriage settlement, give]; ***12N.*** 3.2.35-37: my niece shall take note of it, and assure thyself, there is no love-broker in the world can more prevail [pun on note (contract), assure (promise, insure), broker (economic agent)]; ***CofE*** 3.2.141: swore I was assur'd to her [betrothed]; ***BBush*** 1.2.18-19: assurances of love, / These ties and bonds of friendship; 1.3.33-34: nor lend / Upon the assurance of a well-penn'd letter; ***MofV*** 1.3.28, 29, 30: I will be assur'd I may [pun on be certain and obtain a surety or legal contract]; ***2Hen.4*** 5.2.30: no man be assur'd what grace to find; ***Cym.*** 1.6.159: Her assur'd credit: ***Mac. 4.***1.83-84: I'll make assurance double sure, / And take a bond of fate; ***Fatal*** 5.1.12-13: I must have present moneys, or / Assurance to secure me; ***Killed*** 5.1.106: for thy more assurance, here's a pawn; ***Rich.3*** -i.4.496: his head's assurance; ***Faust.*** 2.1.54: Assure my soul to be great Lucifer's.

ATTACH, v. To arrest for debt; to seize (a person or goods) for imprisonment. *[HWhore1* 1.5.209; ***Hen.8*** 1.1.95-96: hath attach'd / Our merchants' goods; ***EHo*** 4.1.248; ***CofE*** 4.1.6, 73; 4.4.6.

AUDIT, n. Literally, a hearing. A final accounting, extended metaphorically to the spiritual or heavenly realm. Sometimes, in adianoeta, life itself, the debt or account one owes to God or Nature for the gift of life. *[**Hen.8*** 5.2.141: your earthly audit; ***Corio.*** 1.1.144: I can make my audit up; ***Mac.*** 1.6.27: to make their audit; ***Ham.*** 3.3.82: how his audit stands who knows save heaven?; ***Cym.*** 5.4.27-28: If you will take this audit, take this life, / And cancel these cold bonds.

AUD1TOR, n. An accountant; sometimes a consultant in reckoning the settlement of a debt. "Accounts were formerly vouched for orally" *(OED)*. Someone who can monitor and judge economic affairs. *[**1Hen.4*** 2.1.57; ***ToffA*** 2.2.156: Call me before th' exactest auditors.

AURUM, n. Gold, especially in reference to alchemical compounds. Drinkable gold (aurum potabile) was supposed to have miraculous curative or medicinal properties. See ***Restorative.*** *[**Volp.*** 1.4.73: aurum palpabile,; ***MadW.*** 3.3.56: aurum potabile.

B

BAG. n. Represents a sum of money, a large amount, full bags of coins. Metaphorically, scrotum or genitals (Ross). Proverbially, "I wot well how the World wags, he is most loved that has most bags" (Tilley, W874. Postlethwayt notes, "Bags of silver coin in France are generally given and received, without counting their contents." Thus one was able to perpetrate an economic deception, as reported by Wriothesley: "Anthony Fowlkes, a gentleman, set on the pillory in Cheape, and had his eare hard nayled to the pillory, for deceivinge certeine citizens for mercenary wares, hosen. and other, in offringe them a bagge with newe counters sealed for a pawne. sayinge yt was gould, till he would bringe mony" (2:79). Also "to give the bag," to trick or cheat. *[**WTale*** 4.4.263-64: twenty money bags; ***CofE*** 4.4.96: bag of gold; ***TAnd.*** 2.3.280: bag of gold; ***MTerm*** Ind. 24: Where bags are fruitful'st, there the womb's most barren; ***EMOH*** 1.3.122: how plumpe my bags are; ***Gall.*** 235: They must have bags, although my credit crack for't; ***2Hen.6*** 1.3.128-29: the clergy's bags / Are lank and lean with thy extortions; ***Per.*** 3.2.41: tie my pleasure up in silken bags; ***MWives*** 2.2.171: a bag of money; 3.4.16: sums in sealed bags; ***MofV*** 2.8.18: A sealed bag, two sealed bags of ducats; ***Shrew*** 1.2.177: that his bags shall prove; ***John*** 3.3.7-8: shake the bags / Of hoarding abbots, imprisoned angels; ***Oth.*** 1.1.80: Look to your house, your daughter, and your bags!; ***Lear*** 2.3.50-51: fathers that bear bags / Shall see their children kind; ***OldF.*** 1.2.75-76: Twas neuer merie world with vs, since purses and bags were inuented, for now men set lime twigges to catch wealth; 1.2.191; ***WHo*** 4.2.203.

BAGATINE, n. A Venetian coin of copper or billon, of small worth (one-third farthing), a trifle, first issued in the mid-fifteenth century. The obverse shows a winged lion. About twenty millimeters in diameter. [***Volp.*** 2.2.258

Venetian copper bagatine.

BANCO, n. From bench, the surface across which money transactions were made. Literally, simply the bank, a place money was left for safekeeping, without obtaining any interest on the sum deposited. In early banks, first in Venice, a depositor was ostensibly to receive upon withdrawal exactly the same coins that he had deposited. Also may be extended to indicate money of account as opposed to actual currency, *e.g.*, the English pound in the sixteenth century. [***JofM*** 4.1.76: Great sums of money lying in the banco.

BAND, n. A bond; that which binds. This can refer simultaneously to one or more of the following: a contract for a loan, a neckband or restraint, fetters for a prisoner, a wedding ring and the bond of matrimony, a duty or obligation, a debt, a promise, and a bond of kinship, friendship, or tradition. Proverbially, "Death pays all debts [bonds]" (Tilley, D148). See ***Bond.*** *[**CofE*** 4.2.49: was he arrested on a band?; 4.3.30-31; ***Ado*** 3.1.114: To bind our loves up in a holy band; ***Well*** 4.2.56: Now will I charge you in the band of truth; ***Rich.2*** 1.1.2: according to thy oath and band; 5.2.65-66: some band that he is enter'd into / For gay apparel; ***1Hen.4*** 3.2.157: the end of life cancels all bands; ***Ham.*** 3.2.159-60: Hymen did our hands / Unite comutual in most sacred bands.

BANKROUT, n., v., and adj. Also bankrupt. Literally, a broken bank. Broke, financially ruined. Pursued by creditors. A prodigal, or one who has spent all his money quickly and imprudently on riotous living. Metaphorically, perhaps spent of semen; also killed, broke in the account of life; and intellectually or linguistically impoverished. A great scandal occurred in 1563 when "Ser Thomas Lodge (to y[e] great slaundar of y[e] wholl city) in y[e] ende of his maioralitie proffessyd to be banqerowpte" (Stowe, 126). In the statute 13 Eliz. cap. 7, bankrupts are named as those trying to avoid debts by hiding, leaving the country, or staging false arrest (Postleth- wayt). *[**CofE*** 4.2.58: Time is a very bankrout and owes more than he's worth; ***2Gents.*** 2.4.42: I shall make your wit bankrupt; ***LLL*** 1.1.26-27: dainty bits / Make rich the ribs, but bankrout quite the wits [bits as coins, *bon mots,* and cates]; ***MND*** 3.2.85: debt that bankrout sleep doth sorrow owe; ***MofV*** 3.1.44-45: A bankrout, a prodigal; 4.1.122: To cut the forfeiture from that bankrout; ***AYLI*** 2.1.57: that poor and broken bankrupt; ***Rich.2*** 2.1.151: Be York the next that must be bankrout so [killed]; 2.1.257: The King's grown bankrout; 4.1.267: Since it [my face] is bankrout of his majesty; ***R&J*** 3.2.57: O, break, my heart, poor bankrout; ***NHo*** 2.1.25; ***WHo*** 3.2.8-9: I was first a Puritan, then a Banquerout, then a Broker; ***Maid*** 3.3.9: his bankrout merit; ***BBush*** 2.3.60.

BANKRUPT. See ***Bankrout.***

BATE, v. Aphaeresis for (a)bate. To reduce, to diminish, to underrate, usually in reference to the value of a debt or loan. A common practice of Renaissance moneylenders was to reduce the full amount owed, especially to young men with the promise of coming into a fortune, and then to establish a new loan to pay off this reduced amount, at an even higher rate of interest (today called "rolling it over"). While this appeared to be kindness, it was termed "usurer's kindness," for the debtor ended up owing more than he had originally. After a series of these batings, the debtor could easily be financially ruined and pull anyone with kinship or obligation to him down too. In this way moneyed men of the merchant class could also gain lands, by attaching them as payment for these bated debts. Also used to describe the implicit contract between audience and players (including playwright). ***[Per.*** 4.2.51: I cannot be bated one doit of a thousand; ***TofA*** 1.2.206: you bate too much of your own merits; 3.3.26: Who bates mine honor shall not know my coin; ***Temp.*** 1.2.249-50: Thou didst promist / To bate me a full year; ***Well*** 2.3.234: I will not bate thee a scruple; ***2Hen.4*** Ep. 14-15: Bate me some, and I will pay you some; ***Magn.*** 4.8.74-75: I will not 'bate you a single *Harrington,* / Of interest upon interest.

BAWD. See ***Close bawd.***

BEAR, v. Literally, to carry a burden. Economically, to carry money, with the implication of having control or power over that wealth; to support another person financially; to be wealthy; to borrow money; to give birth to heirs. ***[MWives*** 1.3.68: she bears the purse; 2.2.171; ***AYLI*** 2.4.12: bear no cross [pun on coin and hardship]; ***2Hen.4*** 1.2.226: too impatient to bear crosses [coin/hardship]; ***12N.*** 2.4.102: that love a woman can bear me; ***Lear*** 2.4.50: fathers that bear bags; ***CofE*** 5.1.8: bear my wealth [borrow]; ***NHo*** 4.3.18: beare the charge; ***Killed*** 3.2.105-6: that Judas that hath borne my purse, / And sold me for a sin!

BEAUTY. See ***Booty.***

BED-RIGHT, n. The sexual economics of marriage, implying mutual possessory obligations. ***[Temp.*** 4.1.96-97: no bed-right shall be paid / Till Hymen's torch be lighted.

.**BEHOOF**, n. Literally, something useful. Profit, benefit, advantage, with the implication that one offers it as a duty or gift to another. ***[ITamb.*** 2.5.32: we ever aimed at your behoof; ***2Hen.6*** 4.7.77-78: This tongue hath parley'd unto foreign kings / For your behoof; ***Ham.*** 1.3.97; 5.1.63.

BENEFIT, n. Literally, an act well done. Economically, pecuniary advantage. Also a profit or a "bestowal of property" (Schmidt). Proverbially, "Benefits are soon forgotten"

(Tilley, B309). *[CofE* 1.2.25: Of whom I hope to make much benefit; ***1Hen.6*** 5.3.16: In earnest of a future benefit; ***Rich.3*** 3.7.195-96: take to your royal self / This proffer'd benefit of dignity; ***AYLI*** 2.7.186: benefits forgot.

BENEVOLENCE, n. Also called a contribution. Literally, well-wishing. A loan coerced by the king as a show of good will and support toward him by his subjects. Here used anachronistically, since the benevolence was first used by Edward IV in 1473. Wriothesley reports of one in 1545: "the Kinge demaunded of his subjectes ... a benevolence towardes his great charges of the warres . . . after the rate of *2s.* in the pounde" (1:151). One Mr. Richard Rede, who refused to pay, was sent to fight in Scotland. *[**Rich.2*** 2.1.250.

BETTER PENNY. See ***Penny.***

BEZANT. See ***Solidare.***

BEZZO. Also betzo. See ***Farthing***.

BIANCO, n. An Italian silver (i.e., white) coin of the fifteenth century and earlier, issued in various provinces, *e.g.*, Venice, Mantua, Bologna. It is possible that there is an ironic commentary in *Shrew, Beware,* and *Oth.* on the strongly pecuniary nature of the marriage arrangements, with a pun on the women named Bianca and bianco in a general sense as coins, money, especially since the settings are Padua, Florence, and Venice (Cyprus), respectively. In *Oth.* Bianca is a strumpet who performs for silver, and Iago carries through this money/sex/love nexus by calling her "trash," a "creature," and a "customer." See *White Money. [**Shrew*** 2.1.335-36: And I am one that love Bianca more / Than words can witness; 4.4.22: Give me Bianca for my patrimony; ***Beware*** 3.2.166-67: There will I lock my life's best treasure up, / Bianca; ***Oth***. 4.1.93, 95, 119; 5.1.85.

BILL, n. From medieval Latin *bulla,* "a document furnished with a seal" *(OED).* An economic document of various types: a promissory note, or a bill of debt; an account, as at a tavern; a final reckoning of charges; an inventory; an order for work, as with a tailor; a bill of exchange, or a paper that allowed monies of different currencies to be exchanged by an agent (there were several kinds, according to Nissim da Pisa: a bill of absolute exchange, real exchange, dry exchange, *etc.,* and these were often formulated in such complicated ways as to hide interest charges); a payment owed; a contract; a bill of entry, which certified the inventory of goods brought in on a ship. Sometimes a bill of exchange was accepted instead of a tangible valuable as a pawn or security to a goldsmith for a loan. Often appears in puns on other meanings, such as bills as weapons, the bill of a bird, billing as kissing and making a contract (of love). Similarly, bill-men can be gendarmes and moneylenders or merchants and their agents. Metaphorically, death, the contract of life. See ***Bond, Note. [2Hen.6*** 4.7.127: take up commodities upon our bills; ***EMen*** 488, 490: bill of exchange; ***Shrew*** 4.2.89-90: bills for money by exchange / From Florence; 4.3.145: error i' th' bill!; **MND** 1.2.105: bill of properties; ***WHo*** 5.3.81: bill of items; 5.4.24: bill-men; ***Heir*** 148; ***Ado*** 3.3.177-78: We are like to prove a goodly commodity, being taken up of these men's bills.—A commodity in question [weapons and accounts or debts]; ***TofA*** 3.4.49: sums and bills; ***MWives*** 1.1.10-11: bill, warrant, quittance, or obligation; ***Faust.*** 2.1.64, 73; 5.2.64: I writ them a bill with mine own blood; ***JofM*** 1.1.56: bills of entry; ***BBush*** 1.3.16-17: his bill would pass / Unquestion'd for her lading; 4.3.3, 13; ***Mac.*** 3.1.99-100: the bill / That writes them all alike [death]; ***T&C*** 3.2.57: billing again?; ***Cym.*** 4.2.225: charitable bill [pun on ruddock; the robin's bill brings moss to cover a grave, but the charitable bill (will) of the father leaves the son money (ruddocks, gold coins)]; **Maid** 3.3.90: clap up Billes.

BILLON. See ***Bull'on brass.***

BIT, n. Ostensibly a dainty morsel of food, but with possible economic extensions. Bit also refers to money in general or more specifically threepence, fourpence, or sixpence. Especially in metaphorical economic phrases, this latter meaning is probable as an adianoeta. See ***Golden bit. [LLL*** 1.1.26-27: Dainty bits / Make rich the ribs, but bankrout quite the wits [young men spend prodigally on delicacies (?)]; ***TofA*** 2.2.165-66: How many prodigal bits have slaves and peasants / This night englutted! [a bill for a feast footed by prodigal spenders].

BITE. See ***Cross-bite.***

BLACK AND WHITE, n. A written contract, especially for a debt, and therefore enforceable under legal remedies for nonperformance. Emphasis on the desirability of obtaining a "black and white" rather than simply a handshake or a man's word demonstrates increasing contractual economic relations among people in the drama. *[**Drum*** 187: Carefull, I, I, let nothing without good blacke and white, I warrant you [further pun on warrant as a contract or guarantee]; ***Ado*** 5.1.303: white and black.

BLACK DOG, n. According to Tilley, a current Renaissance proverb was "Hee has a face like a blacke Dogge," or "Hee blusheth like a black dogge, hee hath a brazen face" (D 507). This saying seems easily to have adapted itself to certain coins as well, bad shillings or other pieces of silver, which were actually made of a base metal and then lightly washed over or veneered with silver. Because they were not white (silver) or red (gold), these coins were called black; when the veneer wore away, the "blush" of the base metal could be seen beneath. See ***Nose.*** *[**TAnd**.* 5.1.121-22: canst thou say all this and never blush?—Ay, like a black dog, as the saying is.

BLACK MONEY. See ***Bull'on brass.***

BLANC. See ***Charter***.

BLANCH, v. Chemically to turn base metals into something resembling silver, perhaps by veneering the coin with tin or melting it with arsenic and niter (Postlethwayt). A counterfeiting process. In alchemy, albification. *[**EHo*** 4.1.268: blanch copper.

BLANK. See ***Charter***.

BLOODY NOSE. See ***Nose***.

BOB, v. and adj. From Old French *bober*. To trick financially, to swindle, "To make a fool of, deceive, cheat. ... To take by deception, to filch" *(OED)*. With a pun on to cut. Only later does it become slang for a shilling. *[**Ram.*** 358: Throat, thou art bobb'd; ***T&C*** 3.1.68: You shall not bob us out of our melody; ***Oth.*** 5.1.16: gold and jewels that I bobb'd from him; ***Gall.*** 237; ***Rich.3*** 5.3.334: beaten, bobb'd, and thump'd.

BOND, n., **BOUND,** adj. Like ***Bill*** and ***Note,*** an economic contract, an obligation to pay a certain amount of money at an appointed date. The bond may be secured by one's word, by a piece of property, or by a surety, a third party who will be responsible upon forfeiture. A blank charter for taxes collected by agents of the king. A promissory note as a material representation of wealth, assets. A debenture. In general, a duty, a covenant, a moral tie; "uniting force, affinity" (Le Comte). This economic term appears in puns on shackles, constipation (to be bound), servitude, and bound in a moral sense with an economic note, as a literal extension of the rhetorical figure asphalia. Metaphorically, life is the greatest bond. Proverbially, "An honest man's word is as good as his bond" (Tilley, M458). *[**TofA*** 2.1.34; 2.2.37: date-broke bonds [overdue]; ***MofV*** 1.3.145: your single bond; ***Rich.2*** 2.1.64: inky blots and rotten parchment bonds; ***MND*** 3.2.267-68: I would I had your bond, for I perceive / A weak bond holds you. I'll not trust your word; ***12N.*** 3.1.21: words are very rascals since bonds disgrac'd them; ***2Gents.*** 2.7.75: His words are bonds; ***CofE*** 4.4.121: enter'd in bond for you [rope/debt/servitude]; ***Prod.*** 1.1.116-17: you shall haue my bond, Vncle; ***NHo*** 2.1.141-42: to put my father in mind of a bond, that wilbe forfit this night if the mony be not payd; ***MTerm*** 2.3.288- 89: I might make my bond passe for a hundred pound 'ith Citie; ***Mac.*** 3.2.49: Cancel and tear to pieces that great bond; 4.1.83-84: make assurance double sure, / And take a bond of fate; ***1Hen.6*** 4.7.20: bonds of perpetuity; ***1Hen.4*** 3.3.101: three or four bonds; ***WHo*** 3.2.95-96: Wilt thou take my bond Sergeant? Wheres a Scriuener; 4.1.120: the Scrivener is but new gon vp to take her bond; ***MadW.*** 2.4.69-70: one villain binds his fellows. Go, we must be all bound for our own securities; 2.6.63-64: though I were a lord, I must enter into bond; 3.2.211: Bound? No, no, I'd a very comfortable stool this morning; ***DCourt.*** 1.2.70-71: a hard bound Philosopher, when he is on the stoole; 2.1.116: the common bonde of being; ***BBush*** 5.2.35-36: the payment / Of some religious debt Nature stood bound for; ***Well*** 1.3.188-89: my love hath in't a bond / Whereof the world takes note [further pun on bond/note]; ***Rich.3*** 4.4.77: bond of life; ***Cym.*** 3.2.36-37: Lovers / And men in dangerous bonds pray not alike; 5.4.28: cold bonds [life]; ***Killed*** 5.1.74-75: Will you not stand / In joint-bond bound to satisfy the debt?

BONDMAN, n. One bound by contract in service, with a pun on physically bound, constrained. Since we are all bound to life, all men by extension are bondmen. See ***Cancel***. *[**CofE*** 5.1.141, 289-91: Within this hour I was his bondman, sir, / But he, I thank him, gnaw'd in two my cords: / Now am I

Dromio, and his man, unbound; ***JC*** 1.3.101-2: every bondman in his own hand bears / The power to cancel his captivity.

BONNET, n. Perhaps slang for a coin, from "A gold coin of James V of Scotland, issued only in 1539 and 1540. ... It is so called from the king's head being decorated with a bonnet, or square cap, instead of a crown" (Frey). Its possible puns in Shakespeare include hat /coin in hand and unbonneted as exposed/unrewarded or bereft of money. *[**Corio.*** 3.2.73: Go to them, with this bonnet in thy hand; ***Oth.*** 1.2.22-23: my demerits / May speak, unbonneted, to as proud a fortune; ***Lear*** 3.1.14—15: unbonneted he runs, / And bids what will take all; ***Rich.2*** 1.4.31: Off goes his bonnet to an oyster-wench.

Gold bonnet, James V of Scotland.

BOOT, n. and v., **BOOTLESS,** adj. (opp.) Literally, something good or useful. A profit, advantage, unexpected gain, augmentation, or booty. Its double meanings include shoes and mockery. *[**WTale*** 4.4.635-37: Though the pennyworth on his side be the worst, yet hold thee, there's some boot; 4.4.674-76: What an exchange had this been, without boot! What a boot is here, with this exchange!; ***1Hen.4*** 2.1.81-84: they ride up and down on her, and make her their boots.—What, the commonwealth their boots? Will she hold out water in foul way?; 3.1.65-68: have I sent him / Bootless home and weather-beaten back.—Home without boots, and in foul weather too! / How scapes he agues; ***Lear*** 5.3.302: With boot, and such addition; ***A&C*** 2.5.71: I will boot thee with what gift; ***Shrew*** 5.2.176: Then vail your stomachs, for it is no boot; ***2Gents.*** 1.1.25-28: you are over boots in love, / . . .

nay, give me not the boots. / ... it boots thee not [shoes/ mockery/profits].

BOOTY, n. An unexpected profit, usually obtained by pillage or other illegal means. Shakespeare capitalizes on the similar pronunciation of beauty, producing a paronomasia that reflects an underlying mercantilist attitude toward love. Proverbially, "Beauty is made for use" (Tilley, B170.1). *[**R&J*** 1.5.47: Beauty too rich for use; ***AYL1*** 1.3.110: Beauty provoketh thieves sooner than gold; ***1Hen.4*** 1.2.25: thieves of the day's beauty; ***WTale*** 4.4.832: [Fortune] drops booties in my mouth.

BORROW, v. Slang for to steal, to rob. [***NHo*** 1.1.187.

BOTTLE-NOSED, adj. A pejorative description characteristic of money- men, i.e., usurers, misers, unscrupulous merchants. These characters evolved dramatically from a combination of the abstraction of Avarice, Judas, and Roman stage caricatures; later Jewish features also became characteristic. *[**Wily*** 238: base, broking, brabbling, brawling, bastardly, bottle-nosed, beetle-browed, bean-bellied; ***JofM*** 3.3.9-10: secret, subtle, bottle-nosed knave; ***EMen*** 522: Signor Bottle-nose.

BOTTOM, n. Synecdoche for a ship; also for the merchandise that it holds; with a pun on a woman's sexual merchandise, her "bottom." *[**John*** *2*.1.73: the English bottoms; ***12N.*** 5.1.57: The most noble bottom of our fleet; ***MofV*** 1.1.42: My ventures are not in one bottom trusted; ***Temp***. 2.1.226- 27; ***Hen.5*** 3. Pro. 12; ***BBush*** 1.3.15-17: there was never brought to harbour / So rich a bottom but his bill would pass / Unquestion'd for her lading; 5.2.107-8: your merchant-ship / May break; for this was one of your best bottoms [his daughter].

BOUGET. See ***Budget***.

BOUGHT AND SOLD, adj. Economically abused, treated like merchandise, imposed upon, betrayed, ruined. By extension, verbally embarrassed or maltreated. *[**CofE*** 3.1.72; ***John*** 5.4.10; ***1Hen.6*** 4.4.13; ***Rich.3*** 5.3.305; ***T&C*** *2*.1.46-47: thou art bought and sold among those of any wit, like a barbarian slave; ***Wily*** 269: Lelia, she is bought and sold; ***BBush*** 2.3.114; ***Hen.8*** 1.1.292.

BOUND. See ***Bond***.

BOWED, adj. In describing a coin, bent, i.e., worthless. *[**Hen.8*** 2.3.36: A threepence bow'd would hire me.

BRACE, n. A pair, a couple, two things together, used numismatically as a slang measure. *[**Wily*** 302: a brace of angels; ***NHo*** 5.1.192-93: a brace of hundreth pounds; ***Debts*** 1.3.37: a brace of threepences; ***Cym.*** 1.4.90-91: brace of unprizable estimations [a diamond and chastity]; ***WHo*** 3.2.64: hue brace of Angelles: ***Trick*** 3.1.153: a brace of royals.

BRASS, n. Inferior coins, something of little worth, with an adnominatio or misunderstanding of the French *bras,* arm. For a continuation of the joke, see *Moy*. *[**Hen.5*** 4.4.20: Offer'st me brass?; ***Prod.*** 5.1.92: a brasse shilling.

BREAK, v. and adj. To miss a specified day for repayment of a bond and thus to be liable for the forfeit. To go bankrupt. With a pun on to collapse. According to Thomas Adams in his sermon "The White Devil," "for Breakers, such as necessity compels to it, I censure not: if they desire with all their hearts to satisfie the vtmost farthing and cannot: God will then accept votall restitution for totall restitution: . . . *the will for the deed:* ... a sore it may be, no sin." See ***Broke, Longer Day***. *[**Madam*** 1.3.113, 117: Give 'em longer day . . . / But see you break not; 2.1.26: Three such dinners more would break an alderman; ***BBush*** 1.1.37-38: broken, both / In mind and means; 2.2.4: to ha' me break; 5.2.107-8; ***MofV*** 1.3.136-37: if he break, thou mayst with better face / Exact the penalty; 1.3.163: If he should break his day, what should I gain; ***BFair*** 2.5.89-90: would my booth ha' broke if they had fall'n; ***Well*** 2.1.187: If I break time, or flinch in property; ***Debts*** 1.1.182: I in my madness broke my state; ***R&J*** 3.2.57: O, break, my heart, poor bankrout.

BRITAIN'S BURSE. See ***Burse, Old Exchange***.

BROKAGE, n. A commission or fee paid to a broker; profit from being a business middleman and thus suspect, since not derived from true labor, the sweat of the brow. Scriveners often acted as middlemen for financial investment. *[**Madam*** 1.2.53: Nor ever yet paid brokage to his [usurer's] scrivener.

BROKE, v. Also break. To bargain, to act as a middleman, to traffic. When applied to love, sex, and marriage, to pander, to woo, "to barter for a woman" (Partridge). *[**Ado*** 1.1.309-10: I will break with her, and with her father, / And thou shalt have her; 2.1.155-57: Sure my brother is amorous on Hero, and hath withdrawn her father to break with him about it; 2.1.299: I have broke with her father; 3.2.74-75: to break with him about Beatrice; ***Well*** 3.5.71-72: brokes with all that can in such a suit / Corrupt the tender honor of a maid.

BROKER, n. Originally, one who broached or tapped a keg, extended to any retailer or middleman. In merchandising, an agent hired to act, usually abroad, in behalf of the merchant. Thus, metaphorically, a representative, not the real thing, and words, as (false) representatives of reality. Also a pawnbroker. When extended into the realm of love, sex, and marriage, a pander, a "flesh-broker, a procurer, a pimp" (Partridge). *A Barbican broker* is of a certain street in London, famous for selling clothing. See ***Agent, Factor.*** *[**2Hen.6*** 1.2.100: a crafty knave does need no broker; ***Ham.*** 1.3.127: Do not believe his vows, for they are brokers; ***John*** 2.1.582: This bawd, this broker, this all-changing word; ***2Gents.*** 1.2.41: A goodly broker; ***T&C*** 3.2.203-4: brokers-between; ***HWhore2*** 3.2.64-65: Knowest thou never a damn'd broker about the city?; ***WHo*** 3.2.8-9: I was first a Puritan, then a Banquerout, then a Broker; ***OldF.*** 1.2.116-17:1 am mad, to see Schollers in the Brokers shop; ***Madam*** 2.1.132: A Barbican broker will furnish me with outside.

BUDGET, n. Originally, *bouge,* or leather bag. A purse or wallet; a metaphor for the mind, with the implication of words as coins. *[**WTale*** 4.3.20: bear the sow-skin bouget; ***EMen*** 515: who would think my master had so much wit in his old rotten budget?

BULLET, n. Perhaps a reference to bullet-money, pellets of silver used as money in the Orient. Here, in a possible four-level pun: in a paronomasia, bullets as billets, small notes of debt or IOUs; coins; literal bullets as from a Pistol (the character addressed); and semen from the two testicles. Also words as coins, ammunition, and notes of discourse or promise (representative currency). With a hidden pun on Pistol/pistole. See ***Discharge.*** *[**2Hen.4*** 2.4.112-15: do you discharge upon my hostess . . . with two bullets; ***Ado*** 2.3.240: quips and sentences and these paper bullets of the brain; ***BBush*** 3.1.84-85: bullets three . . . —Have ye their moneys?

BULLION, n. "Gold or silver in the lump, as distinguished from coin or manufactured articles; also applied to coined or manufactured gold or silver when considered simply with reference to its value as raw material" *(OED). [JofM* 4.1.67: Whole chests of gold in bullion and in coin.

BULL'ON BRASS, n. Also billon or black money. A base metal consisting of gold or silver mixed with large proportions of copper or tin, used to make coins of debased intrinsic value. "The degeneracy of the pure contents of a coin through an alloy" (Palgrave). In medieval French billon was also used for bullion, "precious metals" (Munro). Generally used disparagingly in the plays to indicate a token coinage. Stow[e] reports of Henry IV, "Y^e^ xj. yere of his reygne [1410] began ye alaye of goulde: & ye kyngs sons betyn in ye Chepe" (1), and that in 1552, "o^r^ mony was so base the exchaunge to Andwarp was vnder 17 s.. the li." (45). *[Wily* 322: golden gain, . . . / That precious pearl, . . . / Is counted refuse, worse than bull'on brass.

BUNG, n. Perhaps from Old English pung; a purse or a pickpocket. *[2Hen.4* 2.4.128: you cutpurse rascal! you filthy bung.

BURSE, n. Originally, a purse or wallet. In general, a place of many shops, a meeting place for merchants and money-men. An exchange. In England, first the Royal Exchange founded and built by Sir Thomas Gresham in 1566, and later the New Exchange, or Britain's Burse, built on the Strand in 1609 by the Earl of Salisbury. Stowe reports that many were hurt in clearing land for the burse in 1566, and, moreover, "all whiche chargis was borne by ye citizens of London" (135). See ***Old Exchange.*** ***[EMen*** 486: our business done here at the Burse; ***Maid*** 1.2.34-35: all the gaudy Shops / In *Gressums* Bursse.

BURSEMEN, n. Merchants and money-men, from burse as purse and a market area. ***[Vex.*** 120.

BUSINESS, n., **BUSY**, adj. In general, a mercantile activity: industry, occupation, employment. When extended into love, sex, and marriage, intercourse (Ross). Proverbially, "Love and business teach eloquence" (Herbert). ***[A&C*** 1.2.173; ***WTale*** 1.2.228-29: Perchance are to this business purblind? Say.—Business, my lord?; ***MTerm*** 1.1.112: They're busye 'bout our wives, We 'bout their Lands; ***Beware*** 1.1.153-54: This day and night I'll know no other business / But her.

BUY, v. To exchange money for an item or service. Specifically applied to love, sex, and marriage; to obtain. Also to earn, to bribe, to kill, and to pay restitution. Proverbially, "Better to buy than to borrow" (Tilley, B783). See ***Bought and sold.*** *[**T&C*** 3.3.28: he shall buy my daughter; ***Mac.*** 1.7.32- 33: I have bought / Golden opinions; ***Rich. 3*** 4.4.290: Having bought love with such a bloody spoil; ***1Hen.4*** 4.2.22-23, 33: bought out their services; ***Beware*** 1.2.176: Men buy their slaves, but women buy their masters; ***BBush*** 3.2.31: ye shall buy me bravely; ***MND*** 3.2.426-27: Thou shalt buy this dear, / If ever I thy face by daylight see; ***12N.*** 3.4.3: youth is bought more oft than begg'd or borrow'd; ***NHo*** 5.1.131-32: hee that buies a woman, must take her as she falls; ***MforM*** 5.1.425: buy you a better husband.

C

CALF. See ***Golden calf.***

CANCEL, v. and adj. From to cross out, to annul (by fulfillment) a contract of debt. Metaphorically, to die, to end the bond of life; and intercourse, as the fulfillment of the marriage debt. *[**Ed.2*** 5.4.51:1 seal, I cancel, I do what I will; ***JC*** 1.3.102; ***3Hen.6*** 5.4.79: His statutes cancell'd, and his treasure spent; ***1Hen.4*** 3.2.157: The end of life cancels all bands; ***Rich.3*** 4.4.77: Cancel his bond of life, dear God; ***Mac.*** 3.2.49: Cancel and tear to pieces that great bond; ***Cym.*** 5.4.28: cancel these cold bonds; ***R&J*** 3.3.97-98: what says / My conceal'd lady to our cancell'd love?; ***EMen*** 540: We'll work our lands out of Pisaro's daughters, / And cancel all our bonds in their great bellies.

CANDLE-RENT, n. Rent or income from a house and property that are not kept in good repair. *[**Volp.*** 5.7.17.

CANT, v. To beg or to steal, from cant, the language spoken by thieves and vagabonds.*[**Scorn.*** 449.

CANTORE. See ***Counting-house.***

CARACT. See ***Carat***.

CARAT, n. Also caract, charract, charect. Originally, a weight, of one-third ob. or one-seventy-fourth solidus. A standard measure of the purity of gold, based on twenty-four as the finest. Metaphorically, value, worth, esteem. *[**CofE*** 4.1.28: How much your chain weighs to the utmost charect; ***2Hen.4*** 4.5.161: Other, less fine in carat, [is] more precious; ***Magn***. 1.1.43- 45: You doe mistake / My Caract of your friendship . . . / Or at what rate 1 reckon your assistance.

CARDECUE, n. Literally, a *quart d'ecu,* one-fourth of a French crown. A silver coin first issued in 1574. Notes to lines in various editions place its value in England in the seventeenth century at 6d., 15d., 18d., and 24d., but Frey says positively that the cardecue was legal tender in England in 1625 for 19 ½ d. *[**Well*** 4.3.278; 5.2.32-33: There's a cardecue for you.

Silver cardecue, Henry IV of France.

CARRACT, n. Also carrect. A large merchant ship with the potential of being full of treasure. Metaphorically, a woman; in a cacemphaton, to board her is to have intercourse. *[**Oth***. 1.2.50: he to-night hath boarded a land carract; ***CofE*** 3.2.137: Whole armadoes of carrects.

CARRECT. See ***Carract***.

CASH, n. As is currently used, coin, ready money, specie, as opposed to bonds or other representations of value. Perhaps from the French *casse,* a chest containing money. *[**Hen.5*** 2.1.114-15: I shall have my noble?—In cash, most justly paid; ***HWhore2*** 3.2.39-40: Must have cash and pictures; ***EHo*** 1.1.58: art thou out in the cash; 4.2.311-13: turned two thousand pounds' worth of good land of hers into cash;

MTerm 2.1.78: I am out of cash my selfe; ***Madam*** 4.2.52: Deriv'd from your brother's cash; ***DCourt.*** 2.3.36; *Vex.* 146: one-half in ready cash, the other seal'd for six months; ***BBush*** 1.3.123.

CASHIER, v. and adj. To dismiss from duty, to fire, to abandon. Also to steal, to relieve one of money. *[**Oth.*** 1.1.48; 2.3.375; ***Case*** 4.5.61:1 cashire thee; ***OldF.*** 1.1.325: I casheire you my companie; ***TofA*** 3.4.60: What does his cashier'd worship mutter?; ***MWives*** 1.1.178-79: being fap, sir, was . . . cashier'd; 1.3.6: Discard, . . . cashier; ***HWhore2*** 4.1.395: cashier'd out of pay; ***NHo*** 3.1.101.

CASKET. See ***Coffin.***

CAST, v. To reckon, to figure a total, to calculate, to estimate value. With a pun on to vomit (cast up). *[**JofM*** 1.2.47; ***2Hen.4*** 5.1.20: Let it be cast and paid; ***2Hen.6*** 4.2.85-86: He can write and read and cast accompt; ***A&C*** 3.2.16-17: hearts, tongues, [figures], scribes, bards, poets, cannot / Think, speak, cast, write, sing, number; ***Ham.*** 2.1.111-12: it is as proper to our age / To cast beyond ourselves in our opinions; ***EMen*** 478: I taught them not / To keep a merchant's book, or cast account; ***TofA*** 1.1.212: plain-dealing, which will not cast a man a doit; ***Scorn.*** 427: thou art able to discharge thine office, / And cast up a reckoning of some weight.

CATCH-POLE, v. Originally, one who chases fowl; a tax-collector. To arrest for debt. *[**HWhore1***4.2.165.

CATERPILLAR, n. Slang for a hypocritical, greedy (financially hungry) person, an extortioner, who devours society for his livelihood. Bernard Gilpin, in his sermon "The New Oppressors," says of caterpillars, "They laugh with the monie which maketh others to weepe, & thus are the poore robbed on euerie side without redresse." *[**Trick*** 1.4.8; ***Rich.2*** 2.3.166: caterpillars of the commonwealth; ***2Hen.6*** 4.4.36-37: All scholars, lawyers, courtiers, gentlemen, / They call false caterpillars; ***EMOH*** 3.2.92.

CATTELS, CHATTELS, n. Originally, capital. Personal property, moveable goods, furniture, any possessions other than land. By extension, a wife or mistress. *[**BBofA*** 1.1.348: His lands and cattels; ***Hen.5*** 2.3.48: Look to my chattels and my moveables; ***Shrew*** 3.2.230: She is my goods, my chattels, she is my house; ***DCourt.*** 1.1.17-18: consorted with his moveable chattle, his instrument of fornication, the bawde.

CATZERY, n. Underhanded ways of making a living; roguery, cheating. *[**JofM*** 4.5.12: one that is employed in catzerie.

CECCHINE, n. Also *sequin, chequin, zecchino.* Same as a *ducat* and sometimes a *moccinigo.* A Venetian gold coin first issued around 1280. The obverse shows the doge kneeling before St. Mark. The reverse sometimes has a portrait of Christ. About twenty millimeters in diameter. See ***Ducat*** and Appendix B. *[**Volp**.* 1.3.65-66: every word / Your worship but lets fall, is a *cecchine!',* ***Per.*** 4.2.26: Three or four thousand chequins.

CHAIN, n. Along with keys, indicates the office of steward or bursar in a household. Stewards in the drama are notably niggardly. *[**EMOH*** 1.2.73: a fellow with a great chaine; ***Ado*** 2.1.189-90: like an usurer's chain.

CHANGE, n. Coins, as we mean today, but with a pun on "something different." The implication is that women constantly have an eye out for new sexual partners and that their favors can be bought with money. *[**Oth.*** 1.3.351-52: she must have change . . . put money in thy purse.

CHANGE, v. and adj. In aphaeresis, to (ex)change money, in species or denomination; sometimes with the implication of prostitution. Also in a coin metaphor, to alter in the sense of obliterating the stamp or impress of the king that makes the coin tender. To converse, i.e., trade or exchange the currency of words. *[**EHo*** 1.1.54; ***Ham.*** 3.4.168: use almost can change the stamp of nature; ***WHo*** *2*.1.174-77: this world is like a Mynt, we are no sooner cast into the fire, taken out agen, hamerd, stampt, and made Currant, but presently wee are changde; ***Ado*** 4.1.183: the change of words; ***LLL*** 5.2.238: Will you vouchsafe with me to change a word?

CHAPMEN, n. Buyers (and sellers). Hagglers over prices. Pejoratively, itinerant merchants. In reference to love, sex, and marriage, suitors or bawds. *[**DCourt**.* 1.2.37: like a petty chapman; ***T&C*** 4.1.76; ***LLL*** 2.1.16: base sale of chapmen's tongues; ***Vex.*** 135; ***Gall.*** 183; ***BFair*** 2.5.16; ***BBush*** 1.3.67, 122; 2.3.108.

CHARECT. See ***Carat.***

CHARGE, n. Cost, expense; financial responsibility, money given in trust for safekeeping; value (of charge). In an aphaeresis, (dis)charge, semen. Perhaps with a pun on "gun-powder load" (Le Comte). Proverbially, "Thou dost not bear my charges that thou shouldst command me" (Tilley, C245). *[**1Hen.4*** 1.3.79: at our own charge shall ransom; 2.1.57-58: auditor [with] abundance of charge; 3.1.111: a little charge will trench him here; 3.2.161: Thou shalt have charge and sovereign trust; ***Lear*** 1.1.9: at my charge; ***MofV*** 4.1.257-58: on your charge; 4.1.367: hang'd at the state's charge; ***Well*** 2.3.114: at my father's charge; ***John*** 1.1.49: This expedition's charge; 1.1.256: to my charge; ***CofE*** 1.2.61: so great a charge; 1.2.70: the gold I gave in charge to thee; ***NHo*** 4.3.18: beare the charge; ***WTale*** 1.2.26: To you a charge and trouble; 4.4.258: parcels of charge; ***T&C*** 4.1.58: world of charge; 4.4.126:1 charge thee use her well, even for my charge; ***Rich.3*** 1.2.255: beat [be at or bear?] charges for a looking-glass; ***Scorn.*** 429: I be at charge to pay the footmen; ***BBush*** 3.4.22; ***IHen.6*** 5.5.92: For your expenses and sufficient charge; ***MWives*** 1.4.98-99: 'Tis a great charge to come under one body's hand.

CHARGE, v. To exact a fee, with a pun on "to assail sexually" (Partridge). *[**2Hen.4*** 2.4.121-22: I will charge you.

CHARGEABLE, adj. Expensive. *[**Debts*** 3.2.9; 5.1.170; ***Vex***. 101.

CHARGE-HOUSE, n. A school. Perhaps a boarding school. *[**LLL*** 5.1.83: Do you not educate youth at the charge-house on the top of the mountain?

CHARRACT. See ***Carat.***

CHARTER, n. Also blank. Document for tax collection given to agents of the king. Blank charters were objectionable, since the agent could fill in any amount. Donne, in "Satire III," refers to them as "Kings blanck- charters to kill whom they hate." Stowe notes that as soon as Henry IV took the throne, "were all the seales of blanke chartours brent at the Standarde in Chepe" (52). A *blanc* is also an originally very pure (thus white) silver coin of the fourteenth century and later, also called a *gros blanque,* worth about 10d., but the term does not appear in the plays. *[**Rich.2*** 1.4.48; 2.1.250.

CHATTEL. See ***Cattels***.

CHEAP, adj. Inexpensive, a bargain, a sale, at almost no cost. Also of small value. Proverbially, "Good cheap is dear" (Herbert). See ***Pennyworth***. *[**OldF.*** 2.2.19: good cheap; ***1Hen.4*** 2.4.360: You may buy land now as cheap as stinking mack'rel; 3.3.45; ***2Hen.6*** 1.1.222: cheap pennyworths; ***2Hen.4*** 5.3.19: flesh is cheap and females dear; ***Hen.5*** 4.3.66: hold their manhoods cheap; ***Per.*** 4.2.60: Such a maidenhead were no cheap thing.

CHEAPEN, v. To bargain, to haggle, to bid for, to buy. Also with the implication of lowering in value or price. According to Wriothesley, the Earl of Warwick "as he rode by Eastcheepe to the Court, he chepned a carcasse of mutton, and the butcher held it at xiii s. and he said that was to much; and another said xvi s. and then he answered that it were better he were hanged" (2:48). Extensions include courtship, bargaining for a woman sexually or connubially. *[**HWhore2*** 3.3.43-44: I'll cheapen wares of the man, whilst Bots is doing with his wife; ***Volp.*** 4.1.144; ***Bond.*** 1.3.78; ***Per.*** 4.6.10: cheapen a kiss of her; ***Ado*** 2.3.31: I'll never cheapen her; ***Fatal*** 4.2.86-87: a woman still is currant ware: / Each man will cheapen.

CHEAPSIDE, n. A district in London where many economic transactions took place. Goldsmiths' row, brokers' shops, the financial district. Proverbially, "Cheapside is the best garden" (Tilley, C260). *[**EHo*** 5.5.62: Cheap-side, famous for gold and plate; ***2Hen.6*** 4.7.126; ***NHo*** 2.1.49; ***Madam*** 4.2.25; ***Maid*** title et passim; ***DCourt.*** 2.3.4-5: to Cheapside, to buy a fair peece of plate; ***BFair*** 1.2.8.

CHEAT. See ***Close bawd.***

CHEQUIN. See ***Cecchine.***

CHINK, n. Also chunk. The sound made by coins in the pocket or purse. Ready cash, coins, money in general. A proverbial saying maintains, "No chink no drink" (Tilley, Ml088). When chinks is used in reference to a woman, it includes not only her dowry, but also a pun on certain portions of her anatomy, i.e., sexual favors. *[**Wily*** 225: rich chink; ***R&J*** 1.5.116-17: he that can lay hold of her / Shall have the chinks; ***NHo*** 2.1.248-49: chinck chink, makes the punck wanton and the Baud to winck; 5.1.114: to make the gold chinke in your pockets; ***Drum*** 197: Theres Chunck that makes the Lawier prate, / Theres Chunck that makes a foole of Fate.

CHUFF, n. A miser or greedy person. One who is wealthy but employs his riches only to his own pleasure instead of in their right use, to benefit society. Anyone alienated from the community; someone unwise in proper economic behavior. A fat person, or a combination of all these traits. *[**HWhore1*** 1.2.45; ***NHo*** 5.1.136: fat Citty chuffes; ***1Hen.4*** 2.2.89: fat chuffs.

CHUNK. See ***Chink***.

CHURCH-MONEY, n. Probably church-seed or church-scot, a tax due to the bishop at Martinmas in Saxon law. See ***Lot, Scot****. [**3Lad.*** 348: For now we neither pay Church-money, subsidies, fifteens, scot nor lot.

CHURL, n. Generally, as a term of contempt, a man of base breeding, a bondman. Economically, a miser, a niggard, someone stingy or sparing of generosity. *[**Faust.*** 2.2.122: Covetousness, begotten of an old churl; ***CofE*** 3.1.24: that [good meat] every churl affords; ***R&J*** 5.3.163: o churl, drunk all; ***2Hen.6*** 3.2.212-13: Thy mother took into her blameful bed / Some stern untutor'd churl.

CIPHER, n. Also O. A paradoxical character (person or number) of no value in itself but able to increase the value of any other figure by a factor of ten when placed next to it. Used quibblingly to indicate a person's value. A proverb states, "He is a cipher among numbers" (Tilley, C391). Sometimes used in a pun on "note," or "nothing," for zero in Latin is *nota. [**WTale*** 1.2.6-7: like a cipher / (Yet standing in rich place), I multiply; ***Hen.5*** Pro. 15-18: since a crooked figure may / Attest in little place a million, / And let us, ciphers to this great accompt, / On your imaginary forces work; ***AYLI*** 3.2.290: either a fool or a cipher; ***Lear*** 1.4.192-94: thou art an O without a figure. . . . thou art nothing.

CIRCLE. See ***(Golden) Circle***.

CLACK-DISH, n. Also clap-dish. "A wooden dish with a lid carried and clacked by beggars as an appeal for contributions" *(OED)*. With its variant form of clap-dish, it is easy to see how the metaphorical extension of the term includes female sexual organs, linking money and sex. Also a tongue that wags noisily, lecturing on economic ethics. *[**MforM*** 3.2.126-27: his use was to put a ducat in her clack-dish [perhaps with an additional pun on use as sexual employment and putting to use, i.e., gaining interest on a woman's sexual principal]; ***Gall.*** 274: Widow, hold your clapdish.

CLAP. See ***Handfast.***

CLAP-DISH. See ***Clack-dish***.

CLIP, v., **CLIPPER,** n. To trim, shave, or file metal from the edges of coins, a process made feasible by the erratic coining manufacture of the Renaissance. Coins were simply hammered into roughly circular shapes with a mold. Sometimes the stamp was off-center or even partially off the coin. Pennies, especially, were of uneven weight, for the only specification was that 240 of them be produced from a pound of silver. Eventually the long cross and ridged or milled edges helped more clearly to define the proper and intended edges of coins. Clipped coins were, of course, less valuable than their whole counterparts. Unscrupulous persons used the metal thus obtained for other purposes, *e.g.,* plate and cups, or turned it into the Mint, for a price, to be made into new coins. Stow[e] reports that in 1532 six men, including a priest, were "hangyd & quarteryd for qwynynge of sylvar & clypynge of gowld" (6), and Wriothesley gives a grisly account of a punishment in 1538: "there was a yonge man, servante to the Ladye Pargetour of London, drawne from Newgate to Tower Hill, and there was hanged, his members cut of and bowells brent afore him, and his head cutt of, and his bodie divided in 4 peeces, which yonge man had clipped goulde to the value of 30/.; his head was sett on London Bridge, and his quarters at diverse gates of the cittie" (1:73-74). The term is also used in Renaissance drama to signify the corruption of language (words as the coins of intellectual exchange, communication), embracing, kissing, fornicating, theft, cutting, and battles in war—and may operate on several levels of meaning simultaneously. Tilley cites "He clips the King's English" (K75) to mean drunkenness; here, it has an additional numismatic pun. See ***Mill-money, Shave***. *[**EMen*** 483: a clipper of the king's English; ***Lear*** 4.7.5-6: All my reports ... / Nor more nor dipt; ***WHo*** 2.1.179-80: King Harry groates . . . feele . . . clipping, and melting; 2.1.233: All wiues loue clipping; ***DCourt.*** 1.2.83: Marry salute my friend, clippe his neck; ***A&C*** 4.8.8: clip your wives; ***MadW.*** 4.5.132: We shall thrive one day, wench, and clip enough; ***Corio.*** 1.6.29-30: let me clip ye / In arms; ***Hen. 5*** 4.1.227- 29: it is no

English treason to cut French crowns, and to-morrow the King himself will be a clipper; ***Gall.*** *257.*

CLOSE, n. and v. Originally, to conclude. To strike a bargain, to end negotiations, to agree, to contract. Pun extensions include to join (unite) and to copulate, again comparing sex to traffic. *[**WTale*** 4.4.800-801: Close with him, give him gold; ***MforM*** 5.1.342: Hark how the villain would close now, after his treason; ***T&C*** 3.2.48-49: And 'twere dark you'd close sooner; ***12N.*** 5.1.158: the holy close of lips; ***2Gents.*** 2.5.12-13: after they clos'd in earnest, they parted very fairly; 5.4.117: to make this happy close; ***2Hen.4*** 2.4.326-27: this virtuous gentlewoman to close with us; ***R&J*** 2.6.6: Do thou but close our hands with holy words.

CLOSE BAWD, CHEAT, COURTESAN, n. A surreptitious and insidious type of cozener; the cozenage is perpetrated by someone intimate and trusted by the victim, or by the rogue himself. *[**Debts*** 2.1.52; ***MadW.*** 1.1.111; ***Beware*** 3.3.267.

COFFER, n. Box or chest for the safekeeping of money. In the drama generally used to indicate available funds or the king's total wealth. Metaphorically extended to mean a wife's sexual treasure, her chastity. *[**1Hen.4*** 1.3.85; ***Oth.*** 2.1.208; ***Rich.2*** 1.4.43; ***MforM*** 1.2.151: in the coffer of her friends; ***JofM*** 3.4.89: my purse, my coffer; ***12N.*** 3.4.347: there's half my coffer; ***MWives*** 2.2.274; 292-93: My bed shall be abus'd, my coffers ransack'd; ***OldF.*** 3.1.246-47: still he spends, / And still his Coffers with abundance swell; ***Shrew*** 2.1.350: In ivory coffers I have stuff d my crowns.

COFFIN, n. Also casket. A synonym for coffer. Knowledge of this usage makes Shylock seem slightly less horrid, more logical, when he wishes that Jessica's stolen ducats were in her coffin. *[**Per.*** 3.1.67: Bring me the satin coffin; 5.3.23-24: I op'd the coffin, / Found there rich jewels; ***MofV*** 3.1.90: and the ducats in her coffin; ***Madam*** 3.3.27.

COIN, n. In addition to a piece of metal bearing an impression of the king's, valuable both for its intrinsic metallic value and for the king's word it bears, a coin in Renaissance drama also signifies money in general, ready cash, all official and current money of a realm, and a device or plan. Also "quoin," pudenda (Carey). *[**1Hen.4*** 2.2.36: all the coin; ***WTale*** 4.4.725: stamped coin; ***3Lad.*** 369: cankered coin [ill-gotten or debased]; ***Hen.8*** 3.2.325: the King's coin; ***JofM*** 5.2.107:

about this coin; ***EMen*** 488: Gentlemen . . . must want no coin.

COIN, v. To produce or mint money, to legitimize, to turn into something valuable. To counterfeit, to plot, to invent. By extension of counterfeiting, to have illegitimate children. Since coins are equated to words, to write, to produce witty sayings. *[**Lear*** 4.6.83: they cannot touch me for [coining]; ***1Hen.4*** 3.3.78: coin his nose, coin his cheeks; ***JC*** 4.3.72: coin my heart; ***Hen.5*** 2.2.98: coin'd me into gold; ***TofA*** 2.1.6: the dog coins gold; ***Corio.*** 3.1.78: Coin words; ***TAnd.*** 2.3.5: coin a strategem; ***Cym.*** 2.1.59: hourly coining plots; ***MforM*** 2.4.45-46: do coin heaven's image / In stamps that are forbid; ***WHo*** 2.1.213: What excuse shall I coyne now?; ***EMOH*** Ind. 204-7: Ile prodigally spend my selfe, / ... Ile melt my braine into inuention, / Coine new conceits, ... my richest words; ***T&C*** 1.3.193: coins slanders like a mint.

COINAGE, n. Generally, available money, or cost. Also invention or production, perhaps in the sense of forgery. *[**1Hen.4*** 4.2.8: I'll answer the coinage; ***Ham.*** 3.4.137: This is the very coinage of your brain.

COINER, n. Inventor, producer, "A man regarded as a coin stamper in the mint of sexual intercourse" (Partridge). *[**Cym.*** 2.5.5-6: Some coiner with his tools / Made me a counterfeit.

COLT, v. To fool or to trick, sexually or economically, with a pun on "horse." *[**1Hen.4*** 2.2.37-39: What a plague mean ye to colt me thus?— Thou liest, thou art not colted, thou art uncolted; *Cym.* 2.4.133: She hath been colted by him.

COME OFF, v. To repay a debt; to hand over money. *[**MWives*** 4.3.11.

COMINGS-IN, n. Income, earnings, total worth or value, revenues. A pun extension includes sexual activity (comings-in as sexual ingress, goings-out as ejaculation, poverty as nudity). Proverbially, "A good Coming in is all in all with a widow" (Tilley, C550). Income can also be "an entrance-fee" (Skeat). *[**MofV*** 2.2.163; ***Ram.*** 364: you do keep a whore. . . . How could she maintain you?—Why, by her comings-in; ***Hen.5*** 4.1.243; ***Faust.*** 1.4.4-6: Sirrah, hast thou no comings in?—Yes, and goings out too. . . .—See how poverty jests in his nakedness; ***NHo*** 1.3.167-69: what are her commings in, what does she liue vpon?—Rents sir, Rents, shee liues vpon her Rents.

COMMISSION, n. A financial job, duty, or responsibility; "authority given to act as agent or factor for another in the conduct of business or trade" *(OED);* a warrant by which such responsibility is held and power exercised; by extension, a writ for levying taxes. See ***Benevolence, Charter****. [****MforM*** 1.1.47; ***Hen.8*** 1.2.56-58: The subject's grief / Comes through commissions, which compels from each / The sixt part of his substance, to be levied.

COMMODITY, n. Originally, a convenience. A benefit, a profit, selfish gain; a supply with ready access; ware or merchandise to be traded; expediency or opportunity; commerce in general. A special meaning in the sixteenth century arose to circumvent anti-usury laws. A moneylender would sell goods (commodities) on credit to a petitioner, who could then resell the commodities to the moneylender at a lower price to raise the cash he needed. The interest charge would thus be hidden in the discrepant prices of the transactions. By the usual extension of the economic concept into sexual affairs, an adianoeta on "Pudend. . . . The sexual sense may spring from the ordinary man's tendency to regard a woman as a sexual convenience . . . reserved for his private *use"* (Partridge). Also a prostitute. A *cracked commodity* is a pregnant maid. *[****Lear*** 4.1.20-21: our mere defects / Prove our commodities; ***WTale*** 3.2.93: To me can life be no commodity; ***EHo*** 1.1.36; ***Per.*** 4.2.30-31: our credit comes not in like the commodity; ***1Hen.4*** 4.2.17-18; commodity of warm slaves [conscripted soldiers]; ***Ado*** 3.3.177: a goodly commodity; ***3Lad.*** 331; ***MofV*** 1.1.178: Neither have I money nor commodity; 3.3.27: the commodity that strangers have; ***John*** 2.1.573: tickling commodity; 2.1.597: kings break faith upon commodity; ***HWhore1*** 1.1.96: dead commodity; ***NHo*** 1.2.63-64: I scorne to bee one of your Low-country commodities, I; 4.1.248-49: barter away their light commodities [sexual favors]; 5.1.11; ***CofE*** 4.3.6: Some offer me commodities to buy; ***2Hen.6*** 4.7.127: take up commodities upon our bills**;** ***BFair*** Ind. 214: take up a commodity; *12N.* 3.1.44: commodity of hair; ***2Hen.4*** 1.2.248: 1 will turn diseases to commodity; ***Wit*** 633: I'll do you this commodity; ***BBush*** 3.4.55: to do thee commodity; ***Magn.*** 4.3.3: a crack'd commoditie; ***Madam*** 3.1.81-82: for marriage, and the other thing too; / The commodity is the same; ***MTerm*** 1.1.85: make my course commodities looke sleeke; 2.3.189-90: he shall take up a commoditie of cloath of me; 2.3.205-6: raise double commoditie by exchange; ***WHo*** 2.2.186-87: the commodity of beauty was not made to lye dead vpon any young womans hands; ***MadW***. 2.6.51: This is the commodity of keeping open house; ***DCourt.*** 1.2.31, 34-35: that trade is most honorable that sells the best commodityes ... so the Baud above all, her shop has the best ware.

COMMON-WEALTH, n. In a general sense, the benevolent economics of nature, which consists of fertility and rational increase, augmentation of all that is good and of benefit to individual men and society. Specifically, used in cacemphaton to mean a common citizen, a woman, a prostitute, since her bounty is held in common, used by all; a brothel as the bank of this commonwealth. *[**Well*** 1.1.126-27: the commonwealth of nature; ***2Hen.6*** 4.2.165: hath gelded the commonwealth, and made it an eunuch; ***LLL*** 4.1.41: Here comes a member of the common-wealth; 4.2.75-77: their daughters profit very greatly under you. You are a good member of the common-wealth; ***Ado*** 3.3.168: lechery ... in the commonwealth; ***Bond.*** 1.3.163-65: He thinks women / No part of the republique.—He shall finde / We are a Common-wealth; 3.3.120: common good [woman]**;** ***MforM*** 1.2.101-5: shall all our houses of resort in the suburbs be pull'd down? . . . here's a change indeed in the commonwealth!; ***MofV*** 3.5.37-39: I shall answer that better to the common-wealth than you can the getting up of the Negro's belly.

COMPOUND, v. To come together with the purpose of increase, augmentation, *e.g.,* interest compounded. Sexually extended to mean to conceive a child, copulation with the intent of increase. *[**Hen.5*** 5.2.207-8: compound a boy, half French, half English; ***Lear*** 1.2.128-29: My father compounded with my mother; ***TofA*** 4.3.271-74: thy father . . . put stuff / To some she- beggar and compounded thee / Poor rogue hereditary.

COMPT, n. A reckoning, a judgment with intent to settle a bill, an accounting. The Last Judgment. *In compt* is the process of figuring the totals. *[**Oth.*** 5.2.273: at compt; ***Well*** 5.3.57: the great compt; ***Mac.*** 1.6.26-27: in compt, / To make their audit; ***TofA*** 2.1.34-35: take the bonds . . . / And have the dates in compt [Theobald emendation].

COMPTER, n. Also counter. A coin or token struck in imitation of legitimate coins but in a base metal. A piece of metal used in calculations and in certain games, i.e., span-counter. A general pejorative term for base money, a coin of no intrinsic value, good-for-nothing men. *[**T&C*** 2.2.28: Will you with compters sum; ***WTale*** 4.3.36: I cannot do't without compters; ***Cym***. 5.4.169-70: Your neck, sir, is pen, book, and counters; so the acquittance follows; ***Faust.*** 1.4.35-36: Mas but for the name of french crownes a man were as good haue as many english counters [A text, 1604]; ***AYLI*** 2.7.63: What, for a counter, would 1 do but good?; ***2Hen.6*** 4.2.157- 58: boys went to span-counter for French crowns; ***JC*** 4.3.80: To lock such rascal counters from his friends; ***BBush*** 3.1.124; ***NHo*** 1.2.21.

COMPTIBLE, adj. Astute at reckoning; therefore aware, sensitive. *[**12N.*** 1.5.175-76: I am very comptible, even to the least sinister usage.

CONDOLEMENT, n. A beneficial consolation for a sorrow or loss; in general, a retributory profit. *[**Per.*** 2.1.150-51: certain condolements, certain vails.

CONSIDERATION, n. A remuneration or exchange. "Anything regarded as recompense or equivalent for what one does or undertakes for another's benefit; especially, in the law of contracts, 'the thing given or done by the promisee in exchange for the promise.' It may itself be a promise. No promise is enforceable without consideration, unless made by deed" *(OED). [**Hater*** 123: send me what you promised me for consideration.

CONTRACT, n., v., and adj. Promise to marry. Sell one's soul. Metaphorically, to seal a physical bargain, to copulate, with payment for services rendered implicit. *[**Temp.*** 4.1.19, 84: A contract of true love to celebrate; ***AYLI*** 3.2.314: the contract of her marriage; ***WTale*** 4.4.390: Contract us; 5.1.203-4: will not have / Our contract celebrated; ***Well*** 2.3.177-78: Good fortune . . . / Smile upon this contract; *12N.* 5.1.156: A contract of eternal bond of love; 5.1.261: You would have been contracted to a maid; ***Rich.3*** 3.7.5: his contract with Lady Lucy; 3.7.179: For first was he contract to Lady Lucy; ***R&J*** 2.2.117: I have no joy of this contract to-night; ***MWives*** 5.5.223: she and I (long since contracted); ***MforM*** 3.2.282: And perform an old contracting; 5.1.375: wast thou e'er contracted to this woman; ***Lear*** 5.3.229: I was contracted to them both; ***Debts*** 5.1.278-79: Thou hadst better / Have made a contract with the king of fiends; ***Beware*** 1.2.115: contract myself at midnight to the larder-woman.

CONTRIBUTION. See ***Benevolence***.

CONVEY, v. Euphemistically, to steal, from to convey as to move or carry from one place to another. *[**MWives*** 1.3.29: "Convey," the wise call it. "Steal"?; ***Cym***. 1.1.63: That a king's children should be so convey'd.

CONVEYANCE, n. A written document transferring property, especially land, from one person to another. With a pun on booty stolen and then handed (conveyed) to another thief in the crowd. *[**Ham***. 5.1.110-11: conveyances of his lands; ***BFair*** 2.4.43-44: All the purses and purchase I give you to-day by conveyance.

CONVEYER, n. A thief, with a pun on "carry." *[**Rich.2*** 4.1.317: Conveyers are you all.

CONY-CATCH, v. Generally, to cheat, to swindle, to trick fools out of money. See ***Pursenet***. *[**HWhore1*** 1.2.183; ***HWhore2*** 2.1.282; ***MWives*** 1.1.124-25; 1.3.33: There is no remedy; I must cony-catch; ***Shrew*** 5.1.98- 99: Take heed, Signior Baptista, lest you be cony-catch'd in this business; ***WHo*** 5.1.158.

COPE, v. From Dutch *koop,* a sale. To buy, to bargain for (in marriage), to exchange, to trade away, to deal successfully with, to requite. By extension, to converse (trade words), and to achieve satisfactory sexual relations with a woman. See ***Cheapen***. *[**3Lad.*** 331: To cope for new broom; ***MofV*** 4.1.412: We freely cope your courteous pains; ***AYLI*** 2.1.67:1 love to cope him; ***WTale*** 4.4.424; ***2Hen.6*** 3.2.230: I'll cope with thee; ***Oth.*** 4.1.86: to cope your wife.

COPEMAN, n. A merchant, or a fence of stolen merchandise. *[**Volp.*** 3.7.143-44: He would have sold his part of Paradise / For ready money, had he met a copeman.

COPPER, n. Coins of little value, made of base metal; baseness, to be hidden, to be gilded over. *[**LLL*** 4.3.383: our copper buys no better treasure; ***T&C*** 4.4.105: copper crowns; ***Killed*** 3.2.104: Is all this seeming gold plain copper?

COPPER NOSE. See ***Nose.***

COPY, n. "The transcript of the manorial court-roll, containing entries of the admissions of tenants, according to the custom of the manor, to land held by such tenants in the tenure hence called COPYHOLD" *(OED).* In general, articles of indenture. *[**HWhore1*** 4.1.5; ***Madam*** 2.2.22.

COPYHOLD, n. The tradition of manorial tenure by which tenants held their lands, including churches and colleges; the documents showing such tenure; nickname for a tenant, as opposed to a landowner. *[**Gall.*** 275: I have not so much / As one poor copyhold to thrust my head in; ***Wit*** 634: Old Copyhold.

COUNTER, n. A prison for debtors. In the seventeenth century there were two in London, in Poultry and Wood Streets. Also mentioned as debtors' prisons in the plays are King's Bench, Fleet, Ludgate, and Newgate. With a pun on encounter, put into the Counter. A proverb says, "God keep me from four houses, a Usurer's, a Tavern, a Spital, and a Prison" (Herbert). See ***Compter***. *[**Wit*** 628; ***NHo*** 1.3.150: the house of praier and fasting—the Counter; 5.1.155-56: he may borrow mony of this Merchant, and be layd vp in the Counter, or Ludgate; ***MTerm*** 3.4.90; ***EMOH*** Ind. 44-45: deuoures / More wretches then the *Counters;* ***MadW.*** 3.2.70; ***Madam*** 1.1.35; ***EHo*** 2.2.331; 4.2.328-30: "You shall be encount'red," that is, had to the Counter.

COUNTER-CASTER, n. An accountant, one who reckons with compters. *[**Oth.*** 1.1.31.

COUNTERFEIT, n. and adj. Originally, made in opposition or imitation. Not real or valid, not legal tender, a counterfeit coin. By extension into the sexual realm, a counterfeit woman is "Virtuous-seeming but actually lewd or wanton" (Partridge) and a counterfeit child illegitimate, a bastard. See ***Slip***. *[**1Hen.4*** 2.4.492; 5.4.116: he is but the counterfeit of a man; ***John*** 3.1.99: You have beguiled me with a counterfeit; ***Well*** 3.6.37: this counterfeit lump of ore; ***2Gents.*** 2.4.12; 5.4.53: Thou counterfeit to thy true friend; ***TofA*** 4.3.113-14: the counterfeit matron, / It is her habit only that is honest; ***Cym.*** 2.5.5-6: Some coiner . . . / Made me a counterfeit; ***OldF.*** 5.2.184: this purse is counterfeit; ***R&J*** 2.4.46; ***T&C*** 2.3.26; ***Shrew*** 4.4.92: a counterfeit assurance.

COUNTERFEIT, v. To produce by stealth that which is illegal or illegitimate. To feign propriety. Stow[e] reports that in 1527 "was one Harman drawyn from Newgate to Tyburn, & there hangyd for qwynynge of false golde" (2), and in 1530, three men were "drawne from Newgate to ye Towerhyll, and ther hangyd & quarteryd for countarfeytynge ye kyngs coyne" (4). In his "Sermon XVIII" of 1623, Donne explains the severity of these kinds of penalties: "A principal reason that makes coining and adulterating of money capital in all states, is not so much because he that coins usurps the Prince's authority (for every coiner is not a pretender to the Crown)... as because he that coins injures the public: and no man injures the public more than he who defrauds him, who is God's steward for the public, the King." See ***Clip***. *[**Oth**.* 2.1.243: can stamp and counterfeit advantages; ***Ado*** 2.3.102: May be she doth but counterfeit.

COUNTERPANE, n. An identical copy of a contract; a part of an indenture the serrated edges of which mesh with its counterpart. [***BFair*** Ind.82-83.

COUNTING-HOUSE, n. Also cantore. A room or separate building devoted to the concerns of business: counting comings-in, keeping the account books, writing up bills or correspondence, perhaps meeting with clients. Similar to a modern office. *[**JofM*** 1.l.l.s.d.; 3.1.18; ***EMOH*** 2.6.106.

COURTESAN. See ***Close bawd.***

COURT-HAND, n. The "style of handwriting in use in the English law-courts from the 16th cent, to the reign of George II" (Onions). A certain script used to write legal bills like bonds obligatory. *[**2Hen.6*** 4.2.93-94: he can make obligations, and write court-hand.

COZEN, v., **COZENER**, n. Originally, to claim kinship for profit. To cheat, to deceive, primarily in economic matters. Also with metaphorical sexual extensions and in puns with "cousin." *[**Lear*** 4.6.163: The usurer hangs the cozener; ***Well*** 4.2.76: To cozen him that would unjustly win; 4.5.27-28: I would cozen the man of his wife and do his service; ***JofM*** 2.3.188-89: cozening, forfeiting, / And tricks belonging unto brokery; ***MWives*** 4.5.77- 78: three cozen-germans that has cozen'd all the hosts; 4.5.94: cozen'd and beaten too; 5.5.166-67: cozen'd of money; ***Maid*** 1.1.30: cozend you with a guilded Two-pence; ***Debts*** 5.1.230: devilish practices you used to cozen; ***1Hen.4*** 1.3.255.

CRACK, v., **CRACKED,** adj. To ruin, to spoil the value. Used in reference to coins which, when struck, obtained a crack in the metal, through the device or inscription, and thus were rendered uncurrent. Many of these coins made their way out of the mint but were considered undesirable. When extended into the realm of love and sex, the term has similar implications: to crack virginity is to ruin it; a crack in a wife is a sexual flaw, "a rupture of chastity" (Partridge); a maiden *crack'd within the ring* is deflowered, like a coin of no intrinsic value or legal tender; a *crack'd commoditie* is a pregnant miss; *love sans crack or flaw* is, like a good coin, valuable. Similarly, *crack'd crowns* are broken heads, i.e., ruined soldiers and ruined coins. *[**Corio.*** 1.5.5: a crack'd drachme; ***Cym.*** 4.4.50: a crack'd [life]; ***Per.*** 4.6.142: Crack the glass of her virginity; ***WTale*** 1.2.322: this crack ... in my dread mistress; ***HWhore1*** 3.1.35; ***Ham.*** 2.2.428; ***Magn.*** 4.3.3; ***LLL*** 5.2.415; *1Hen.4* 2.3.93; ***WHo*** 2.1.178-79: the old crackt King *Harry* groates; ***Maid*** 1.1.32-35: there is no woman made without a Flaw . . .—But 'tis a Husband sowders up all Crackes; ***DCourt.*** 1.1.115-16: In Land, the title may be crackt; ***EHo*** 3.2.385: crack'd credits; ***Vex.*** 167: these two crack'd gallants / Are in several bonds.

Silver tester, Henry VIII, cracked in the ring.

CREATE, v. To endow with a patrimony; to set up financially. See ***Make***. *[**HWhore1*** 1.3.100: I'll create thee half mine heir.

CREATURE, n. Used pejoratively to indicate one who becomes dehumanized for economic gain. Applied to women, a prostitute. *[**Well*** 2.3.142: If thou canst like this creature as a maid; ***DCourt.*** 1.1.97-98: a money Creature, One that sels humane flesh; 2.1.83: A creature of a publique use; ***MWives*** 4.2.129-31: the honest woman, the modest wife, the virtuous creature; ***Per.*** 4.2.6: We were never so much out of creatures; 4.6.78: creature of sale; ***Rich.2*** 5.3.17: from the common'st creature pluck a glove; ***Oth.*** 4.1.95.

CREDIT, n. Originally, belief. Honesty, trust, reliability, reputation, advantage, credulity, borrowing power; often with an equivocation on many meanings simultaneously. Proverbially, "Credit lost is like a Venice glass broke," and "He that has lost his Credit is dead to the world" (Tilley, C814, C817). *[**Lear*** 3.1.35: on my credit; ***CofE*** 3.2.22: compact of credit; 4.1.68: Consider how it stands upon my credit; 5.1.6: credit infinite; ***Oth.*** 1.3.97; ***MadW***. 1.1.30-31: how can they keep their countenance that have lost their credits; 1.1.123: for my credit; ***MforM*** 5.1.244: his worth and credit; ***MofV*** 1.1.180: try what my credit can . . . do; ***Shrew*** 4.2.107: His name and credit shall you undertake; ***1Hen.4*** 1.2.55-56: I have used my credit; *TofA* 2.1.23; ***Per.*** 4.2.30-31: our credit comes not in like the commodity; ***Faust.*** 4.7.63: I'll gage my credit, 'twill content your grace; ***JofM*** 1.1.57: credit in the custom-house; ***WHo*** 4.1.20: Who are you, some man of credit?; ***AYLI*** 1.1.126-27: I wrastle for my credit.

CREDIT, v. To believe one's word, to trust. *[**MadW***. 3.1.83: credit me; ***Per***. 5.1.123: make [my] senses credit thy relations; ***Temp.*** 1.2.102: To credit his own lie.

CREDITOR, n. One to whom a debt, usually of money, is owed. By extension, an audience at a play, for the author owes them a debt for their admission price. Metaphorically, a friend or lover. *[**CofE*** 4.4.120; ***MofV*** 3.1.113; ***TofA*** 3.4.104; ***2Hen.4*** Ep. 12; ***John*** 3.3.21-22: a soul counts thee her creditor, / And with advantage means to pay thy love.

CREDITRESS, n. A woman to whom one owes a debt (semen) or who owes the man her treasure (sexual favors); one's mistress. *[**Fatal*** 3.1.92, 94: In recompense of all my dutious service, /. . . Become my Creditresse.

CROESUS, n. King of Lydia, he conquered most of the Greeks in Asia. He had inherited great wealth from his father and augmented it by his own successes, so that he became a legendary figure of prosperity. Solon, the wise man, however, warned him that money could not buy him kinship, contentment, or a happy death, and, indeed, he came to an unhappy end in 546 B.C. A proverb states, "As rich as Croesus" (Tilley, C832). *[**Ram***. 273: Able to spend the wealthy Croesus' store.

CROSS, n. and v. A general term for any number of coins with the popular cross stamped on the reverse. Sometimes a penny, sometimes a coin of greater value. In England from 1180 to 1247 all silver pennies carried a short cross, which did not reach to the edge of the coin. Since these were easy to clip metal from without marring the device, in 1248 the long cross penny was first issued to help remedy the clipping problem. Coins with crosses were also minted in the other major European countries. This coin lends itself to many puns: bearing a hardship or burden; a disagreement, or to be contrary, to thwart; to reward, i.e., give a cross; to cross out or cancel a debt; and a religious symbol (cf. ***Angel)***. Cross and pile means heads or tails. (See Tilley, C834). ***[JofM*** 2.3.293: golden cross; ***Vex.*** 149: your good husband will leave you ne'er a cross i' th' house to bless you with; ***AYLI*** 2.4.12-14: I should bear no cross if I did bear you, for I think you have no money in your purse; ***2Hen.4*** 1.2.225-26: too impatient to bear crosses; ***LLL*** 1.2.34: crosses love not him; ***Cym.*** 5.4.101: Whom best I love, I cross; ***TofA*** 1.2.162: he'ld be cross'd; ***Gall.*** 216: the cross of this silver; ***WHo*** 2.3.59-60: I haue not one crosse about me, onely you two; ***MadW.*** 3.2.150: the thought of joys, and sight of crosses; ***BFair*** 1.4.123; ***Killed*** 2.3.30: I cannot get a cross of you; 3.3.3: I cannot spare a cross; ***Lear*** 5.3.279: these same crosses spoil me [fencing move/hardship/coin]; ***BBush*** 3.2.20: to-morrow's cross'd [financially ruined],

CROSS-BITE, v. To enact a double ploy, to cheat the original cheater. In reference to coins, possibly to bite off their edges, to clip. [***JofM*** 4.5.12- 13: one that is employed in catzerie / And cross-biting.

CROWN, n. An English gold coin first issued in 1526, worth 5s., called the Crown of the Double Rose. This was the first English coin to be minted from twenty-two rather than twenty-four carat gold. The twenty-two carat gold thus became known as crown gold and has been the standard of fineness since 1634. Under Elizabeth the gold crown reached a low value of 3s. 4d. and was discontinued in 1601. A crown is also an English silver coin first issued in 1551, also worth

5s. The obverse shows the king mounted on a horse; the reverse has a shield and the long cross. About forty millimeters in diameter. A silver half-crown from 1601 shows a portrait of the Queen, with the long cross and shield on the reverse.About thirty-four millimeters in diameter. A double crown (coined by James I) is worth 10s. A thistle crown of James I is worth 4s., later valued up in 1611 to 4s. 4 ¾ d., and discontinued in 1612. Crown also refers to the French crown, the *ecu d'or,* first issued in 1336 and later imitated in England. Stow[e] reports: "The same yere [1526] ye vj. day of September was proclamyd of goulde ye frenche crowne iiij.s. vj.d., ye halffe noble iij.s. ix.d., ye angell noble vij.s. vj.d., and ye riall xj.s. iij.d., & so every pese affter yt valewe" (2). In 1554 Mary valued French crowns at 6s. 4d., and in 1562 Elizabeth devalued them to 4s. *(TRP).* See ***Appendix E***. This term lends itself to many puns in the drama: the two halves of an eggshell; a diadem; cracked crowns as debased coinage, illegitimately held sovereignship, and heads split by war; payment (sometimes a half-crown) for a prostitute and the syphilis (French crown) that she gives in return; in this vein dollars are like crowns, for they are the pains (dolours) of syphilis (the French crown); treacherous crowns are bribes; crowns (like coins) are often compared to words. Guilders are equated to French crowns. Half a crown buys a pair of gloves, is a week's allowance for a maiden, and is a high price to pay for a seat in the theater; two crowns is the price for a minstrel song; five hundred crowns is blood-money for a murder; one thousand crowns is a substantial reward; and a store of crowns indicates great wealth. See ***Ecu, Gridiron***. *[**Lear*** 1.4.156; ***1Hen.4*** 1.2.132: stuff your purses full of crowns; 2.3.93: crack'd crowns; ***T&C*** 4.4.105: some with cunning gild their copper crowns; ***Case*** 5.1.24-25: bid thy hands shed golden drops, / Let these bald french crownes be vncouered; ***Maid*** 4.3.23; ***Drum*** 200; ***Prod.*** 4.3.59; ***Well*** 2.2.22; ***LLL*** 2.1.129; 3.1.141; ***MND*** 1.2.95- 96: your French-crown-color . . . , your perfit yellow; 1.2.97: Some of your French crowns have no hair; ***BBush*** 2.1.68; 3.5.27; ***Scorn***. 430; ***MforM*** 1.2.50-52; ***Oth.*** 2.3.90: King Stephen . . . His breeches cost him but a crown; ***Rich.2*** 2.1.293: Redeem from broking pawn the blemish'd crown; ***2Hen.4*** 2.4.174: give crowns like pins; ***Hen.5*** 2. Pro. 22: treacherous crowns; 2.2.89: light crowns; 4.1.227-28: it is no English treason to cut French crowns; 4.4.38: brave crowns;

2Hen.6 2.1.20: a crown, the treasure of thy heart; 4.2.157-58: boys went to span-counter for French crowns; 4.10.27; ***3Hen.6*** 2.5.57; ***Faust.*** 1.4.33-34 [A text, 1604]; ***JofM*** 4.5.46: Here's many words, but no crowns; 4.6.45; ***Dido*** 4.3.53: Each word she says will then contain a crown; ***1Tamb.*** 4.2.92-94: Not all the kings and emperors of the earth, / If they would lay their crowns before my feet, / Shall ransom him; ***Heir*** 130; ***Wit*** 628, 633; ***HWhore1*** 3.1.71-72: I'll so batter your crown that it shall scarce go for five shillings; ***Case*** 5.1.62: a golden crowne [coin], *laques* shall be a king; ***WHo*** 3.3.16: lauish halfe a Crowne on his Leachery; ***BFair*** Ind. 17; ***DCourt.*** 1.1.122-23: doe you give them, the french Crowne, they'le give you the french.

Gold crown of the single rose, Henry VIII.

Gold crown of the double rose, Henry VIII.

Silver crown, Edward VI.

CRUSADO, n. Also *cruzado*. A Portuguese gold coin first issued in 1457. The reverse shows a short or a long cross, hence the name of the coin. This was the first coin struck from gold from the new world. About twenty-four millimeters in diameter. The inscription reads, "IN HOC SIGNO VINCES" ("In this sign shall you conquer"), said by Constantine about the sign of the cross. Current during the Renaissance in England for about 6s. 8d. (the long cross crusado for 6s. 4d.). *[**Case*** 5.3.36; ***Oth.*** 3.4.25-26: purse / Full of crusadoes; ***HWhore1*** 3.1.257; ***OldF.*** 2.2.60.

CRUZADO. See ***Crusado***.

Portuguese gold crusado.

CUE, n. Also Q. Slang for a farthing, probably an abbreviation for quadrans, as a farthing is one-fourth of a penny. Stow[e] uses the abbreviation qr. to indicate a farthing (24). With a pun on an actor's cue. See ***Cardecue***. *[**Ram***. 298: And took I not my cue?

CURRENT, adj. Originally, running. "Passing from hand to hand; in circulation; in general use as a medium of exchange"

(OED). Genuine, as opposed to counterfeit; widespread; authoritative; recognized, known. By extension, in reference to women, current ware, in demand, sexually willing, available. See ***Ware***. *[**OldE*** 1.1.301-02: ten pieces of bright gold, / Currant in any Realme; ***1Hen.4*** 2.3.94: crack'd crowns, / And pass them current; 4.1.5; ***2Hen.4*** 2.1.120-21: The one you may do with sterling money, and the other with current repentence; ***Rich.2*** 1.3.231: Thy word is current with him for my death; ***Rich.3*** 1.3.255: Your fire-new stamp of honor is scarce current; 2.1.95: go current from suspicion; 4.2.9: try if thou be current gold; ***Fatal*** 4.2.86: currant ware; Ass 3.1.12: His name is currant; ***HWhore1*** 5.2.515: The cuckold's stamp goes current in all nations; ***NHo*** 1.2.82-83: a woman is mans stampe, wee are not currant till wee passe from one man to another; ***WHo*** 2.1.174-77: this world is like a Mynt, we are no sooner cast into the fire, taken out agen, hamerd, stampt, and made Currant, but presently wee are changde.

CURRENT GOLD. See ***Gold***.

CUSTOM, n. and v. Also customage. Common usage, habit, tradition; a tax, toll, or duty levied on commercial activities like the movement of merchandise, or exacted by tradition; habits of trade, patronage; the merchandise itself. By extension, sexual habits and sex as commerce. See ***Form***. *[**Gall.*** 184: I'll buy your custom; ***JofM*** 1.1.52-53: yourself / Will come and custom them; 1.1.63: The very custom barely comes to; ***Debts*** 4.2.24: He owes us, and his custom; ***Shrew*** 4.3.99: you shall hop without my custom; ***Per.*** 3.1.52: strong in custom; 4.2.138-39: you'll lose nothing by custom; ***Ham.*** 3.4.161: That monster custom; 4.5.105: custom not known; ***Oth.*** 3.3.122: tricks of custom; ***Vex***. 99: safe deliver'd with our customage; 111: what woman can have a husband, but you must have custom for him?; ***DCourt***. 1.2.132-33: Can custome spoile, what nature made so good? /. . . Beauti's for use.

CUSTOMAGE. See ***Custom***.

CUSTOMER, n. One who makes a living by traffic or custom; by extension, a prostitute or perhaps "a male frequenter of brothels" (Partridge). *[**Well*** 5.3.286: some common customer; ***Oth***. 4.1.119: I marry [her]! What? a customer!; ***MforM*** 4.3.4.

CUSTOM-HOUSE, n. A place of business transactions or the settling of taxes on imported merchandise. *[**JofM*** 1.1.57; ***WHo*** 2.1.124.

CUSTOM-SHRUNK, adj. Decreased in patronage, reduced trade, shortage of customers, here with reference to a brothel. *[**MforM*** 1.2.84.

CUT, v. Like clip, to shave or trim the edges of coins for fraudulent profit. Also to be cut off, left without an inheritance; economically to diminish; and to steal a purse. This term has wonderful pun extensions, all used in addition to the coin meaning: to cut or kill humans in battle; to castrate; to abuse or use someone badly; to perform a barber's task. See ***Clip**, **Geld**, **Shave***. *[**AYLI*** 2.3.25: to cut you off; ***Hen.5*** 4.1.228; ***TAnd**.* 5.1.95: wash'd, and cut, and trimm'd; ***JofM*** 2.3.112:1 can cut and shave; ***TofA*** 3.4.92: Cut my heart in sums; ***WTale*** 4.4.614-15: cut most of their festival purses; ***Well*** 4.3.279-80: cut th' entail from all remainders; ***MWives*** 1.4.111-12: I will cut all his two stones; ***John*** 2.1.96: Cut off the sequence of posterity; ***JC*** 4.1.9: cut off some charge in legacies.

D

DANDIPRAT. See ***Pence.***

DATE-BROKE, adj. Bonds obligatory on which payment is overdue; the agreed date for payment has been broken. See ***Break**. [**TofA*** 2.2.37: date- broke bonds.

DATELESS. See ***(Longer) Date.***

DAYS. See ***Golden (and Silver) Days, (Longer) Date**.*

DEAR, adj. Valuable, expensive, important, highly esteemed. With an adnominatio on deer. Ross "suspects something grimy here, but . . . [is] not sure what it is." *[**Lear*** 1.1.20-21: no dearer in my account; 3.1.19: Commend a dear thing to you; ***TofA*** 1.1.124: at my dearest cost; ***1Hen.4*** 5.4.107-8: Death hath not strook so fat a deer to-day, / Though many dearer, ***1Hen.6*** 4.2.54: they shall find dear deer of us; ***OldF**.* 2.2.18-19: Motley so deere, and fooles so good cheape.

DEBASE, v. Also abase, abate, diminish. Numismatically, the government's way to reduce the value of coins, by proclaiming each coin worth a lower nominal exchange (see ***Appendix E***) or by reducing the intrinsic value of the metal (through weight or alloy) while still allowing the coin to circulate at the same nominal rate. Wriothesley reports of a "deminishing of the coyne of shillinges and grotes" on 8 May 1551, to 9d. and 3d., respectively, "After which proclamation made the people within the cittie of London murmured sore and sett upp booth their wares and victuales at higher prices" (2:97). This practice did much to undermine the concept of true and inviolable value. In the plays used only figuratively, as applied to persons, to lower in status or position (social and physical), to demean (to kneel), to lessen in value. Appears in aphaeresis with (de)base. *[**Rich.2*** 3.3.127: We do debase ourselves; 3.3.190-91: you debase your princely knee / To make the base earth proud; ***Corio***. 3.1.135-36: we debase / The nature of our seats; ***Rich.3*** 1.2.246: will she yet abase her eyes on me.

DEBITOR AND CREDITOR, n. A bookkeeper or accountant; also the register of debits and credits, an account book. By extension, the final accounting, death. *[**Oth.*** 1.1.31; ***Cym***. 5.4.168.

DECAYED, adj. Financially ruined or declined in fortunes, with the implication that pecuniary irresponsibility or inexpertise is the cause. *[**Well*** 5.2.24; ***CofE*** 4.3.26-27: takes pity on decay'd men and gives them suits of durance; ***Corio***. 5.2.44: a decay'd dotant; ***Madam*** 1.3.83; ***DCourt***. 1.1.102-05: A poore decayed mechanicall mans wife, her husband is layd up, may not she lawfully be layd downe, when her husbands onely rising, is by his wifes falling?; ***Vex***. 101: twice have I rais'd / His decayed fortunes to a fair estate; ***Debts*** 2.1.78-79: ladies / Of errant knights decay'd.

DEED (OF GIFT), n. A legal document that specifies the exchange of property or donation to be made. Its presence in the drama is representative of increased contractual relations between men, indeed, encroachment of written bonds into arenas where human bonds by tradition should suffice. Sometimes with a pun on document/action and gift/act, especially in reference to sexual relations: "deed of love, copulation" (Ross). *[**EMen*** 555:Hath made a deed of gift of all his lands; 557; ***MofV*** 4.1.394; 5.1.292; ***Faust.*** 2.1.88: A deed of gift of body and of soul; *T&C* 3.1.131-32: hot blood, hot thoughts, and hot deeds; 3.2.55: Words pay no debts, give her deeds; 4.5.98: Speaking [in] deeds, and deedless in his tongue; 5.3.111-12: My love with words and errors still she feeds, / But edifies another with her deeds; ***OldE*** 1.2.94-95: cannot borrow fiue shillings of him neither in word nor deede; ***Ham.*** 4.3.39-42: this deed . . . must send thee hence; ***MforM*** 3.2.177: dark deeds darkly answer'd; ***1Hen.4*** 3.2.148: To engross up glorious deeds; ***Per.*** 4.6.29: she'd do the deeds of darkness.

DEFACE, v. To cancel or obliterate, with reference to bonds, financial contracts, and coins. *[****MofV***** 3.2.299: deface the bond; ***1Hen.6*** 5.5.28-29: How shall we then dispense with that contract, / And not deface your honor.

DEFEATED, adj. Frustrated, in the sense of losing out on hoped-for or expected wealth. *[****Fatal***** 1.1.146.

DEFEATURE, n. Undoing, defeat, ruin in financial matters, with an aphaeretic adnominatio on facial features. *[****CoE***** 2.1.98: the ground of my defeatures; 5.1.300: written strange defeatures in my face.

DELIVER, v. Release from debt or prosecution for default by remitting a certain amount; to hand money (or valuables) over. *[****Gall.***** 245: But forty shillings will deliver me; ***MofV*** 3.3.22-23: I oft deliver'd from his forfeitures / Many; 4.1.416: I, delivering you, am satisfied; ***CofE*** 5.1.285: pay the sum that may deliver me; ***Rich.3*** 1.4.247.

DEMESNES, n. Domain. Land ownership as an indication of wealth, sometimes with an aphaeretic adnominatio on "means." Also a woman's sexual wealth, portions of her anatomy. *[****Ram.***** 271, 283; ***Prod.*** 2.4.170: of great demeanes and wealth; ***R&J*** 2.1.19-20: quivering thigh, / And the demesnes that there adjacent lie; 3.5.180.

DENIER, n. A French copper penny or silver-billon penny, first coined by Charlemagne in 768, originally with a short cross on the obverse *and fleur-de-lis* on the reverse. About sixteen millimeters in diameter. Named after the Roman denarius; a douzain is *duo-denarius.* Usually used pejoratively, as something of minuscule value. Also a measure of weight and fineness (in silver), although not in the plays. *[****Killed***** 5.1.39: In all the world I have not one denier; ***Ass*** 3.3.188: Not a deneer more; ***1Hen.4*** 3.3.79: I'll not pay a denier; ***Shrew*** Ind. 1.9: not a denier; ***Rich.3*** 1.2.251: a beggarly denier; ***Ram.*** 273: Not a denier is left; ***Prod.*** 4.2.4.

Denier tournois, Charles II, Arches Principality.

DESPATCH, v. Slang for to spend. *[**Wit*** 630.

DIMINISH, See ***Debase***.

DING-DONG, n. The sound of coins in the pocket or purse. See ***Chink.*** *[**Wit*** 645.

DISABLE, v. To injure or impair one's fortunes, to spend too much in a frivolous and unthinking manner. *[**MofV*** 1.1.123: disabled mine estate.

DISCHARGE, n., v., and adj. To pay a debt; to fulfill an obligation; to make a financial settlement. A special pun occurs on pay/discharge a bullet (billet)/ejaculate (Le Comte suggests defecate). Also to vomit. See ***Bullet.*** *[**CofE*** 4.1.13: discharge my bond; ***TofA*** 2.2.12: Would we were all discharg'd; ***MofV*** 3.2.273: The present money to discharge the Jew; 4.1.208: to discharge the money; ***T&C*** 3.2.86-87: vowing more than the perfection of ten, and discharging less than the tenth part of one; 4.4.41: With the rude brevity and discharge of one; ***3Hen.6*** 5.5.87-88: Discharge the common sort / With pay and thanks; ***HWhore1*** 1.2.57-58: I'll discharge at my day; ***MTerm*** 4.1.48; ***WHo*** 3.1.6: had discharged his bond; ***2Hen.4*** 2.4.112- 15: do you discharge upon my hostess . . . with two bullets; ***Scorn.*** 427: discharge thine office, / And cast up a reckoning.

DISPOSSESS, v. To disinherit an heir, with the implication of abandonment. *[**TofA*** 1.1.139: dispossess her all; ***John*** 1.1.131: To dispossess that child.

DOG. See ***Black dog***.

DOIT, n. Also *duit.* A copper penny from the Low Countries, first issued around 1580, worth about half a farthing, or 1/8 d. About twenty-two millimeters in diameter. In the plays used contemptuously, as a coin of almost no value. [***MofV*** 1.3.140-41: take no doit of usance; ***TofA*** 1.1.212: not. . . a doit; ***Temp***. 2.2.32; ***Corio.*** 1.5.6: irons of a doit; 4.4.17: dissension of a doit; 5.4.57; ***Per***. 4.2.51; ***A&C*** 4.12.37: For poor'st diminutives, for doits; ***2Hen.6*** 3.1.112: That doit that e'er I wrested from the King; ***2Hen.4*** 3.2.19: little John Doit; ***Killed*** 5.1.28; ***BBush*** 2.1.173: One little doit; 4.3.33: I'll do it to a doit.

Doit, Low Countries, 1598, copper alloy.

DOLOR, DOLLAR, n. Probably from the German *thaler,* a silver coin first struck in 1525, then worth about three marks, or 2s. 11d. Also refers to the Spanish silver piece of eight, worth eight *reales,* in the seventeenth century current for 4s. 6d. See ***Appendix B.*** It generally appears in a pun on dolors, pains or sorrows or disease. Forty dollars is a cheap price for a horse. [***Lear*** 2.4.54-55: thou shalt have as many dolors for thy daughters as thou canst tell in a year; ***MforM*** 1.2.50: three thousand dolors a year; ***Temp***. 2.1.18-19: A dollar.—Dolor comes to him; ***Mac.*** 1.2.62; ***Faust.*** 4.5.13-14.

Silver thaler, Philip IV of Brabant, 1562.

DOPPIA. See ***Cecchine, Double ducat.***

DOUBLE DUCAT, n. An Italian gold coin struck in the early sixteenth century, worth twice the value of a *ducat,* or about 18s. See ***Appendix B.*** *[**MofV*** 2.8.19; ***Drum*** 198.

DOUZAIN. See ***Denier.***

DOWER, n. Also dowry. Originally, to give or to endow. The economics of marriage: money left to a widow by her deceased husband; money and property that the bride brings into a marriage; a price that a groom gives to relatives of the bride to obtain her; or an endowment. Proverbially, "A great dowry is a bed full of brambles" (Herbert). *[**Lear*** 1.1.44; 1.1.241: She is herself a dowry; ***Temp.*** 3.1.53-54: my modesty / (The jewel in my dower); ***Well*** 2.3.143-44: she / Is her own dower; 5.3.328: Choose thou thy husband, and I'll pay thy dower; ***1Hen.6*** 5.1.44; ***3Hen.6*** 3.2.72: mine honesty shall be my dower; ***MWives*** 1.1.239; ***Shrew*** 2.1.343; 4.4.45; ***MforM*** 1.2.150; ***Beware*** 1.1.53-54: Little money sh' has brought me; / View. but her face, you may see all her dowry; ***AYLI*** 3.3.55: [horns] is the dowry of a wife.

DOWRY. See ***Dower.***

DRACHMA, n. "As much as one can hold in the hand" *(OED).* The ancient Greek unit of value, and a silver coin equal to the *franc,* six *obols,* and about 10d. Also the Jewish one-quarter *shekel,* and a general term for a 'mall quantity. A cracked *drachma* is entirely worthless. *[**Bond.*** 3.3.32: Discouer to a Drachma; ***JC*** 3.2.242; 4.3.73: drop my blood for drachmaes; ***Corio.*** 1.5.5: a crack'd drachme.

DRAUGHT, n. Today, a check; a document that is an order to present money to the bearer or person named. With a pun on a potion to drink. *[**Scorn.*** - . 7: I have presented the usurer with a richer draught than ever Cleopatra swallowed; he hath sucked in ten thousand pounds worth of my land more than he paid for; ***BFair*** 2.4.58: Drink your draught of indenture.

DREAM. See ***Golden dream.***

DROP, n. and v. The smallest possible amount. Metaphorically extended to mean slang for a coin. Perhaps in oblique reference to a proverb, "His money comes from him like drops of blood" *(The Oxford Dictionary of English Proverbs [ODEP]),* referring to a niggard. See ***Golden drops***. ***[TofA*** 3.4.96: Five thousand drops pays that [blood as money]; **JC** 4.3.72- 73: coin my heart, / And drop my blood for drachmaes.

DROP-HEIR, n. A nickname that probably indicates a prodigal who has spent his current funds or proven himself too irresponsible for his patrimony. ***[MforM*** 4.3.15.

DROSS, n. Dregs. Refuse, or the worthless part of metals. A pejorative term for money. A proverb holds, "No Gold without dross" (Tilley, G289). ***[John*** 3.1.165: vile gold, dross, dust; ***Faust.*** 5.1.105: all is dross that is not Helena; ***Heir*** 113: a man that never lov'd / For any thing call'd good, but dross and pelf; ***OldF.*** 1.1.309-10: for the loue of drosse thou hast despised / Wisedomes diuine embrace.

Gold ducat, Venice, 1606-1612.

Gold double ducat, Ferdinand and Isabella, Low Countries.

DUCAT, n. An Italian gold coin first issued in 1284 (the *zecchino d'oro* from *zecca,* the mint [Munro]) and widely copied, current through the Renaissance. The reverse shows the doge kneeling before St. Mark, and the reverse of some ducats pictured Christ. These are probably the "Christian ducats" referred to by Shylock, *i.e.,* the coins themselves, not their method of having been earned. About twenty millimeters in diameter. The inscription on many ducats reads "SIT TIBI XRE DAT Q TV REGIS ISTE DVCAT" ("To thee, O Christ, be dedicated this duchy which you rule"). The name of the coin was erroneously thought to have derived from the last word of the inscription, but it in reality derived from the Apulian *ducat* (first issued in 1140 in silver), after which the Italian coin was modeled. The gold *ducat* was worth about 9s. Also a money of account in Venice in the fifteenth century and an Italian silver coin worth about 3s. 6d. See ***Appendix B***. A European *ducat* current in Holland during the Renaissance was worth 9s. 4d. Also a general term for any coin or piece of money. In the plays a single ducat or three odd ducats is a small, trifling sum; forty ducats can buy enough poison for suicide or a beautiful ring; one thousand ducats is a substantial fee; two thousand ducats is the price of a diamond or, per annum, a good marriage settlement; three thousand ducats a year is a good income; and ten thousand ducats is a breathtaking wager. In cacemphaton, perhaps, testicles. *[**3Lad.*** 313; ***CofE*** 4.1.30; 4.1.105; 4.3.83; ***2Gents.*** 1.1.137: not so much as a ducat; ***R&J*** 5.1.59; ***Ham.*** 3.4.23: Dead, for a ducat, dead; *Ado* 2.2.53; ***MofV*** 1.3.1; 2.8.16: Christian ducats; 2.8.19; 2.8.22: she hath the stones on her and the ducats; 3.1.86; ***Shrew*** 2.1.369; ***Faust.*** 5.1.4; ***12N.*** 1.3.22; ***Cym.*** 1.4.150-51; ***HWhore1*** 1.1.76; 1.2.29; ***OldF.*** 1.2.180; ***Beware*** 2.2.304; ***MforM*** 3.2.126-27: his use was to put a ducat in her clack-dish.

DUCK-EGG, n. A silly and apparently meaningless pun on *ducat.* One proverb refers to the taking of eggs for money (Tilley, E90). *[**3Lad.*** 313: carry her three or four ducats from me. . . .—Duck-eggs? yes, I'll carry 'em; ***WTale*** 1.2.161: Will you take eggs for money?

DUIT. See ***Doit.***

DUNGHILL, n. A derogatory term for a merchant and his money, indicating the low repute in which traders were held, partly because middlemen were suspect since they made profit from no labor, and partly because most were unscrupulous and would cheat anyone for profit. In his sermon on "The Rich Man" Thomas Adams says, "When the sunne of prosperitie heates the dunghill of riches, there is engendered the snake of pride." *[**BBush*** 2.3.75-77: a dunghill ... a merchant! / A petty fellow! One that makes his trade / With oaths and perjuries!; ***John*** 4.3.87: Out, dunghill!; ***2Hen.6*** 1.3.193: Base dunghill villain and mechanical.

DUNGHILL-MUCK, n. A general derisive term for money; filthy lucre. One proverb states that "Muck and money go together" *(ODEP),* another, that "Money, like dung, does no good till it is spread" (Tilley, M1071). See ***Muck.*** *[**Vex*** 191.

DURANCE, n. Imprisonment; to be under arrest for forfeited bonds or other debts. With a pun on durable cloth. *[**CofE*** 4.3.27: suits of durance; ***12N.*** 5.1.275-76: He upon some action / Is now in durance; ***2Hen.4*** 5.5.34: in base durance and contagious prison.

DUST, n. Because it is made of metal taken from the ground, a metaphorical term for money in general. *[**John*** 3.1.165-66: By the merit of vile gold, dross, dust, / Purchase corrupted pardon; *[**T&C*** 3.3.178: Give to dust that is a little gilt, / More laud than gilt o'erdusted.

DUTCH GOLD. See ***Arsedine***.

DYE, n. A mold used for stamping a coin, with a pun on color or appearance (with an extended pun on investments/vestments, clothes, and the typical equation of words and coins). *[**Ham***. 1.3.127-28: Do not believe his vows, for they are brokers, / Not of that dye which their investments show.

E

EARNEST, n. Also earnest money. "A sum of money paid down on conclusion of a bargain as a security for its due performance. . . . [It] establishes the validity of a contract for the sale of goods of a value exceeding £10, which might otherwise be void under the statute of frauds" (Palgrave). A down payment, an advance, with a pun on sincere; a down payment for a bride, as sealing a betrothal; a material representation of a promise. *[**Lear*** 1.4.94: there's earnest of thy service; ***CofE*** 2.2.24-25: your jest is earnest, / Upon what bargain do you give it?; ***WTale*** 4.4.642-46: Are you earnest, sir? . . . Indeed I have had earnest, but I cannot with conscience take it; ***Ado*** 2.1.40: take sixpence in earnest; 5.1.195; ***Per.*** 4.2.44-45: I have lost my earnest; ***Hen.5*** 2.2.169: golden earnest; 5.1.63: I take thy groat in earnest of revenge; ***1Hen.6*** 5.3.16: In earnest of a further benefit; ***Gall.*** 273: I'll leave a kiss with you, / As earnest of a better gift to-morrow; ***HWhore2*** 1.1.215; ***Fatal*** 5.1.51-52: I must have ernest: /1 cannot pay my debts so; ***2Gents.*** 2.5.12-13: after they clos'd in earnest, they parted; ***Rich.3*** 5.1.22: given in earnest what I begg'd in jest; ***TofA*** 4.3.168; ***Mac.*** 1.3.104: an earnest of a greater honor; 1.3.132: earnest of success; ***Cym.*** 1.5.65: an earnest of a farther good.

ECU, n. A French gold coin deriving its name from the device of a shield which it bore, first issued in 1266 and reissued as the *ecu d'or* in 1336. About twenty-five millimeters in diameter. The *ecu a la couronne* was issued in 1385; the *ecu a la croisette* was coined in the sixteenth century. "Crowns named Porpynes, at four shillings and four pence Sterling" value in England in 1522 were probably *ecus au porcepic,* French silver coins bearing the device of a porcupine (Frey). Also called a scute, from Latin *scutum,* shield. Foreign coins were declared current in England and assigned certain values because of a shortage of native coins. See ***Appendix B.*** *Ecus* were supposedly equivalent to English crowns. See *Cardecue, Crown, Pistolet. [**Hen.5*** 4.4.42: *deux cents ecus;* ***Mass.atP.*** 1.2.61: sends Indian gold to coin me French ecues.

French ecu d'or, Francis I.

Porpyne ecu, Louis XII of France.

French ecu a soleil, Francis I.

EGG. See ***Duck-egg***.

EMPLOY, v., **EMPLOYMENT**, n. To hire, to use sexually, "to be sexually intimate with (a woman)" (Partridge). *[**John*** 1.1.98: he employ'd my mother; ***Rich.2*** 1.1.90: lewd employments; ***DCourt.*** 1.1.117-18, 122-23: employ your money upon women . . . doe you give them, the french Crowne, they'le give you the french.

ENCLOSE, v. In reference to the enclosure acts, which allowed the fencing off of commons land for private use. The problem with enclosures was that they often stole livelihood from the poor, who had no other place to graze their livestock, and that sometimes land would be termed "common" and claimed by a landholder who wanted to increase his estate, when in reality the land enclosed was already privately owned. *[**2Hen.6.*** 1.3.21-22: enclosing the commons of Melford; *Scorn.* 428: I, in a year, have put up hundreds; / Inclos'd, my widow, / Those pleasant meadows, by a forfeit mortgage.

ENDOW, v. and adj., **ENDOWMENT**, n. "Possessing a secured income from property bequeathed or given" *(OED)*. Provided with a dowry or marriage portion. Increased. *[**Rich.2**.* 2.3.139: Base men by his endowments are made great; ***TofA*** 1.1.139: How shall she be endowed; ***Rich.3*** 4.4.250: endow a child of thine; ***Ado*** 2.1.250-51:1 would not marry her, though she were endow'd; ***HWhore2*** 5.2.11-12: endowed it / With lands; ***Lear*** 2.4.180-81: Thy half o' th' kingdom . . . / Wherein I thee endow'd.

ENFEOFF, v., **FEOFF**, n. To give lands to another by means of a fee-simple, or sole ownership. To surrender or give up (previous rights). *['**Wily** 256:* to enfeoff her in forty pounds a year; ***1Hen.4*** 3.2.69: Enfeoff'd himself to popularity; ***BFair*** 5.2.92: being made feoff in trust.

ENGENDER, v. To propagate or breed. With money, this is considered an unnatural activity. See ***Interest***. *[**HWhore2*** 2.1.114-15: I cannot abide to have money engender.

ENGROSS, n., v., and adj. To buy all of an available commodity at wholesale prices, thus creating a shortage on the market and driving up prices; the intent of engrossers is to resell the merchandise for an easy profit once the price is raised. To accumulate, to monopolize. Also that which is accumulated, a store or supply, and to write in large, clear letters, as in a legal document. See ***Forestall***. *[**Volp.*** 1.1.82; ***1Hen.4*** 3.2.148: To engross up glorious deeds on my behalf; ***2Hen.4*** 4.5.70-71: engrossed and pil'd up / The cank'red heaps of strange-achieved gold; 4.5.79: Yields his engrossments; ***MadW.*** 1.1.159: They engross all the market; ***Well*** 3.2.65: If thou engrossest all; ***R&J*** 5.3.115: engrossing death; ***MWives*** *2.2.*196: engross'd opportunities to meet her; ***Rich.3*** 3.6.2-3: in a set hand fairly is engross'd / That it may be to-day read; *Wit* 630: Your sister has engross'd all the brave lovers; ***Bond.*** 1.3.195-96: the treasure of the City is ingros'd / By a few priuate men.

ENLARGE, v. To add to one's wealth, to give bountiful gifts, to increase an estate or grant sole ownership. Sometimes with a pun on to release or set free. *[**Fatal*** 5.2.215; ***1Hen.4*** 3.2.115: Enlarg'd him and made a friend of him.

ENRICH, v. and adj. To increase or augment in value; to enhance one's wealth. Metaphorically applied to love and marriage. *[**AYLI*** 1.1.102: lands and revenues enrich the new duke; *1Hen.**6*** 5.5.51: to enrich his queen; ***R&J*** 1.5.41: enrich the hand [marry]; ***Cym.*** 2.2.30: t' enrich mine inventory; 2.4.130: did outsell her gift, / And yet enrich'd it too; ***Rich.2*** 2.3.61-62: enrich'd / Shall be your love; ***1Hen.4*** 3.3.161: thy pocket were enrich'd; ***TofA*** 5.1.6: enrich'd poor straggling soldiers.

ENSTATE. See ***Estate.***

ENTAIL, n. and v. To carve out a prescribed order of succession for ownership of property in posterity. To grant lands in gift to an individual and others specified to follow in ownership after his death. *[**Well*** 4.3.279- 80: cut th' entail from all remainders; ***3Hen.6*** 1.1.194-95: I here entail / The crown to thee and to thine heirs forever.

ENTER, v. To register a law suit, often in the plays for economic reasons: breach of (marriage) contract or non-payment of debt. *[**2Hen.4** 2.*1.1-2, 9.

ENTERTAIN, v., **ENTERTAINMENT**, n. To employ or hire. Funds, support, financial maintenance. Room and board, accommodation. Sexual and economic profit. See ***Jack Drum's Entertainment**.. [**Rich.3*** 1.2.256: entertain a score or two of tailors; *Fatal* 1.2.211: He had from the state sufficient entertainment for the Army; ***2Gents.*** 2.4.110: entertain him for your servant: 4.4.63: I have entertain'd thee; ***AYLI*** 2.4.72; ***Lear*** 2.4.206; 3.6.79; ***MWives*** 1.3.44:1 spy entertainment in her.

ESCOT, v. To support; to patronize. *[**Ham.*** 2.2.345-46: Who maintains 'em? How are they escoted?

ESTATE, n. and v. Also enstate. Holdings, assets, lands; one's economic condition, implying his worldly rank, fortunes, or social class. To bestow or endow with money and possessions. *[**Lear*** 5.3.210; ***MofV*** 1.1.43;.123; 3.2.316; ***Well*** 3.7.4; ***WTale*** 4.2.40: an unspeakable estate; ***Temp.*** A 1.85: some donation freely to estate; ***MND*** 1.1.98: I do estate unto Demetrius; ***AYLI*** 5.2.11-12: will I estate upon you; ***Prod.*** 1.1.193: I hope he dyed in good estate; ***MforM*** 5.1.424-25: We do enstate and widow you with all, / To buy you a better husband; ***TofA*** 2.2.141-42: the ebb of your estate / And your great flow of debts; 3.2.7: estate shrinks from him; ***Mac.*** 1.4.37-38: We will establish our estate upon / Our eldest; ***LLL*** 5.2.845: you on all estates will execute.

ESTIMABLE, adj. Valuable, important, costly. *[**MofV*** 1.3.166: not so estimable, profitable neither.

ESTIMATE, n. Value, worth, reputation; used to refer to persons. *[**1Tamb.*** 1.2.61: These lords perhaps do scorn our estimates; 3.2.53-54: higher would I rear my estimate / Than Juno; ***Rich.2*** 2.3.56: of name and noble estimate; ***T&C*** 2.2.53-55:

value . . . / holds his estimate and dignity / As well wherein 'tis precious of itself.

EXCHANGE, n. and v. To trade; to deal, as in merchandising. Applied to women, with sexual connotations; "to coit" (Partridge). To seal a bargain of love. To change denominations of money by means of representative currency, or a "bill" carried by a factor from one country to another. A meeting place for merchants and money-men. See ***Burse***. *[**1Tamb.*** 1.2.215-16: to make exchange for that / We are assured of; ***T&C*** 3.3.21: Desir'd my Cressid in right great exchange; ***R&J*** 2.2.126-27: What satisfaction canst thou have to-night? /—Th' exchange of thy love's faithful vow; 2.3.62: We met, we woo'd, and made exchange of vow; ***WTale*** 4.4.280: she would not exchange flesh; ***2Gents.*** 2.2.6: we'll make exchange [of love vows]; ***Cym.*** 1.1.119: I my poor self did exchange for you; ***Shrew*** 4.2.89:1 have bills for money by exchange; ***Gall.*** 183, 214, 263; ***HWhore2*** 3.2.11; 'T is put over by exchange; ***MTerm*** 2.3.205-6: raise double commoditie by exchange; ***WHo*** 1.2.30: I was offred forty yesterday vpon the Exchange; ***EMOH*** 4.6.90-91: cost me three pound in the exchange; ***BFair*** 1.2.9-10.

EXCHANGE BELL, n. A bell tolled at Exchange time to call the participants. *[**EMen*** 496 s.d.: The Exchange bell rings.

EXCHANGE TIME, n. The operating hours of the Burse: around lunch and dinner. *[**EMen*** 480: 'tis past eleven; Exchange time full; ***NHo*** 5.1.283-84: the exchainge time, twelue at noone and six at night.

EXCHANGE WALK, n. A stage direction, probably indicating that the characters are to walk back and forth, arm-in-arm, as if discussing a financial venture or as if looking into the shops in the Exchange. *[**HWhore2*** 1.1.32 +s.d.

EXCHEQUER, n. An office of the English king, established in Norman times, which was responsible for all the financial dealings of the crown. Also the treasury, or a general term for a store of money. Since words are often metaphorically equated with coins, one's vocabulary. Also a woman's sexual and financial favors. *[**1Hen.4*** 2.2.36-37: all the coin in thy father's exchequer; ***2Gents***. 2.4.43-44: an exchequer of words; ***MTerm*** 1.1.5; ***Killed*** 2.3.119: His purse is your exchequer; ***MWives*** 1.3.68-72; ***Hen.5*** 3.6.130.

EXECUTE, v., **EXECUTION**, n. Enforcement of a writ against a debtor by a sheriff; the seizing of the debtor or his goods upon forfeit or default. To administer a will. With a pun on to be killed. See ***Attach. [Debts*** 5.1.361: I'll fall to execution; ***DCourt***.. 5.3.68-70: do not lead me to execution through Cheapside, I owe M. *Burnish* the goldsmith monie, and I feare heele set a Seijant on my back for it; ***OldF.*** 1.2.82-84: if a poore wretch steale but into a debt of tenne pound, they lead him straight to execution.

EXECUTOR, n. Also sectour. One who has a financial trust to carry out the provisions of a will and dispense the wealth according to the wishes of the deceased. Proverbially, "A fat housekeeper makes lean executors" (Herbert). ***[Rich.2*** 3.2.148: Let's choose executors and talk of wills; ***Prod.*** 2.4.161: Executors of all his wealth.

EXPECTATION, n. Prospects for spiritual or material reward, an inheritance. Metaphorically, sexual anticipation. ***[2Hen.4*** 5.2.31: You stand in coldest expectation: ***Mac***. 2.3.5: expectation of plenty; ***Oth.*** 2.1.280: expectation of our prosperity; ***T&C*** 3.2.18: expectation whirls me round.

EXTENT, n. Originally, an assessment of value for the purposes of taxation, but here "in execution of a writ; the condition of being seized and held in satisfaction for debt" *(OED)*. ***[AYLI*** 3.1.17: make an extent upon his house and lands.

F

FACTOR, n. Doer, maker. A merchant's hired representative, usually abroad. An agent; a servant. See ***Agent, Broker***. ***[JofM*** 1.1.82: bid my factor bring his loading in; ***1Hen.4*** 3.2.147: Percy is but my factor; ***CofE*** 1.1.41; ***A&C*** 2.6.10: factors for the gods; ***Cym***. 1.6.188:1 (the factor for the rest); ***Rich.3*** 3.7.134: lowly factor for another's gain; 4.4.71-72: Richard . . . hell's black intelligencer, / Only reserv'd their factor to buy souls; ***Fatal*** 1.2.156: May all your wives prove whores, your factors theeves.

FAIRIES' TREASURE, **FAIRY GOLD**, n. Money given by the fairies. It either "crumbles away rapidly" *(OED)* on its own or disappears when its secret is revealed to others. Sometimes used as a metaphor for the prodigal's coffers. [***Fatal*** 4.1.214-15: 'tis Fairies treasure; / Which but reveal'd, brings on the blabbers, ruine; ***WTale*** 3.3.123-24: This is fairy gold, boy, and 'twill prove so. / Up with't, keep it close.

FARM, n. and v. To rent; to let out land on a lease; to receive a fixed payment. [***Ham.*** 4.4.20: To pay five ducats, five, I would not farm it; ***Rich.2*** 1.4.45: We are enforc'd to farm our royal realm; 2.1.256: The Earl of Wiltshire hath the realm in farm.

FARTHING, n. Originally feorthing, an English silver coin, later copper, equaling one-fourth of a penny, first minted by Edward I. The name also derives from the earlier practice of cutting pennies into quarters when no smaller coinage existed. A copper farthing from the reign of Charles I measures fourteen millimeters in diameter; one from the coinage of James I, sixteen millimeters. Token coins called *Harringtons* issued in 1613 had the value of a farthing. A farthing also indicates an extremely small amount. Sometimes it appears with a pun on farting. In the plays three or four farthings represents a normal charitable contribution. Three farthings is the price of a bit of hay, and "remuneration" for a clown. A *bezzo* or betzo is a "small Venetian coin; worth about a farthing" (Skeat). See ***Harrington.*** [***Prod.*** 5.1.24: not a farthing, not a myte; ***EHo*** 4.2.183-85: we shall "as soon get a fart from a dead man as a farthing" of court'sy here; ***Vex.*** 133; ***LLL*** 3.1.137-38; 3.1.148; ***Faust.*** 4.6.23-24; ***Heir*** 104; ***Wit*** -30; ***Madam*** 4.3.51: To the utmost farthing; ***Scorn.*** 436.

English farthing, James I.

FEDERY. See ***Feodary***.

FEE, n. Originally, cattle, property, money. Generally, a payment for services, remuneration, but also income; a perquisite; a wage; a portion; value; a bribe; or possessions, wealth, money. *In fee* means in fee-simple, as absolute possession and ownership; or, "held by lease for a long term, under small rents" (Postlethwayt). A fee is also an estate held on the condition of certain homage and obligation paid to a superior lord. Sometimes appears in a pun on fee as livestock. By extension, also a "reward consisting in gratification of sexual lust" (Partridge). A bawd's usual fee is sixpence. *[**Lear*** 1.1.163; ***CofE*** 4.1.76: Here is thy fee; ***Ham.*** 1.4.65: at a pin's fee; 4.4.22: sold in fee; ***3Hen.6*** 3.1.22: a deer whose skin's a keeper's fee [income/perquisite/job to keep safe]; ***2Gents.*** 1.2.48: To plead for love deserves more fee than hate; ***John*** 2.1.170; ***TAnd.*** 2.3.179-80; ***Rich.3*** 3.5.96: golden fee [King's crown]; ***MND*** 3.2.113: a lover's fee; ***Well*** 2.1.189: death's my fee; ***MTerm*** Ind. 66-67: ours have but sixpenny fees all the yeare long, yet wee dispatch you in two howers; ***TAnd.*** 2.3.179—80: should I rob my sweet sons of their fee. / No, let them satisfice their lust on thee.

FEE, v. To hire, to pay, to buy, to employ or make use of. *[**MofV*** 3.1.126: fee me; ***Hen.8*** 3.2.213: fee my friends in Rome; ***MWives*** 2.2.197: fee'd every slight occasion; ***Drum*** 189: he that fees me best, speeds best.

FEE-FARM, n. Land held in one's possession with implied ownership for perpetuity, so long as a certain rent, tax, or homage is paid. *[**T&C*** 3.2.50.

FEE-GRIEF, n. A private sorrow, over which a single individual has absolute ownership. *[**Mac**.* 4.3.196.

FEE-SIMPLE, n. Under Common Law, "an estate of inheritance in land" *(OED).* Usually used in the sense of absolute possession and ownership. The property involved. *[**3Lad**.* 259: he lent my father a little money, and for breaking one day / He took the fee-simple of his house and mill quite away; ***Well*** 4.3.278-79: for a cardecue he will sell the fee-simple of his salvation; ***R&J*** 3.1.31-34: any man should buy the fee-simple of my life. . . .—The fee-simple! O simple!; ***MWives*** 4.2.210-11: the devil have him not in fee-simple, with fine and recovery; ***2Hen.6*** 4.10.25: entering his fee-simple; ***Magn.*** 2.6.153: the house were their Fee-simple in Law.

FEODARY, n. Also federy, feudary. In the strict sense, a slave, a vassal, a feudal tenant; here used to indicate a confederate or accomplice. [***Cym.*** 3.2.21; ***MforM*** 2.4.122; ***WTale*** 2.1.90.

FEOFF. See ***Enfeoff.***

FETTER LANE, n. A site in London of many pawn shops. *[**EMOH*** 4.2.99.

FEUDARY. See ***Feodary***.

FIFTEENS, n. Also called a subsidy. A tax of one-fifteenth the value of all personal possessions, first used in England by Henry II (1154-1189) to raise money for the Crusades. A fifteenth and a tenth was initiated by Edward I (1272-1307) to tax city residents more heavily than country folk, i.e., a tenth rather than a fifteenth. These were levied for the last time in 1626, but the assessments were revised under Henry VII (1485-1509). Wriothesley chronicles one under Henry VIII in 1512-13: "was grawnted to the Kinge two fifteens and [four] dimes, and head money for everie man; for a Duke 10 markes, for an Earle *5l..,* for Lord *4l..,* a knight 4 marks, . . . and everie man was valued that was worth in goods 800*l.* to pay 4 marks, 400*l.* 4 nobles, 200*l.* 2 nobles, 40*l.* a noble, 20*l.* to pay 40*d..,* and everie man valued worth 40s. [wages] to pay 12*d.,* and servantes, prentises, weomen, and all other [of 15 years and upwards] to pay 4*d.* a peece" (1:8). *[**3Lad.*** 348: For now we neither pay Church-money, subsidies, fifteens, scot nor lot; ***Ram.*** 299: these are tricks of the long fifteens; ***2Hen.6*** 4.7.21-22: he that made us pay one and twenty fifteens, and one shilling to the pound, the last subsidy.

FIGURE, n. The impression or portrait on a coin, which, combined with the intrinsic value of the metal and the king's word or promise of worth on the coin, makes it legal tender. By extension through adianoeta, the stamp of divinity that God puts on every man. Sometimes a synecdoche for the coin itself. Also a number of value, one through nine. See ***Cipher.*** *[**MofV*** 2.7.56: A coin that bears the figure of an angel; ***Cym..*** 5.4.25: take pieces for the figure's sake; ***2Gents.*** 3.2.6-7: This weak impress of love is as a figure / Trenched in ice; ***MforM*** 1.1.16: What figure of us think you he will bear? [How will he manage economics (coins)?/How will he represent me?]; ***EMOH*** 2.1.113-14: You should giue himafrench crowne for it: the boy would finde two better figures i' that; ***Hen.5*** Pro. 15: a crooked figure; ***Lear*** 1.4.192-93: an O without a figure.

FINE, n. Also fine and recovery. "A legal process by which an entailed estate could be converted into a fee-simple" (Riverside); the transference of property from hereditary tenancy to absolute ownership. In law, any friendly settlement of a suit. Appears in puns on "end" and on paying a "fee" (for a wig) and thus "re-covering" a bald head. See ***Pay a fine***. *[**MWives*** 4.2.210-11: in fee-simple, with fine and recovery; ***MofV*** *4*.1.381: To quit the fine for one half of his goods; ***Ham..*** 5.1.106: Is this the fine [end] of his fines; ***CofE*** 2.2.72-74: There's no time for a man to recover his hair that grows bald by nature.—May he not do it by fine and recovery?

FINGER, v. To steal, to filch, to touch money with "unworthy motives" *(OED)*. Appears in puns on to touch or to feel (sexually) and to play a musical instrument. *[**Ram.*** 357: stole you my daughter?—. . . I fingered have your daughter; ***3Hen.6*** 5.1.44: The king was slily finger'd from the deck; ***Ham.*** 5-2.15: finger'd their packet***; 1Tamb.*** 4.4.105-6: here are the cates you desire to finger; ***JofM*** 1.1.12: The needy groom that never fingerred groat*:* 4.6.47-48**:** he fingers very well.—So did you when you stole my gold.

FIRK, v. To get money by robbing or cheating. To give someone a beating. "To copulate" (Partridge). Sometimes all three meanings simultaneously. *[**HWhore1*** 5.1.60: from poor clients lawyers firk money; ***Ram.*** 291: firking the posteriors; ***Hen.5*** 4.4.28; ***EHo*** 3.2.368: show me a quirk, while I firk others; ***Vex.*** 165: these brisk factors are notable firkers; ***BBush*** 3.1.141; ***NHo*** 5.1.26.

FISHMONGER, n. One who trades dubiously in fish; by extension, probably a bawd. Proverbially, "a fishmonger's wife may feed of a conger" (Tilley, 355>. *[**Ham.*** 2.2.174.

FIT, v. and adj. Economically, to supply or pay, to settle an account; with many puns on suitable, harmonious, of the right size. Sometimes with an implication of payment as more than one has bargained for, a punishment. *[**BBush*** 3.2.116: I'll fit ye; ***2Gents.*** 2.7.42: fit me with such weeds; ***MWives*** 2.1.161: she'll fit it; ***Well*** 2.1.90: I'll fit you; 2.2.15-21: a bountiful answer that fits all questions. / —It is like a barber's chair that fits all buttocks. . . . As fit as ten groats is for the hand of an attorney; ***Ado*** 2.3.42: We'll fit the [hid]-fox with a pennyworth; ***Hen.8*** 2.1.98-99: See the barge be ready; / And fit it; ***Lear*** 1.1.97: Return those duties back as are right fit; 3.2.76: make content with his fortunes fit.

FLESHMONGER, n. "One who carries on a contemptible or discreditable trade' or 'traffic' in flesh" *(OED);* therefore, a prostitute or her pimp. *[**MforM*** 5.1.333-34.

FLORIN. See ***Guilder.***

FOOL. See ***Golden fool.***

FORESTALL, v. Similar to engross. To buy up all that is available of a single commodity before it reaches the retail market, with an eye toward driving up the price and making a better profit. *[**Vex.*** 165: forestall the market; ***Mass.atP.*** 1.13.4.

FORFEIT, n., v., and adj. A penalty for a transgression. Financially, failure to fulfill a monetary obligation, the penalty to be exacted, and the person who fails to pay. Evidently lists of those who defaulted on minor bonds were posted at the barbershop; or else young prodigals, who most often defaulted on financial obligations, gathered at the barber's, still interested most of all in cutting fine figures in fashion and personal appearance. Remember, for example, Young Novall in ***Fatal*** (4.1), who, after spending five hours a day dressing, repairs to the barber accompanied by his tailor and perfumer. Forfeiting is generally committing a crime or transgression, but economically it may refer specifically to confiscation of another's money or property. Those caught cheating on or avoiding their debts were sometimes nailed to the pillory by the ear (see description under ***Bag.)*** Metaphorically, default on God's contract of life or on any contract. *[**MofV*** 4.1.37: the due and forfeit of my bond; ***1Hen.4*** 1.3.87-88: Shall we buy treason? and indent with fears, / When they have lost and forfeited themselves? [given themselves up as captives]; ***MforM*** 2.3.73: all the souls that were were forfeit once; 5.1.321: stand like the forfeits in a barber's shop; ***Well*** 3.6.32: the divine forfeit of his soul; 5.3.142-43: his vows are forfeited to me, and my honor's paid to him; ***R&J*** 1.4.111: some vile forfeit of untimely death; ***JofM*** 2.3.188-89: cozening, forfeiting, / And tricks belonging unto brokery; ***Faust.*** 5.2.6-7: The time is come / Which makes it forfeit; ***MTerm*** 2.3.121-22: bonds lye forfette in my hands; ***LLL*** 5.2.425: Our states are forfeit; ***NHo*** 2.1.141-42: to put my father in minde of a bond, that wilbe forfit this night if the mony be not payd; ***Debts*** 5.1.182-83: make a forfeit of / Thy ears to the pillory.

FORFEITURE, n. The penalty, previously agreed upon, to be exacted for nonfulfillment of an economic obligation. This could be an additional fine, or goods, lands, properties, or even something seemingly worthless, like a pound of flesh. *[**MofV*** 1.3.164; 3.3.22; 4.1.335; ***TofA*** 2.2.30: due on forfeiture.

FORM, n. Also custom. In an economic bond, *for form* refers to the convention of having a second signer to the obligation, ostensibly as a witness to the character of those contracting the bond. Unscrupulous moneylenders would use this ruse to get the unsuspecting actually to engage their own wealth and property in case of forfeiture of the original debtor, who was probably a confederate of the moneylender. *[**Fatal*** 5.1.4: for forme onely; ***MTerm*** 2.2.264-66: no Cittizen must lend money without two bee bound in the bond, the second Man enters but for custome sake.

FRACTED, adj. Broken, referring to a financial bond whose date of payment has passed. See ***Break.*** *[**TofA*** 2.1.22: fracted dates.

FRANC. See ***Frank***.

FRANK, adj. Originally, free. Financially generous, liberal, bountiful, freely given, with the implication of natural, innocent, socially responsible, as opposed to materialistic, individualistic, and economically sophisticated. The *franc* is also a gold coin of France, first issued in 1360, but this coin disappeared from circulation in 1450, and there seems to be no reference to it in these plays. The *franc* became a synonymous money of account with the *livre*. The term also implies sexually free and generous. *[**WHo*** 4.1.141: some franker customer is come; ***Well*** 1.2.20: Frank Nature; ***Corio***. 3.1.130: frank donation; ***R&J*** 2.2.131: to be frank and give it thee again; ***Lear*** 3.4.20: frank heart gave all; ***Oth***. 3.4.43-45: 'Tis a good hand, / A frank one. . . . / —'twas that hand that gave away my heart.

FREE, adj. As an extension of financial liberality, wanton, generous with bodily favors. *[**1Hen.6*** 1.3.64: O'ercharging your free purses with large fines; 5.4.82: liberal and free; ***2Hen.6*** 4.7.124: we charge and command that their wives be as free; *2Gents.* 5.4.82: that my love may appear plain and free.

FRENCH CROWN. See ***Crown.***

FRUIT. See ***Golden Fruit.***

FUR, n. The traditional garb for a stage usurer was austere clothing with a lining or trim of fur as his only ornament. Furred gowns, then, indicate moneylenders, misers, cozeners, or other economic abusers. *[**Lear*** 4.6.165: furr'd gowns; ***Wily*** 221: fox-furred slave; ***WHo*** 5.3.43: furr'd Gownes; ***MTerm*** 3.4.11: furde Gowne; ***MforM*** 3.2.7; ***Staple*** 5.3.38: Wrapp'd up in furs.

FURNISH, v. and adj. To provide funds, clothes, or other materials. To supply, to lend, to accommodate, to equip. *[**MofV*** 1.1.182; ***2 Gents***. 2.7.85: To furnish me upon my . . . journey; ***Rich.2*** 1.4.46: revenue whereof shall furnish us; ***2Hen.4*** 1.2.224: to furnish me forth; ***Hen.5*** 2.2.87: To furnish him; ***TofA*** 3.1.19; ***Madam*** 2.1.13 keeps no account of his expenses, and comes ever furnish'd; ***Temp.***2.2.143: furnish it anon with new contents; ***T&C*** 3.3.33: furnish'd with the present money.

G

GAGE, v. and adj. In aphaeresis, (en)gaged, bound in debt, in pawn. *[**MofV*** 1.1.129-30: my time something too prodigal / Hath left me gaged; ***EMOH*** 2.5.24: I ha' left my gowne in gage; **Faust. 4.1.63:** *I'll gage my credit.*

GAINER, n. Also questuary, from Latin *quaestus,* gain. Slang for a good deal, a bargain. Also one who gets money by labor or by some advantage obtained through trickery. Proverbially, "Light gains make heavy purses" (Tilley, G7). *[**Vex.*** 158: you must look / To be little gainer; but lose you cannot; ***MWives*** 2.2.140-41: Wilt thou, after the expense of so much money, be now a gainer.

GALL, v. To injure or to sicken one's economic fortunes. See ***Heal.*** *[**MWives*** 3.4.5: my state being gall'd with my expense.

GALLEY-HALFPENNY. *See **Sol.***

GAZET, n. Also gazzetta, gazette. A Venetian copper or billon coin of small value, issued in the seventeenth century. Probably the price of the first newspaper published, hence gazette. *[**Volp.*** 2.2.233.

Venetian billon gazetta.

GELD, v. To castrate, thus by extension, to cut the strings of a purse, which was usually carried by men near to or connected to the codpiece, for safety. To rob of money; to deprive of something essential, i.e., funds, income. Perhaps with a pun on the original meaning of payment or tribute. *[**WTale*** 4.4.610-11: 'twas nothing to geld a codpiece of a purse; ***2Hen.6*** 4.2.165: Lord Say hath gelded the commonwealth; ***Rich.2*** 2.1.237: gelded of his patrimony; ***NHo*** 4.2.9: Shee gelded my purse of fifty pounds in ready money.

GEM. See ***Jewel.***

GET, v. To work, make money, make a living, perhaps with an aphaeresis on (be)get, i.e., copulate. Proverbially, "Money begets money" (Tilley, M1053). *[**Per.*** 4.2.28-29: Is it a shame to get when we are old?; ***AYLI*** 2.5.41: pleas'd with what he gets; ***3Lad.*** 254:1 care not whom I serve—the devil, so I may get pence.

GET-PENNY, n. An attraction or good ware, something that pulls in trade and income. *[**EHo*** 4.2.100.

GETTINGS, n. Prospects for acquiring wealth; potential for profit; income. *[**Ram.*** 287: good gettings; 293: bare gettings.

GILD, v. and adj. To counterfeit, to cover over something base with an appearance of richness; to steal or to pay, in the sense of supplying (oneself) with money, gold. With a paronomasia on "guilt." *[**T&C*** 4.4.105: Some with cunning gild their copper crowns [pun on coins/diadems/ heads]; ***Hen.8***

3.2.411: gild again the noble troops; ***MofV*** 2.6.49: gild myself; *John* 4.2.11: To gild refined gold; ***Maid*** 1.1.30: cozend you with a guilded Two-pence; ***2Hen.4*** 4.5.128: double gild his treble guilt.

GILT, n. and adj. A general term for gold or money, from gelt. Also the result of gilding; counterfeit or covered with a veneer of gold. Often with adnominatio on "guilt." *[**MadW.*** 2.2.28: Though guilt condemns, 'tis gilt must make us glad; ***TofA*** 4.3.302: in thy gilt and thy perfume; ***2Hen.4*** 4.3.51: gilt twopences; ***T&C*** 2.3.25: a gilt counterfeit; ***3Hen.6*** 2.2.139: Iron of Naples hid with English gilt; ***Hen.5*** 2 Pro. 26: the gilt of France (O guilt indeed!).

GOD OF GOLD. See ***Gold, Pluto, Plutus.***

GOLD, n. Aside from referring to the most precious metal and to money or wealth in general, the term occurs in many combinations. *Angel gold* is the purest or best gold, a standard of purity. *Current gold* indicates coins, or wealth in a form to be counted and exchanged. *God of gold* is another nickname for a miser. *Good gold* is gold of great fineness, not debased. *Indian gold* was supposed to be endless, from the vast mining and spoilage of the newly discovered lands. *Light gold* refers to coins somewhat debased or clipped as well as to prostitutes. *Old gold,* like good gold, is fine, undebased, perhaps in reference to the Renaissance practice of reducing the standard of purity for coins of legal tender. Old gold coins were thus worth more, even if they carried the same nominal designation as new coins (see ***Appendix E***). *Stamps in gold* are coins; stamped in gold refers to the legitimizing word of the king—the figure, device, and legend on a coin that make it legal tender—in addition to its intrinsic worth. *Tested gold,* like *tried gold,* is pure, having been rubbed on the touchstone or melted in the fire. *True gold* distinguishes the debased, veneered, or counterfeit from a coin (or a person) pure all the way through. *Virginian gold,* from the new world, and *Venice gold,* from the old world banking and economic center, were both thought to be pure and fine. Proverbially, "All is not gold that glisters," "That is gold which is worth gold," and "If gold knew what gold is, gold would get gold, I wis" (Herbert). Tilley includes "Gold speaks" (G285a) and "He that has gold may buy land" (G286). *[**Wily*** 241; ***Scorn.*** 417, 428, 429; ***Rich.3*** 4.2.9; 4.2.34: corrupting gold; ***HWhore1*** 3.2.27; ***Mass.atP.*** 1.2.61; ***HWhore2*** 3.2.168; 5.2.229; ***WHo***

1.2.9; ***EHo*** 1.1.52; 3.2.392; ***MWives*** 3.4.16; ***MofV*** 2.7.53; ***MforM*** 2.2.149; ***Shrew*** 2.1.354; ***Gall.*** 212; ***OldF.*** 1.1.289: Gold is the strength, the sinnewes of the world; 4. Chor. 14-15: what treacherie / Cannot this Serpent gold intice vs to?; ***R&J*** 5.1.80-81: gold, worse poison to men's souls, / Doing more murther in this loathsome world.

GOLD-END MAN. See ***Gold ends.***

GOLD-ENDS, n. and adj. Ambiguous usage. Apparently refers to platitudes or proverbial sayings, as well as to small pieces of gold left over from goldsmithing and the ambitions of a person who seeks wealth. A *gold-end man* is a goldsmith, one who lives in the gold end (section) of the city, or one who buys ends of gold and silver. *[**EHo*** 2.1.167; 4.2.192; 5.1.169; ***BBush*** 3.1.130 +s.d.

GOLDEN (AND SILVER) DAYS, n. Like the Golden Age, refers to better financial times, days of great wealth, with extremely pleasant connotations. *[**NHo*** 4.3.65; ***MTerm*** 3.4.13; ***MadW.*** 1.1.155; ***3Hen.6*** 3.3.7.

GOLDEN BIT, n. Slang for a coin; also used to mean a bribe. With a pun on horse's bridle. See Bit. *[**HWhore1*** 2.1.440; ***Heir*** 135.

GOLDEN CALF, n. Refers to the devoted worship of money as an end in itself, from the story of the Israelites worshipping the idol of the golden calf in Exodus 32. Moses melted the golden calf, powdered it, sprinkled it upon water, and made the Israelites drink this potion as a punishment for their misguided devotion. Similarly, a standard punishment for a miser or usurer is to drink molten metal. Drinkable gold (***aurum potabile***) also appears in the drama as a miraculous curative potion or aphrodisiac, and the character Gresham in *If you know not me, 2*, drinks a powdered pearl to show that he understands that wealth is not what is most important to a man. Thomas Adams, in his sermon "The Gallant's Burden," compares usury, luxury, lechery, and pride to worship of the golden calf. *[**Fatal*** 2.1.86.

(GOLDEN) CIRCLE, n. Usually refers to a coin, an angel, but sometimes to a ring as a token of love and fidelity. [***EMen*** 475; ***BFair*** 4.4.174-75: Can you lend me a piece, a Jacobus, in circle?

GOLDEN DREAM, n. A dream of money or great riches or the aspiration thereto. [***Gall.*** 277: thou'st had a golden dream, / Which gilded over thy calamity; ***Madam*** 5.3.132-33: What a golden dream you have had in the possession / Of my estate!

GOLDEN DROPS, n. Also shower. A general term for coins; refers specifically to the shower of gold as raindrops which fell on Danae. Those who use the term in the latter sense skew their interpretation of the myth so that the shower is viewed as a reward from God, but it retains the connection between sex and money. See ***Drop***, ***Golden shower***. ***[Case*** 5.1.24-25: bid thy hands shed golden drops, / Let these bald french crownes be vncouered; ***WHo*** 2.2.48-49: This showre shall fil them all: raine in their laps, / What golden drops thou wilt.

GOLDEN FOOL, n. A rich man easily parted from his wealth; one who has no conception of the responsibility or right use of money, *e.g.,* Bartholomew Cokes, Timon. ***[TofA*** 4.3.17-18: The learned pate / Ducks to the golden fool.

GOLDEN FRUIT, n. Like the golden apples that deterred Atalanta from winning her race, this term refers to the enticing and distracting bodily charms of a beautiful woman and obliquely to semen, which produces heirs and allows one to pass his riches on. Appropriate to the image, the apples allowed Melanion to win Atalanta as his wife. ***[Per.*** 1.1.28; ***Maid*** 3.3.10-11: Get but his Wife with Child, perch at tree top, / And shake the golden fruit into her Lap; ***Heir*** 112.

GOLDEN GULL, n. Like a golden fool, this person is unlearned, perhaps stupid, as well as wealthy and economically foolish. He is soon parted from his money. ***[HWhore1*** 2.1.508.

GOLDEN HOOK, n. From a fishing analogy, economically something beautiful or enticing that lures a man to seek wealth or entraps him into parting with his money. This could also refer to a prostitute. See ***Angle. [OldF.*** 1.2.51: poysned baits, hung vpon golden hookes; ***HWhore1*** 2.1.393: this golden hook and lascivious bait; ***WHo*** 2.2.118.

GOLDEN JOY, n. Financial prosperity achieved through unexpected remuneration or reward. ***[2Hen.4*** 5.3.100.

GOLDEN LETTER, n. Gold was the color used to mark Sundays on a calendar. By extension, any special day became a golden letter day. It may also be used to indicate the day a debt is due. [*John* 3.1.85; LLL 5.2.44.

GOLDEN LORD, n. One who has wealth as well as nobility; spiritual and material congruence. [***OldF.*** 3.1.230.

GOLDEN MESH, n. Blonde hair, with the implication that it can ensnare or entrap men, obliquely equating seeking love to seeking money. [***MofV*** 3.2.122.

GOLDEN OPINION, n. A good reputation, good credit, high praise or esteem. [***Mac***. 1.7.33.

GOLDEN PROMISE, n. A hint of a reward, which could be pecuniary or sexual. [***TAnd.*** 4.4.97.

GOLDEN RUBBISH, n. A general disparaging term for money. [***Vex.*** 187.

GOLDEN SERVICE, n. An interaction that is valuable, necessary, helpful, like good advice. [***12N***. 4.3.8.

GOLDEN SHORES, n. Women, referred to economically and sexually. To reach the shore is to cash in on the profit. [***MWives*** 1.3.80.

GOLDEN SHOWERS, n. The acquisition of great riches as a boon of fortune or a gift from God, with oblique reference to Danae. See ***Golden drops.*** [***OldF.*** 1.2.146; ***EHo*** 5.1.128.

GOLDEN STAMP, n. Generally, any coin, with reference to its two crucial attributes: the metal, which is intrinsically valuable; and the stamp of the portrait and word of the sovereign, which ensures that the assigned value of the coin will be accepted in trade. Here, probably specifically the angel. In a practice initiated by Edward the Confessor, the king would pass through the streets healing the sick, those suffering from scrofula or the king's evil, by giving each a touch-piece, a coin, to hang around his neck with a white ribbon. This practice, called "touching," was revived by James I. The superstition may be based on the miracle described in Mark 1:40-41, where the king of the Jews, Jesus, is shown to have healing powers through touching. [***Mac***. 4.3.153.

GOLDEN THIGH, n. Part of the legend surrounding Pythagoras was that he was the son of Apollo and had a golden thigh, which he revealed to a throng of Greeks at Olympia. *[Volp*. 1.2.27.

GOLDEN TIME, n. Like golden days, this term refers to economic prospects. It is a happy, carefree, prosperous time or the vision of a prosperous future. *[12N*. 5.1.382; ***2Hen.4*** 5.3.96; ***3Hen.6*** 3.2.127.

GOLDEN TONGUE, n. The attribute of one who talks well, who perhaps uses wit and language to gain wealth. A material sign of success with words. The ability to praise and flatter, a valuable skill, contrasted quibblingly with a copper nose, a worthless gilded coin. Also an oblique allusion to Midas. ***[EMen*** 496: thou golden tongue, thou good-news teller; **Ed.2** 1.4.327: I'll hang a golden tongue about thy neck; **T&C** 1.2.105: Helen's golden tongue.

GOLDEN TRAFFIC, n. Love. This term indicates the acceptance of friendship and courtship as mercantile transactions, although golden traffic is the highest form of commerce. *[Vex*. 100.

GOLDEN WAVES, n. A synecdoche for laden ships returning to the merchant's home port. Stow[e] reports that in 1557 three London merchant ships returning from Antwerp, laden, were taken by Scots and Frenchmen; their loss was set at £20,000 (47). ***[Vex.*** 164.

GOLDEN WORDS, n. Praise or flattery. Words are to coins given as a reward for praise as the mind is to a purse, containing the wit and vocabulary which, when coined into words, become the legal tender of intellectual exchange. ***[Ham***. 5.2.130-31: His purse is empty already: all's golden words are spent.

GOOD, adj. Originally, pleasing or suitable. Economically, a man of sound credit and financial reputation, one capable and reliable in meeting his expenses and paying his debts. See ***Sufficient***. ***[MofV*** 1.3.16-17: he is a good man . . . he is sufficient: ***DCourt*** 3.2.3: your bill had ben sufficient y'are a good man: ***BBush*** 1.3.17-18: Yet he still / Continues a good man [financially able];:***MWives*** 1.3.37: he is of substance good; 2.2.11: good soldiers and tall fellows [economically reliable].

GOOD FELLOW, n. A cant term for a thief or a rogue, with a pun on its meaning. *[EHo* 5.2.43-44; ***Hen.5*** 5.2.242-43: thou shalt find the best king of good fellow s.

GOOD GOLD. See ***Gold***.

GREEK, n. A merry fellow, a carouser, one of loose morals, especially in the : combination merry Greek. The Romans thought the Greeks to be fond of luxury and liquor. Used in the Renaissance to indicate a cheater; one who gains money by his wits. *[**Case*** 4.7.163; ***HWhore1*** 5.1.10; ***MadW.*** 1.2.19-20: ***T&C*** 1.2.109; 1.3.276; 4.4.56; ***12N.*** 4.1.18.

GRIDIRON, n. A slang term for a guilder or French crown, perhaps from the appearance of cross-hatching in its device. *[**Faust.*** 1.4.32—34 [A text]: take these gilders.—Gridyrons, what be they?—Why french crownes..

GROAT, n. An English silver coin worth 4d., the first English silver coin of greater value than a penny. It was first proposed at Parliament in 1227 but probably not coined until 1351. The name derives from *groot* or *grossus,* thick. A groat from 1561 shows the portrait of the Queen on the obverse and a long cross and shield on the reverse. About twenty-three millimeters m diameter. In the plays usually used as a reference to something inexpensive or, disparagingly, cheap. One groat is a cheap admission price for three to the theater, three groats buys cheap bread, ten groats will bribe a promoter or pay off an attorney, and a suit of fourteen groats is shabby attire. *Ten-grot-Rimers* are lesser, mercenary poets. *A* gray groat is a pejorative term, opposed, of course, to gold. *King Harry-groates* as old groats were probably valued higher than the new groats because of a purer silver content. *An* old Harry-groat is a steward. *To* buy and sell with groats is an insignificant activity. *To offer* me a groat is an insult. A *shove-groat shilling* was a coin used in a game similar to shuffleboard. Because it was large and flat, it could easily be aimed at a certain mark on a flat surface. *A* half-fac'd groat refers to the king's portrait in profile on the coins and also to half-brothers who are sons of the king and thus his issue or coinage and of his stamp, i.e., resembling him. Ten groats is the difference in value between a royal and a noble. *[**3Lad.*** 315; ***JofM*** 4.4.110; ***WHo*** 2.1.179; ***Volp.*** 2.2.70: one poor groat's-worth; ***Maid*** 2.2.152; ***Gall.*** 186; ***Scorn.*** 421; ***Wit*** 652; ***Bond.*** 5.3.246; ***Debts*** 2.2.108; ***Corio.*** 3.2.10; ***Hen.5*** 5.1.60;

2Hen.4 2.4.192; ***Well*** 2.2.21-22; ***John*** 1.1.94; ***Prod.*** 3.3.87-88: Not worth a groat, not worth a halfepenie; ***MWives*** 1.1.155; ***Rich.2*** 5.5.67-68.

English groat, Edward IV.

Elizabethan groat, c. 1561.

GROSS, n. and adj. The total amount, the full sum. Also refers to a wholesale transaction. *[**MofV*** 1.3.55: raise up the gross; 3.2.158: in gross; ***LLL*** 1.2.46: gross sum; 5.2.319: sell by gross; ***2Hen.4*** 2.1.84: gross sum.

GROW, v. Economically, to mature and prosper, as a marriage contract. *[**Temp**.* 4.1.19: To make this contract grow; ***CofE*** 4.4.121: the debt grows; 134.

GROWING, v. and adj. In an economic sense, accruing, as interest on a debt. Money soon to be due to be repaid. *[**CofE*** 4.1.8.

GROWN, v. Economically, indicates the process of gaining or losing money, credit, or reputation. Grown into means acquired, obtained. *[**Rich.2*** 1.4.44: coffers . . . grown somewhat light; 2.1.257: grown bankrout; ***1Hen.6*** 4.1.36:

grown to credit by the wars; ***WTale*** 4.2.40: is grown into an unspeakable estate; ***R&J*** 2.6.32-34: They are but beggars that can count their worth, / But my true love is grown to such excess /1 cannot sum up sum of half my wealth.

GUILDER, n. A general term for money. Specifically, a Dutch measure of value; ten guilders equal a florin. Also a silver coin equal to one florin, a gulden, struck in 1600 and worth about Is. 8d. See ***Appendix B.*** A leopard is a gold coin of Edward III, struck in 1343, worth one-half florin, named for its device on the obverse. Also in reference to any foreign coins circulating in England, *e.g.*, French crowns. *[**CofE*** 1.1.8; 4.1.4; ***Faust.*** 1.4.32-34 [A text]: take these gilders.—Gridyrons, what be they?—Why french crownes; ***BBush*** 1.3.72: thirty thousand gilders.

GULL. See ***Golden gull.***

H

HALFPENCE. See ***Pence.***

HANDFAST, n. Also clap. A handshake to seal a bargain; the bargain itself; earnest given to insure a contract; manacles; stinginess. By extension, sealing of a marriage bargain; a betrothal. Often several meanings simultaneously. *[***Vex**. 132: promise me marriage, and give me earnest in a hand-fast; ***WTale*** 1.2.104: clap thyself my love; 4.4.768: in handfast; ***Cym.*** 1.5.77-78: to hold / The hand-fast to her lord.

HANSEL, n. and v. Several possible meanings. Handsel is a gift given on an auspicious occasion or earnest money offered to seal a bargain. It also refers to the handshake that concludes a transaction, or the first money a trader earns in the day. Skeat suggests "to use for the first time." A hand- seller is an itinerant merchant, probably adept at cheating his customers or overselling his wares. To be handselled, then, may ironically mean to receive a worthless gift or to be cheated in an economic transaction. *[**Beware*** 1.2.10; ***BFair*** 2.2.180.

HARP. See ***Shilling***.

HARRINGTON, n. A copper farthing patented by James I in 1613 to John Harington of Exton, who minted the coin, also called a Royal Token. In the plays it refers to a coin of minuscule value. A proverbial saying was "Not worth a Harrington" (Tilley, H178). See ***Farthing***. *[**Magn.** 4.8.74.*

HARRY GROAT. See ***Groat.***

HEAL, v. To mend, metaphorically, one's economic fortunes; to regain money squandered prodigally. See ***Gall.*** *[**MWives** 3.4.6: I seek to heal it only by his wealth.*

HIRE, n. Payment, wage, reward. *[**AYLI** 2.3.39: the thrifty hire I sav'd; **MofV** 1.3.80: should fall as Jacob's hire.*

HOLD-DOOR, adj. In reference to a pander or a bawd, the hold-door trade. *[**TandC** 5.10.51.*

HOLDFAST, n. Nickname for a miser, indicating stinginess, tenacity. An old proverb says that "Brag is a good dog, but Holdfast is a better" (Tilley, B588), indicating a general approval of thrift over prodigality. *[**Wily** 268: my old grandsire Holdfast; **Hen. 5** 2.3.52: Hold-fast is the only dog.*

HOOK. See ***Golden hook.***

HOOP OF GOLD, n. A ring; a cup or goblet by which a pledge of loyalty or obligation is sealed during a toast, from the hoops that held a quart vessel together. Therefore, also the amount of liquid contained therein. *[**NHo** 1.3.114; **MofV** .1.147; **2Hen.4** 4.4.43: A hoop of gold to bind thy brothers in.*

HOSPITAL MONEY, n. Probably money intended as a charitable donation, perhaps with a pun on hospital as "a house of entertainment" (OED). *[**MTerm** 5.1.78.*

HOT, adj. Quick and excessive, full, wasteful, prodigal, as opposed to cold purses. *[**Gall.** 287: hot in expense; **WTale** 4.3.118-19: Your purse is not hot enough to purchase your spice; **1Hen.4** 2.4.323: Hot livers and cold purses; **Hen.5** 1.2.151: Galling the gleaned land with hot assays.*

HOUSE OF SALE, n. A merchant's shop; by extension, a brothel, a place where sex is merchandised. *[**Ham.** 2.1.58.*

HUNDRED, n. Percent; used to indicate interest charges and rates of repayment. Also a nickname for a usurer. See ***Interest.*** *[**Drum** 219: thirty in the hundred; **Wily** 225: ten in the hundred; **Scorn.** 436: twelve i' the hundred; **Staple** 2.3.41-43: When monies went at ten i' the hundred, I / And such as I, the* servants of Pecunia, / Could spare the poor two out of ten and did it; ***EMen*** 540: You take ten in the hundred more than law; 555: I take two- and-twenty in the hundred, / When the law gives but ten; ***EHo*** 2.2.123-26: I, and such other honest men as live by lending money, are content with moderate profit, thirty or forty i' th' hundred.

HUSBAND, v., **HUSBANDRY,** n. In a financial sense, to economize, to manage, to nourish or nurture a profit, with the implications of thrift and prudence, proper knowledge of the right use and obligations of wealth. Metaphorically, that nurtured or produced, *e.g.,* offspring. Proverbially, "Frugality and good husbandry is an income," but "Usurers are always good husbands" (Tilley, F776, U30). *[**Volp.*** 1.3.44: Husband your goods; ***MWives*** 4.6.52: husband your device; ***Hen.5*** 5.2.39: All her husbandry doth lie on heaps [the sons of Nature, the soldiers, are dead]; ***Staple*** 3.4.37: good husbands [thrifty]; ***Gall.*** 243; ***MforM*** 1.4.43-44: her plenteous womb / Expresseth his full tilth and husbandry; 3.2.70-71: You will turn good husband now, Pompey, you will keep the house; ***Shrew*** 5.1.68-70: while I play the good husband at home, my son and my servant spend all; ***2Hen.4*** 5.3.10-11: your servingman and your husband [steward]; ***MofV*** 3.4.25: The husbandry and manage of my house; ***Mac.*** 2.1.4-5: There's husbandry in heaven, / Their candles are all out; ***Ham.*** 1.3.77: borrowing dulleth [th'] edge of husbandry.

I

IMPOST, n. A customs duty levied on imported goods. Metaphorically applied to the selling of value and the marriage exchange. *[**Ram.*** 339: I would I had the monopoly of them, / So there were no impost set upon them; ***Hater*** 103: there is an impost set upon knighthoods, and your friend shall pay a noble in the pound; ***Vex.*** 111: what woman can have a husband, but you must have custom for him? and often the ware proves naught too— not worth the impost.

INCLOSE. See ***Enclose***.

INCLOSER, n. One who encloses, i.e., is greedy for the lands or possessions of others; thus, the nickname for a usurer. See ***Enclose***. ***[Scorn***. 428.

INCOME. See ***Comings-in***.

INCREASE, n. Accumulation, augmentation, growth, with a dichotomy of meaning that illustrates the Renaissance concept of natural and artificial economics. Children, progeny, heirs, as the natural consequence of marital intercourse are a positive boon from Nature, a fulfillment of her economic system. Increase as interest, making money breed unnaturally, because it is innately barren, is tampering with Nature and thus constitutes artificial economics. Also implied in the distinction is social welfare versus individual materialism. See ***Interest***. ***[Well*** 1.1.127-28: loss of virginity is rational increase; 1.1.148: a goodly increase; ***Rich.3*** 4.4.297: To quicken your increase [fertility]; ***Corio.*** 3.3.114: her womb's increase; ***Temp.*** 4.1.110: Earth's increase; ***TAnd.*** 5.2.191: Like to the earth swallow her own increase; ***JofM*** 1.1.180: the Turks have let increase; ***3Hen.6*** 2.2.164.

INDENT, v. To make a bargain, to contract, from the practice of indenting documents involving two parties by cutting a zigzag pattern on the edge so that the duplicates were exactly the same and thus unlikely to be altered or forged. See ***Indenture***. ***[1Hen.4*** 1.3.87: Shall we buy treason? and indent with fears; ***MTerm*** 4.1.105-6: I have indented with a couple of searchers; ***BFair*** Ind. 84; ***Debts*** 5.1.185.

INDENTURE, n. A contract formed by the process of indenting, serrating the edge. Any bond or obligation; a love contract. More specifically, an apprentice's bond of service to his master. Sometimes with a pun on dentures, from the teeth-like protuberances indenting or serrating the edge of a contract would produce. See ***Counterpane, Indent. [Drum*** 218; ***EHo*** 1.1.29-30: dost thou jest at thy lawful master, Contrary to thy indentures?; ***John*** 2.1.20: this indenture of my love; ***1Hen.4*** 2.4.47; 3.1.79: indentures tripartite; ***Per.*** 1.3.8: he's bound by the indenture of his oath; 4.6.176: serve by indenture; ***Ham.*** 5.1.110: a pair of indentures; ***Scorn.*** 449; ***Magn.*** 1.6.44-45: You may perceive the Contract in their faces; / And read th' indenture; ***EMOH*** 3.6.110; ***BFair*** 2.4.58.

INDIA, n. and adj. Represents an endless supply of extremely pure metal from the Indian mines. By extension, a particularly fine, beautiful, or bountiful woman (as precious as gold). See ***Gold.*** *[**1Hen.4*** 3.1.166-67: as bountiful / As mines of India; ***Hen.8*** 1.1.20-22: they / Made Britain India: every man that stood / Show'd like a mine; ***12N.*** 2.5.14: metal of India; ***1Tamb.*** 2.5.41: Indian mines; ***JofM*** 1.1.19-20: merchants of the Indian mines / That trade in metal of the purest mold; ***T&C*** 1.1.100: Her bed is India; ***Mass.atP.*** 1.2.61: Indian gold.

INDITE, v. Perhaps an intentional mistake for indict. If so, a three-level pun using paronomasia is possible: arrest for debt, ask to dinner (invite), ask by invitation (in writing). Probable because of the mention of Lombard Street, a place of many pawnshops. *[***2Hen.4** 2.1.28-29: indited to dinner to the Lubber's Head in Lumbert street; ***R&J*** 2.4.129: She will indite him to some supper.

INESTIMABLE, adj. Priceless; of an extent or value beyond estimation; "transcending all price" (Schmidt). *[**T&C*** 2.2.88; ***Rich.3*** 1.4.27: Inestimable stones; ***Per.*** 2.4.8: inestimable value.

IN FARM. See ***Farm***.

IN FOR, prep. In debt; the extent of one's financial obligations. *[**MforM*** 4.3.4-5.

INGAGEMENT, n. To be indebted. A debt or a pawn, a financial liability. A bond, an obligation. *[**Fatal*** 1.1.144; 1.2.79-81: fayling . . . / Of meanes to free himselfe, from his ingagements, / He was arrested.

IN HAND, adj. Actual money, not credit or an IOU, usually paid as a down payment in a transaction. See ***Earnest.*** *[**EHo*** 5.1.94-95: I would lend it. . . for forty pounds in hand.

IN POSSE. See ***Posse.***

IN QUESTION, adj. Questionable, or an issue to be tried in court to determine proper ownership. Refers punningly to men as commodities. *[**Ado*** 3.3.179: A commodity in question.

INTERESSED, adj., **INTEREST,** n. To have a legal claim or title to; to share in, to be concerned; to be self-interested in the sense of desiring a personal profit. Also, in reference to seeking a wife. *[**Lear*** 1.1.85; ***Faust.*** 2.2.86.

INTEREST, n. A charge for the use of money. Usury. Profit. In the Middle Ages profit was objected to primarily if it derived from any action not requiring human labor, the sweat of the brow. Interest fell into this category, and it resulted, moreover, from an "unnatural" process. Teleologically, money was invented for exchange, according to Aristotle. Any other use perverted this original, natural function, since God had not given barren metal the natural ability to breed and propagate. The New Testament (Luke 6:34-35) also offered advice against taking interest. Thus the taking of interest seemed to ally the moneylender with the devil or the forces of evil, especially since many were non-Christian. In the reign of Alfred, one convicted of charging interest would forfeit his chattels, his lands, and his right to Christian burial, while under William the Conqueror the penalties ranged from loss of all substance to whipping, pillory, and banishment. In 1571 Parliament legalized the taking of interest up to 10 percent, as had the government of Henry VIII in 1545, a bill that had been rescinded by Edward VI because of the many abuses inherent in the system. Generally any gain, increase, or advantage. Also venereal disease, extra payment from copulation. See ***Hundred***, and ***Appendix*** A. *[**JofM*** 2.3.195: I with interest tormented him; ***TofA*** 1.2.200: Pays interest for't; his land's put to their books; 3.5.106-7: let out / Their coin upon large interest; ***MofV*** 1.3.50-51: my well-won thrift, / Which he calls interest; 1.3.75, 76, 77, 94; ***1Hen.4*** 4.3.49: You shall have your desires with interest; ***Rich. 3*** 4.4.323-24: Advantaging their love with interest / Of ten times double gain of happiness; ***2 Gents***. 2.1.102; ***Madam*** 5.2.69-70: The interest / Will eat faster in't, than aquafortis in iron; ***HWhore1*** 3.3.68-69: That usury's worst of all, / When th' interest will eat out the principal [venereal disease].

INVENTORY, n. One's total wealth or estate. A list of all such material possessions made upon the owner's death, so that a sale or the carrying out of his will can take place. *[**Cym.*** 2.2.30; ***Volp.*** 5.3.3; ***Hen.8*** 3.2.451.

INVESTMENT, n. Money ventured in hopes of a profit, with a pun on vestment, clothes (French *investir,* Italian *investire*). Extended metaphorical puns in this passage on dye (color/mold for a coin), vows (words as coins), brokers, and bonds. *[Ham.* 1.3.127-28, 130: Do not believe his vows, for they are brokers, / Not of the dye which their investments show /. . . Breathing like sanctified and pious bonds.

ISSUE, n. Originally, that which goes out. A certain mint of coins, with a pun on progeny, as the coins of copulation, and concerns, as issues. Also the line of descent for an inheritance. *[MforM* 1.1.36; ***Well*** 5.3.197: Confer: : by testament to th' sequent issue.

J

JACK DRUM'S ENTERTAINMENT, n. Also John Drum's entertainment To be paid or furnished with a beating; to be drubbed and dismissed *[3Lad.* 324; ***Well*** 3.6.38-39.

JACOBUS, n. Slang for the unite of James I, previously called a sovereign a gold coin worth 20s. Used with piece and circle as other slang terms for coins. ***[BFair*** 4.4.174-75: Can you lend me a piece, a Jacobus, in circle.

JANE. See ***Pence.***

JAR, v. Originally, to make a harsh noise. To have a conflict in regards to price; to haggle. With a pun on to be musically discordant (the base [bass] knave will haggle about a marriage contract). *[JofM* 2.3.66: We will not jar about the price; ***Shrew*** 3.1.47: 'tis the base knave that jars..

JEBUSITE, n. Literally, one of a tribe of Canaanites driven out of Jerusalem by King David. Generally, then, an outcast, a pariah, anyone religiously or economically different. In the seventeenth century Dryden used the term to indicate a Roman Catholic. In the plays it refers to a Jew or a moneylender. *[***Drum** 185; ***JofM*** 2.3.298: this offspring of Cain, this Jebusite.

JEW, n. Aside from its religious denotation, this term took on an economic significance. In England the practice of moneylending was forbidden by law initially, but since most found a source of ready money to be imperative to business and sometimes even to survival, Jews were allowed to act in this capacity. In fact, they were denied all other means of livelihood, in essence forced into usury, which was at least as odious under Old Testament law as it was to the Christians, and then taxed heavily on their profits whenever the Crown was short of funds. A very Jew, then, is a term of derogation for one who practices his moneylending trade with a shrewd eye for profit: a crafty dealer, a miser, a grasping usurer, one who is crazy for profit. A *sweet Jew* is a prostitute; *a Jew's trump* is an ingenious economic trick; a *Jew's courtesy* is treason or betrayal, perhaps because money is offered not out of kinship or friendship, but instead for profit (and revenge). Like a usurer's kindness, such courtesy was aimed at bringing the debtor into even heavier debt. Stowe uses the phrase "falser than a Jewe or Sarasyn" to indicate ultimate infidelity. *[**HWhore1*** 2.1.274; 5.1.537; ***EHo*** 2.2.261; ***MTerm*** 2.3.305; ***MofV*** 2.2.104-5; 2.3.11; ***JofM*** 5.5.109.

JEWEL, n. Also gem. A thing of great beauty and value; a form of wealth, a friend; by extension, a woman, her chastity, or her maidenhead, as the hidden treasure of her father or husband. Proverbially, "None can guess the jewel by the casket" (Tilley, J55). *[**Per.*** 4.6.154-55: To take from you the jewel you hold so dear; ***Temp.*** 3.1.53-54: my modesty / (The jewel in my dower); ***Beware*** 1.1.55-56: hidden virtues, / Like jewels kept in cabinets; ***HWhore1*** 5.2.474-80: I had a fine jewel once, a very fine jewel, and that naughty man stole it away from me, a very fine [and a rich] jewel.—What jewel, pretty maid?—Maid? Nay, that's a lie. Oh, 't was a very rich jewel, call'd a maidenhead; ***HWhore2*** 1.2.47-50: our friends! they ought to be unto us as our jewels, as dearly valued, being locked up and unseen, as when we wear them in our hands; 3.1.168-69: that jewel / Of my chaste honor; ***MTerm*** 5.1.70: A modest wife is such a Jewell; ***MadW.*** 4.4.79-80: Two dear rare gems this hour presents me with, / A wife that's modest, and a friend that's right; ***Maid*** 4.4.33: I have brought your Jewell by the Hayre; ***DCourt.*** 1.2.36-37: shee sels divine vertues as virginitie, modestie and such rare Jemmes; ***Killed*** 5.1.48: With that rich jewel you my debts may pay [virginity]; ***Trick*** 1.1.44-45: the jewel which / I prodigally gave you, my virginity; ***MWives*** 3.3.45.

JOHN DRUM'S ENTERTAINMENT. See ***Jack Drum's Entertainment.***

JOINTURE, n. Legally, property held in the name of both husband and wife, with a provision that the wife become sole owner in the event of the husband's death. Thus, anything material bestowed upon a wife as sole owner. In general, a dowry, a marriage portion, the economic settlement concerning a marriage (union or conjunction). With a pun on pregnancy, the result of such "joining." *[**Wily*** 242: land conveyed to her by jointure; ***Prod.*** 2.4.9; ***MWives*** 3.4.49; ***AYLI*** 4.1.55-56; ***3Hen.6*** 3.3.136***;*** ***R&J*** 5.3.297; ***Shrew*** 2.1.369-70: two thousand ducats by the year / Of fruitful land, all which shall be her jointer; ***Wit*** 633: she lies with your land and not with you, / Grows great with jointures; ***Madam*** 1.2.59-61: I can make my wife a jointure of such lands too / As are not encumber'd, no annuity / Or statute lying on 'em; ***Heir*** 105; 106: marry a beggar! / What jointure canst thou make her?

JOY. See ***Golden joy.***

JULIO. See ***Pence***.

JUMP, n. and v. To gamble, stake: "venture, hazard, risk" (OED). Applied metaphorically to the Last Judgment. *[**Mac.*** 1.7.7: We'ld jump the life to come; ***A&C*** 3.8.5-6: Our fortune lies / Upon this jump; ***Cym.*** 5.4.182: jump the after-inquiry on your own peril.

K

KENTALL, n. A quintal, a hundredweight of gold; a measure of what a ship can carry (Postlethwayt). *[**BBofA*** 1.1.76.

KINDNESS. See ***Usurer's kindness.***

L

LAUNDRESS, n. Slang for a prostitute, from the women who cared for rooms at the Inns of Court, with a possible hidden pun on a trickster, one who "washes" another, i.e., deceives, probably from the practice of washing or counterfeiting coins. *[**Ram.*** 275: no puisne Inn-a-Court / But keeps a laundress at his command / To do him service; 317: And give their linen to their laundresses; / By tail they now can save their purses ... / now a twelvepenny weekly laundress / Will serve the turn to half a dozen of them; ***MWives*** 1.2.4-5: his laundry—his washer and his wringer; 3.3.148: a twelve penny . . . laundress; 3.3.153.

LAUREL. See ***Sovereign***.

LAVENDER, n., adj. In lavender is slang for something in pawn, perhaps because dried lavender flowers were used like moth balls, to keep stored clothes safe and fresh. See Tilley (L96), "To lay in Lavender." *[**EMOH*** 3.3.40; ***Debts*** 1.5.131: Dragg'd in your lavender robes to jail.

LAY, n. and v. To wager, bet, or gamble. To spend or pay frivolously. To incur debts; to give responsibility; to ambush. Sometimes several meanings at once, with a pun on to fall. *[**EMen*** 553: I'll lay my cap to twopence; ***12N***. 3.4.396: I dare lay any money; ***R&J*** 1.3.12: I'll lay fourteen of my teeth; ***Cym***. 1.1.174: I dare lay mine honor; 1.4.127-28: I will lay you ten [thousand] ducats to your ring; 1.4.147: I will have it no lay; ***MofV*** 3.5.80: on the wager lay two earthly women; ***T&C*** 3.1.87: I'll lay my life; ***2Hen.4*** 5.5.105: I will lay odds; ***2Hen.6*** 5.2.27: a dreadful lay; MWives 2.2.6: lay my countenance to pawn; 3.1.110: lay their swords to pawn; Temp. 2.2.32- 33: lay out ten [doits] to see a dead Indian; ***Ado*** 5.1.223: lay to their charge; ***Hen.5*** 4.1.225-26: lay twenty French crowns to one; ***TofA*** 3.5.114: lay for hearts; ***Oth.*** 4.2.12-13: I durst, my lord, to wager she is honest; / Lay down my soul at stake.

LEASH, n. A set of three, used numismatically as a slang measure. See ***Brace.*** *[**Trick*** 2.1.163: a leash of angels.

LECHERY, n. A metaphorical extension of the idea of interest, that the coins actually bred together and propagated more coins, thus were lecherous. One proverb maintains, "Lechery and covetousness go together" (Tilley, L173), and another that "Money begets money" (Tilley, M1053). See ***Interest.*** *[HWhore2* 2.1.115-16: fie upon this silver lechery, fie.

LEGUM PONE. See ***Ready Coin*** or ***Money***.

LEOPARD. See ***Guilder.***

LET OUT, v. To lend at usury; to allow money the freedom to breed (unnaturally). *[**TofA*** 3.5.106-7: they have told their money, and let out / Their coin upon large interest.

LETTER. See ***Golden letter.***

LIBERAL, adj. Originally, free. Economically generous, bountiful, with the purse and the person as the only two options. Thus, when done in excess, loose or wanton, out of control. Also talkative, free with words. Proverbially, "The miserable man maketh a penny of a farthing, and the liberal of a farthing sixpence" (Herbert). See ***Frank, Free. [1Hen.6*** 5.4.82: she hath been liberal and free; ***2Gents.*** 3.1.349: She is too liberal; ***Ham.*** 4.7.170: liberal shepherds; ***Rich.2*** 1.4.44: liberal largess; 2.1.229: a liberal tongue; ***Oth.*** 3.4.38: fruitfulness and liberal heart; 3.4.46: A liberal hand; ***Shrew*** 1.2.149: Baptista's liberality; ***Rich.3*** 1.3.123: A liberal rewarder of his friends; ***MofV*** 2.2.184-85: they show / Something too liberal; 4.1.438: You are liberal in offers; ***Magn***. 1.3.62-63: But Mr. Steele, was liberall, / And a fine man.

LIBRA. See ***Pound.***

LIFTER, n. A thief; a sexually active man. ***[T&C*** 1.2.117: Is he so young a man and so old a lifter?

LIGHT, adj. Something less than the real thing or the full amount. The proper number of coins could be exchanged in a transaction, but if the coins were light, i.e., had been clipped, then the full amount would not actually be remitted. Similarly with a woman, less than a full marital relationship: sexually wanton, irresponsible. Le Comte suggests "unsteady, fickle," Ross, "undependable, faithless." With a pun on light (as from a lamp). ***[Rich.2*** 1.4.43-44: coffers ... / grown somewhat light; ***Hen.5*** 2.2.89: a few light crowns; ***2Hen.4*** 1.2.165: your ill angel is light; 2.4.295: this light flesh and corrupt blood; Ep.20: light payment; ***Dido*** 3.1.14-15: Dido hath been counted light / In being too familiar; ***Oth.*** 4.1.102: light behaviors; ***MforM*** 5.1.279-80: women are light at midnight; ***R&J*** 2.2.99: thou mayest think my behavior light; ***HWhore1*** 2.1.91: Here's another light angel; ***Cym.*** 5.4.25: Though light, take pieces for the figure's sake; ***Temp.*** 1.2.452-53: lest too light winning / Make the prize [bride] light.

LIGHT GOLD. See ***Gold***.

LIGHT WENCH, WIFE, OR WOMAN, n. Usually, a prostitute. Many possibilities for puns on multiple meanings: wanton/sorrowful (light/heavy); merry; fair (light in complexion); illuminated, as from a candle; and light in weight, irresponsible, trifling. ***[NHo*** 1.3.154; ***CofE*** 4.3.52,

54-55, 57; ***LLL*** 1.2.123-24; 4.3.382; 5.2.15; 5.2.25; ***MofV*** 5.1.130: A light wife doth make a heavy husband; ***Drum*** 195: women of levitie and lightnesse, are soone downe; ***EHo*** 4.2.352.

LIRA. See ***Pound.***

LIVING, n. Income, property (income from land), livelihood, earnings, trade, occupation, indicating the close link of economics and the basics of life. *[**Lear*** 1.4.107; ***2Gents.*** 3.1.316: spin for her living; ***LLL*** 5.2.495-96: get your living by reck'ning; ***AYLI*** 2.3.33: a thievish living; 3.1.8: to seek a living; 3.2.79-80: to get your living by the copulation of cattle; ***WTale*** 4.3.98: my land and living; ***MofV*** 5.1.286: life and living; ***MTerm*** 2.3.279: hee's a Gentleman of a prettie living; ***BBush*** 4.1.8.

LIVRE, n. A French money of account until 1803, consisting of twenty sous of twelve deniers each. See ***Pound.*** *[**Volp.*** 4.1.110-11: thirty livres—/ Which is one pound sterling..

LOMBARD, n. A native of Lombardy; in England the Lombards took over most banking,, money-changing, and pawn-broking functions when the Jews were expelled in 1290. Therefore, a person dealing in money affairs or his place of business, Lombard Street in London, the area of most brokers and goldsmiths. Also called lumber, a pawnshop. *[**NHo*** 5.1.184: his apparell lie ith' Lumbard; ***2Hen.4*** 2.1.28-29: indited to dinner to the Lubber's Head in Lumbert street.

(LONGER) DATE, DAY, n. An extension of time specified in a contract, *e.g.,* the payment date of an obligation or the term of life's contract. The loan itself. Dateless means never to be free or redeemed of debt. *[**Madam*** 1.3.113; ***1Tamb.*** 5.2.214; ***Trick*** 4.5.103; ***BBush*** 1.3.123; ***R&J*** 5.3.115: a dateless bargain to engrossing death.

LORD. See ***Golden lord.***

LOT, n. Originally, a rendering. A city tax supporting the bailiff and other municipal workers, originally lot and scot (shot). See ***Scot.*** To pay scot and lot means to settle with, to pay the whole amount or debt. Also one- sixteenth of a mark, 10d. *[**3Lad.*** 348: For now we neither pay Church-money, subsidies, fifteens, scot nor lot; ***1Hen.4*** 5.4.113-14: that hot termagant Scot had paid me scot and lot too.

LOUR. See ***Lucre***.

LOWRE. See ***Lucre.***

LUCRE, n. Also lour, lowre. In a derogatory sense, money in general, profit, greed, or ill-gotten gain. ***[1Hen.6*** 5.4.141: for lucre of the rest unvanquish'd; ***Cym.*** 4.2.324: Malice and lucre in them; ***JofM*** 4.1.55: That would for lucre's sake have sold my soul.

LUDGATE, n. A prison in London for debtors and bankrupts, located near the city gate. See ***Counter. [Madam*** 1.3.26-28: other men's moneys / Took up at interest, the certain road to Ludgate in a citizen.

LUMBER. See ***Lombard.***

LUNA, n. In alchemy, silver, as represented by the moon. Gold was thought to be represented by the sun and the value ratio of the two metals to be dependent upon the relative sizes of the heavenly bodies. See ***Argentine. [EHo*** 4.1.271.

LUXURY, n. Originally, abundance, sumptuousness. Excess, both economic and sexual. Costly tastes, usually involving prodigal expense. Sensuality, lust, lechery, lasciviousness. A capacity for refined, decadent pleasures. ***[Rich.3*** 3.5.80-81: his hateful luxury / And bestial appetite; ***MWives*** 5.5.94: Fie on lust and luxury; ***Ham.*** 1.5.83: A couch for luxury and damned incest; ***Hen.5*** 3.5.6: The emptying of our fathers' luxury; ***T&C*** 5.2.55: the devil Luxury; ***Lear*** 4.6.117.

M

MAINPRIZE, n. Originally, "to take in the hand, ... to assume responsibility, to pledge oneself." Surety or bail, especially in economic matters. "The action of making oneself legally responsible for the fulfilment of a contract or undertaking by another person" (OED). ***[Debts*** 3.2.212: without bail or mainprize.

MAKE, v. and adj. To set up financially (or sexually); to endow with funds. In economic usage, a possible humorous inversion of the proverb "The tailor makes the man" (Tilley,

T17). *[1Hen.*4 2.2.58: enough to make us all; ***A&C*** 3.11.65: Making and marring fortunes; ***Oth.*** 1.2.51: If it [Desdemona] prove a lawful prize, he's made forever; ***Madam*** 1.2.46: I have made my tailor; ***Lear*** 2.2.55: a tailor made thee; ***MND*** 4.2.18: made men; ***Faust.*** 4.5.31-32: Now am I a man made forever; ***WTale*** 3.3.120-22: You're a [made] old man; . . . Gold, all gold!

MARE, n. Probably from cattels or chattels, a slang term for a woman or wife. Extended to include, contemptuously, nuns. *[**NHo*** 1.3.39; ***JofM*** 3.5.107: a drench to poison a whole stable of Flanders mares; ***MND*** 3.2.463: The man shall have his mare again.

MARK, n. and v. Originally, perhaps, standard. An Anglo-Saxon money of account, valued at 13s. 4d. or two-thirds of a pound, "reckoned in either gold or silver" (Palgrave). A weight of gold and silver in Germany from the eleventh century on. A silver coin of the sixteenth century current in several European countries, worth one-half a *thaler* or 1s. 5½d. See ***Dolor.*** In the plays thirty thousand marks is an enormous royal dowry, one thousand marks is a large sum, and one hundred marks is an ample amount, the value of a costly jewel. Something costing forty marks is expensive, while twenty marks for a suckling pig is an extravagant purchase. Puns occur on marks as scars on the body from lashings and on to mark as to notice. *[**John*** 2.1.530; ***1Hen.4*** 2.1.55-46: 300 marks ... in gold 3.3.42; ***Maid*** 2.1.139-40: sure thou shalt not misse so faire a marke, / For thirteen shillings foure pence [mark as target]; 2.1.153; 4.1.265; ***CofE*** 1.1.21, 24; ***2Hen.6*** 5.1.79; ***2Hen.4*** 1.2.193; ***Shrew*** 5.2.34; ***1Hen.4*** 3.3.82 ***Madam*** 2.1.12; ***MforM*** 4.3.7; ***Ham.*** 3.2.110-11: metal more attractive . . .—do you mark?; ***HWhore2*** 4.1.250; ***OldF.*** 3.1.220; ***MadW***. 5.2.170: chain of a hundred mark; ***EHo*** 2.2.380-81: thousand-mark jointures; ***Trick*** 3.1.160: five mark a year.

MARKET, n. Originally, the act of trading. The conditions of exchange, the action of buying and selling. Commodities sold at market, an occupation or a profit. Often applied to women and to marital transactions. A *reasonable market* is a good price with good trading prospects, an acceptable profit; *to make or end the market* is to make a bargain, close a deal; *not for all markets* means not in demand—when applied to a woman, unattractive, not marriageable; *at any market* means omnipresent, here applied to husbands; *idle markets* sell frivolous goods; *the market of his time* is one's occupation, one's profit. Proverbially, "Three women make a market (Herbert). *[**Drum*** 225: my markets are cleane spoilde; ***JofM*** 2.3.159; ***Bond.*** 1.3.79; ***LLL*** 3.1.110; ***AYLI*** 3.5.60; ***Mac.*** 4.2.40; ***12N***. 3.3.46; ***Ham.*** 4.4.2 ***EMen*** 509: all our market will be spoil'd and marr'd.

MARKET MEN, n. A derogatory term for merchants, middle-men, traders. *[**1Hen.6*** 3.2.4: the vulgar sort of market men; 5.5.53-54: peasants bargain for their wives, / As market men for oxen.

MARKET-PRICE, n. The going rate, the usual price, in reference to a dowry or marriage bargain. Oblique reference to "a prostitute's fee" (Partridge). *[**Well*** 5.3.219.

MART, n. and v. From Dutch *markt,* the marketplace and its duration of trading time. To have business, to bargain, to exchange or be exchanged. By extension, to barter for a wife. *[**CofE*** 1.2.27: upon the mart; 3.1.7: he met me on the mart; ***MofV*** 3.1.47: upon the mart; ***BBush*** 1.3.96: letters of mart; ***Per.*** 4.2.4: We lost too much money this mart; ***Case*** 4.8.4: basely marted; ***Shrew*** 2.1.327: a desperate mart; ***WTale*** 4.4.352: nothing marted with him: ***Cym.*** 1.6.151-52: to mart / As in a Romish stew.

MATTER, n. Substance, i.e., profit. *[**WTale*** 4.4.842; ***2Gents.*** 1.1.129-30: Open your purse, that the money and the matter may be both at once deliver'd..

MEANS, n. Financial holdings; liquid assets; wealth at one's disposal; a living; an occupation or trade; principal; financial opportunity; prosperity; essential needs. *[**TofA*** 1.1.96: His means most short, his creditors most strait; ***MforM*** 2.2.24: needful but not lavish means; 3.2.21: means to live; ***Temp.*** 2.1.50-51: Here is every thing advantageous to life. / —True, save means to live; ***Ado*** 4.1.195: fortune made such havoc of my means; 4.1.199: Ability in means; ***MofV*** 1.1.125: my faint means; 1.1.138: My purse, my person, my extremist means; 1.1.173: had I but the means; 1.3.17: his means are in supposition; 4.1.376-77: you take my life / When you do take the means whereby I live; ***AYLI*** 1.2.247: could give more, but that her hand lacks means; 3.2.24-26: he that wants money, means, and content is without three good friends; ***Well*** 1.3.251-52: thou shalt have my leave and love, / Means and attendants; 4.3.339: There's place and means for every man alive; 5.1.35: Our means will make us means; ***Rich.2*** 2.1.39: Consuming means, soon preys upon itself; ***2Hen.4*** 1.2.140: Your means are very slender, and your waste is great; 5.5.66: competence of life I will allow you, / That lack of means enforce you not to evils; ***Hen.5*** 1.2.125: your Grace hath cause, and means, and might; ***Rich.3*** 4.2.36-37: a discontented gentleman / Whose humble means match not his haughty spirit; ***TofA*** 2.2.126-27: That I might so have rated my expense / As 1 had leave of means; 2.2.169: the means are gone that buy this praise; 4.3.310-14: What man didst thou ever know unthrift that was belov'd after his means? / —Who, without those means . . . didst thou ever know belov'd?; ***JC*** 4.1.44: our means stretch'd; 4.3.200: So shall he waste his means; ***Mac.*** 2.4.28-29: Thriftless ambition, that will ravin up / Thine own live's means; ***Ham.*** 2.1.8: how, and who, what means; ***Lear*** 4.1.20: our means secure us; ***Oth.*** 4.2.185-86: I have wasted myself out of my means; ***Cym.*** 3.4.177: Your means abroad; 3.5.114: my means for thy relief; ***BBush*** 1.1.37-38: broken, both / In mind and means.

MEED, n. Originally, reward or pay. Recompense, wages, payment or punishment for good or bad deeds. Also a gift; one's intrinsic mettle or desert; a bribe; a reward in love. *[**2Gents***. 2.4.112: duty never yet did want his meed; 5.4.23: for my meed, but one fair look; ***AYLI*** 2.3.58: sweat for duty, not for meed; ***Rich.3*** 1.3.138; 1.4.228: hir'd for meed; 1.4.282; ***Cym.*** 3.5.162: labor be his meed; ***Corio.*** 2.2.97-98: He prov'd best man i' th' field, and for his meed / Was brow-bound with the oak; ***TAnd.*** 1.1.215-16: thanks to men / Of noble minds is honorable meed; 5.3.66: meed for meed, death for a deadly deed!; ***LLL*** 1.1.266-67: the meed of punishment; ***TofA*** 1.1.277-78: No meed but he repays / Sevenfold; ***Ham.*** 5.2.142-43: in his meed he's unfellow'd; ***3Hen.6*** 2.1.36; 4.8.38: my meed hath got me fame; ***MWives*** 2.2.203-4: meed I am sure I have receiv'd none.

MEND, v. To recompense, to improve the fortune of, to increase in economic value. *[**TofA*** 1.1.172: You mend the jewel by the wearing it; ***AYLI*** 2.4.94: we will mend thy wages; ***Shrew*** 1.2.150: I'll mend it with a largess.

MESH. See ***Golden mesh***.

METAL. See ***Mettle.***

METAL-EATER, n. One devoted to money and who spends it freely, i.e., eat as to hoard, and eat as to consume, go through. See ***Midas.*** *[**OldF**.* 5.2.226.

METTLE, n. Originally the same as metal, generally applied to a person's substance or character, with a play on metal as of a coin. Inner value, worth. Proverbially, "All Men are made of the same metal" (Tilley, M501). *[**MforM*** 1.1.48; ***Beware*** 4.2.36-39: To call thee to account for a wound lately / Of a base stamp upon me.—'Twas most fit / For a base mettle. Come and fetch one now / More noble; ***Hen.5*** 4.8.60, 62-64: Give him the crowns. . . .—the fellow has mettle enough in his belly. Hold, there is twelvepence for you; ***Oth.*** 4.2.204: now I see there's mettle in thee [equivocation on spirit/monetary profit]; ***1Hen.4*** 2.4.12: a lad of mettle, a good boy; ***Rich.3*** 4.4.302: of your metal, of your very blood; 4.4.382: th' imperial metal [gold].

MICHER, n. A thief, a sneak, a pander, or one who counterfeits poverty. *[**Ram.*** 332; ***Scorn.*** 425; ***1Hen.4*** 2.4.407-8: Shall the blessed sun of heaven prove a micher and eat blackberries?

MIDAS, n. The Phrygian king who gained from Bacchus the power of transforming all he touched into gold. Thus, *Midas-like* is expecting profit everywhere. Even food turned to gold when Midas touched it with teeth or tongue. The symbol represents the dualistic attitude toward wealth. *[**Ed.2*** 1.4.407; ***MofV*** 3.2.101-2: gaudy gold, / Hard food for Midas.

MILL-MONEY, n. Milled money, machine-made coins with ridged edges. Early coins were, of course, hand-hammered and, since naturally irregular, greatly approved of by corrupters of the coinage. Beginning in 1561 some English coins were manufactured by the new process, but they did not receive wide acceptance and thus were discontinued in 1575 and not again attempted until 1662, when all coins were milled rather than hammered. Referred to disparagingly. *[**Scorn.*** 421: his cast-off mill-money; ***MWives*** 1.1.155: mill-sixpences.

Elizabethan milled sixpence.

MINE. See ***India.***

MINT, n. A coin factory, under the purview of the crown, or slang for a store of coins. All references here are metaphorical, with words as the coins of conversation or intellectual exchange and the mind or the wit as the mint that creates or fabricates these word/coins. *[**LLL*** 1.1.165: a mint of phrases in his brain; ***12N.*** 3.2.22: excellent jests, fire-new from the mint; T***&C*** 1.3.193: coins slanders like a mint.

MITE, n. "The lowest denomination of English money of account" (Frey). A minuscule sum, perhaps one-sixteenth of a farthing. See Tilley, M1026. *[**Prod.*** 5.1.25: not a farthing, not a myte; ***Per.*** 2 Gower 8: Losing a mite, a mountain gain.

MOCCINIGO, n. Also mocenigo. Sometimes a synonym for ducat. Also a Venetian silver coin worth ten soldi, first minted in 1474. Its inscription reads, "GLORIA TIBI SOLI" ("Glory to thee alone"). About thirty-two millimeters in diameter. *[**Volp.*** 2.2.255.

MOEDA D'UORO. See ***Moy***.

MOIDORE. See ***Moy***.

MOIETY, n. A half or a portion. *[**MofV*** 4.1.26: a moi'ty of the principal; ***T&C*** 2.2.106-7: Let us pay betimes / A moi'ty of that mass of moan to come; ***Cym***. 1.4.108-09: pawn the moi'ty of my estate to your ring; ***Staple*** 3.4.27-28: I have a moiety / We will divide, half of the profits.

MONEY, n. Metal (intrinsic value) verified by the king's word (extrinsic value) as a store of value and a medium of exchange. In the Renaissance representative currency first became acknowledged, i.e., actual coins were not necessary to indicate wealth or even to change hands in a transaction. *For money* means for any price; *any money* means any sum; *certain money* is a profit confidently expected; *sterling money* is good money, legal tender, with a pun on "current." A proverb warns, "Would you know what money is, Go borrow some" (Herbert); Gresham's law is "Bad money drives out good." Another states, "He that wants money wants all things" (Tilley, M1046). See ***Church-money***, ***Earnest***, ***Hospital money, Mill-money, Odd money***, ***Out-money***, ***Present money***, ***Press-money, Ready coin or money***, ***White money***. *[**MofV*** 3.5.26; ***12N.*** 3.4.396; ***TofA*** 3.4.46; ***2Hen.4*** 2.1.120; ***WHo*** 2.3.57-58: the silly husbands might heere ha' beene guld with Flemish mony; ***MWives*** 2.2.168-70: if money go before, all ways do lie open.—Money is a good soldier, sir, and will on; 2.2.272; 5.5.233: Money buys lands, and wives are sold by fate; ***NHo*** 5.1.20-22: the sequell of the iest shall come like money borrowed of a Courtier, and paid within the day, a thing strange and vnexpected.

MONEY-BAG. See ***Bag.***

MONEY CREATURE. See ***Creature***.

MONEY MEN, n. Those who deal in the money market: merchants, brokers, moneylenders. *[**MTerm*** 2.3.248.

MONEY-MONGER, n. A lender of money, a money changer, with disreputable or underhanded connotations. *[**Prod.*** 1.2.149; ***Madam*** 1.3.9.

MONKEY, n. Slang for £500, a racetrack betting term. Perhaps Shylock's reference in "a wilderness of monkeys." *[**MofV*** 3.1.119.

MONOPOLY, n. The exclusive right to sell a certain product or to trade with a specific nation, sometimes granted by the sovereign. Often compared to engrossing the market. Because a monopoly indicated favor with the ruler and was lucrative, it was viewed as a real boon. According to Postlethwayt, Elizabeth I first allowed monopolies on playing cards so that her subjects would spend time on husbandry and import rather than manufacture; but "all monopolies are contrary to the ancient and fundamental laws of this realm." Under Elizabeth, moreover, monopolies became a severe problem for the national economy: the monopoly on salt drove the price up from 16d. to 15s. a bushel. Other commodities monopolized were currants, iron, ashes, and gold wire. Under pressure, Elizabeth promised to cancel abusive monopolies and no longer to grant any; James I, however, again issued them freely to his favorites. Sir Giles Mompesson by 1620 was claiming a monopoly on the licensing of pubs, validating only those whose owners gave him substantial bribes. In 1624 the monopoly bill made all monopolies illegal, but the issue continued to crop up until the Civil War. A recent economic theory calls the fight for monopolies "rent-seeking" and pinpoints this desire as the basis of much micro- and macroeconomic policy and behavior. *[**Lear*** 1.4.153; ***Ram.***

339: I would 1 had the monopoly of them, / So there were no impost set upon them; ***Maid*** 5.3.34; ***NHo*** 5.1.170.

MOORFIELDS, n. A swampy field outside the London city gates where people gathered for recreation on holidays and where the troops were drilled. Eventually it became known as the haunt of beggars and rogues. *[**Hen.8*** 5.3.33: Is this Moorfields to muster in?; ***EHo*** 1.1.184-89: methinks I see thee already walking in Moorfields without a cloak . . . borrowing and begging threepence.

MOUNTEBANK, n. and v. An itinerant quack doctor who peddled his potions by climbing upon a bench (hence the name) and cajoling his audience with wit and fast-talk. A pejorative term, used to indicate a charlatan or fraud. *[**WHo*** 5.3.56; ***Volp.*** 2.2.4; ***CofE*** 1.2.101: prating mountebanks; 5.1.239; ***Ham***. 4.7.141: I bought an unction of a mountebank; ***Oth.*** 1.3.61: medicines bought of mountebanks; ***Corio.*** 3.2.132: I'll mountebank their loves.

MOVEABLES, n. A general term for personal property other than land. One's mobile possessions, furnishings for a house, furniture. Property that cannot be passed on in an inheritance. A wife or mistress. *[**NHo*** 5.1.485; ***Volp.*** 4.1.41; ***Shrew*** 2.1.197; ***Rich.2*** 2.1.161; ***Rich.3*** 3.1.195; 4.2.90; ***Cym.*** 2.2.29; ***Hen.5*** 2.3.48: my chattels and my moveables; ***DCourt.*** 1.1.17-18: consorted with his moveable chattle, his instrument of fornication, the bawde.

MOY, n. Properly moidore or *moeda d'uoro*, the prototype of a later popular and widely current gold coin of Portugal, first issued in the mid-sixteenth century and in that coinage about equal in value to a crusado, or around 7s. A moy was also a measure for salt, a bushel. Pistol puns on *moi* as a mistake for a coin, the moy, and extends this pun into a ton of moys as a mistake for *pardonnez moi.* The pun takes on extra depth when we realize the connection between ton and bushel. Here used anachronistically. *[**Hen.5*** 4.4.13, 22.

MUCK, n. A general derogatory word for gold and money, filthy lucre. See ***Dunghill-muck***. *[**Bond***. 1.3.231.

N

NAIL. See ***On the nail***.

NEW EXCHANGE. See ***Old Exchange.***

NOBLE, n. and adj. An English gold coin first minted in 1344 and originally valued at 6s. 8d., but in 1527 also issued at a value of 11s. 3d. Coins of the issue of 1465 were called *royals* or *ryals* (*rose nobles*, worth 10s.) and those of 1526 *George nobles.* Those minted between 1412 and 1464 were called *Henricus nobles.* Of the 1465 issue, Stowe says, "Also this yere the kynge lete smyte a newe noble with a roose standyng there as the crosse shulde at the value of x s. ster. And the olde nobill was valued, and so to goo for viij s. iiij d. And ther was newe grotes and pensse made after the valewe of the nobyll, that is to sey, lighter then they were a fore. Also he lete make a pece of gold valued at vj s. viij d., that is to sey an angell, and oÞer smaller peces of golde of les valure" (80). In the *London Chronicle* he reports of 1526 that the half-noble was valued at 3s. 9d. and the angel noble at 7s. 6d. (2). See ***Appendix E.*** A *double ryal* is a sovereign (20s.), an appropriate metaphor. The name "noble" derives from the purity of the gold, noble in having only half a grain of alloy: "As yellow as the golden Noble," a proverb says (Tilley, N193). The obverse shows the crowned king in a ship, holding a sword and a shield; the reverse has a flower and a short cross. About thirty-two millimeters in diameter. Often appears in a pun on the coin and a person's value, i.e., character, social rank, birth. *[**1Hen.4*** 2.4.287: noble man; ***MofV*** 1.1.127: a noble rate; ***MadW.*** 3.3.18: Two hundred pounds in fair rose nobles; ***Fatal*** 1.1.17-18: But give me (sir) my fee.—Now you are Noble; ***Prod.*** 2.1.33-35: he is [a] man of reckoning . . . / he hath the nobles; ***Hater*** 103: there is an impost set upon knighthoods, and your friend shall pay a noble in the pound; ***Madam*** 5.2.68-69: You are a noble man, / Pray you pay in my moneys; ***MforM*** 1.1.49; ***Ado*** 2.3.33: noble, or not I for an angel; ***Hen.5*** 1.2.126-27: Never king of England / Had nobles richer; 3.1.29-30: there is none of you so mean and base, / That hath not noble lustre in your eyes [character, coin, greed]; ***1Hen.6*** 5.4.22-23: to obscure my noble birth.—'Tis true, I gave a noble to the priest; ***Rich.3*** 1.3.80-81: ennoble those / That scarce . . . were worth a noble; ***Beware*** 4.2.36-39: To call thee to account for a wound lately / Of a base stamp upon me.—'Twas most fit / For a base mettle. Come and fetch one now / More noble; ***Rich.2*** 5.5.67-68: Hail, royal prince!—Thanks, noble peer! / The cheapest of us is ten groats too dear; ***John*** 5.2.61-64: Into the purse of rich prosperity / ... so, nobles, shall you all, / . . . methinks an angel spake.

English noble, Henry V.

NOMISMA. See ***Solidare.***

NOSE, n. Copper noses or bloody noses refer to coins of a debased issue, probably of Henry VIII. His large portrait was reproduced on these coins with a prominent nose. With very little wear the silver veneer disappeared first from the nose and allowed the base metal to show through. The term sometimes appears in a pun on war wounds, i.e., bloody noses and cracked crowns, also worthless as coins. The cracked crowns have an added level of significance as shaky kingship. *To coin his nose* refers to the custom of reproducing the king's portrait on coins; therefore, the nose itself (as a synecdoche for the face) is innately valuable. This would also mean that the king or prince could use his fame, position, and recognizability as credit for loans. Usurers are notorious for having large noses, one of their major distinguishing stage characteristics—because they are caricatures with distorted features of humanity. In *EMen* (481) Pisaro is said to have a nose "Able to shadow Paul's, it is so great." See ***Bottle-nosed***. *[**1Hen.4*** 2.3.93-94: We must have bloody noses . . . / And pass them current; 3.3.78; ***T&C*** 1.2.106; ***BBush*** 3.1.76.

NOTE, n. and v. Generally, anything written: a contract, an inventory, a list, a bill, an obligation of debt. Also profit or advantage. Appears in puns on bond, to observe, and to contract. Cf. ***Mark.*** ***[CofE*** 4.1.27; ***MWives*** 4.2.63; ***MofV*** 3.2.140: I come by note, to give and to receive; ***Well*** 1.3.188-89: a bond / Whereof the world takes note; ***2Hen.4*** 5.1.18: the smith's note; ***TofA*** 2.2.16: a note of certain dues.

O

O. See ***Cipher***.

OB. See ***Obulus.***

OBLIGATION, n. A financial duty, a debt, a bond, written up as a legal contract with specified terms of performance. In the plays it is representative of money or wealth in reference to the person holding the obligation. By extension, marriage. See ***Bill***, ***Bond***, ***Note.*** ***[Drum*** 218; ***MWives*** 1.1.10- 11: bill, warrant, quittance, or obligation; ***2Hen.6*** 4.2.93-94: he can make obligations, and write court-hand; ***HWhore1*** 4.1.170-71: that obligation / Where my soul's bound in heavy penalties.

OBOL. See ***Obulus***.

OBULUS, n. Also ob. or obol. A half-penny, from its Greek and Roman numismatic predecessors. An obol was the coin placed in the mouth of a corpse to pay Charon for ferrying him over the Styx. Stow[e] reports a devaluation of 17 August 1551, "a shyllyng to be currant for vj.d., a grote for ij.d., a peny of ij.d. for a peny, a peny for a ob., & a ob. for a qr." (24). ***[1Hen.4*** 2.4.539.

OCCUPIER, n., **OCCUPY**, v. Probably from the Latin *occupare pecuniam,* a merchant, a person who trades in money or goods; also slang for a cohabitor. To occupy the market was the same as to forestall: to buy up all available stocks of a single item, thus creating a shortage and a price increase. Stow[e] reports that in 1551 immediately following a coin devaluation, "ensewed great death [dearth] of all thynges; for y[e] people, couetinge to rayse y[e] losse of theyr money vppon soche kynd of wares or victualles as they occupyed, dyd dayly inhaunse & encrease y[e] prises both of wares &

victualles, most miserably oppressynge y[e] poore" (22). *[**Ram**.* 308.

ODD MONEY, n. A remainder, an amount over an even sum, *e.g.*, a shilling and odd pence (less than two shillings). *[**Gall**.* 257.

OFFERING, n. Also offering piece. A certain coin from the reign of Alfred the Great, of shilling value, much larger than other circulating coins of the time. With a pun on religious pledge or sacrifice. *[**1Hen.4*** 1.2.126-27: rich offerings, and ... fat purses.

OLD EXCHANGE, n. The Royal Exchange, built by Thomas Gresham in 1566. The New Exchange or Britain's Burse was built in 1609. See ***Burse.*** *[**Madam*** 1.1.128; 3.1.13: the Burse, or Old Exchange.

OLD GOLD. See ***Gold.***

ON THE NAIL, prep. Immediate payment; cash on the spot. *[**Madam*** 1.1.6.

ON THE PRESENT, prep. Money to exchange hands immediately, as an earnest or bargain for more money to follow. *[**TofA*** 1.1.141.

OPINION. See ***Golden opinion***.

ORANGE-TAWNY, adj. A traditional color for a stage usurer, the color of his cloak, his badge (required for all Venetian Jews), or his hair and beard. *[**Gall.*** 210: orange-tawney velvet; ***MND*** 1.2.94: orange-tawny beard, 3.1.126: orange-tawny bill [supported by the econolinguistic complex following: note, quill, and angel];***Beware*** 3.1.26-29: She talks of things here my whole state's not worth—Never a green silk quilt is the in the house, Mother, / To cast upon my bed?—No, by troth is there, / Nor orange tawny neither.

ORKYN. See ***Stiver***.

OUCH, n. Also owch. Originally, a buckle, often inset with jewels; hence the setting or stone on a brooch or the clasp itself. *[**2Hen.4*** 2.4.48: brooches, pearls, and ouches.

OUTCRY, n. An auction or public sale in the street. *[**Madam*** 1.3.76: The goods of this poor man sold at an outcry; ***Maid*** 3.3.84: I'le sell all at an Out-cry.

OUT-MONEY, n. Non-liquid assets; money invested or lent out. *[**Trick*** 2.2.62: Let my out-monies be reckon'd.

OUTSELL, v. To obtain a higher price for, thus to exceed in value. *[**Cym*** 2.4.102: Her pretty action did outsell her gift; 3.5.73-74: she . . . / Outsells them all.

OVERCHARGE, v. To exceed the *justum pretium;* to impose a heavy financial burden; to tax exorbitantly. *[**1Hen.6*** 1.3.64: O'ercharging your free purses with large fines: ***Per***. 3.2.54: if the sea's stomach be o'ercharged with gold.

OVERHOLD, v. To overestimate in value; to esteem beyond its true worth. *[**T&C*** 2.3.133: overhold his price.

OWCH. See ***Ouch.***

P

PACKING, n. Fraud, conspiracy, underhanded plotting, with reference to economic profit. *[**EHo*** 5.2.7: there may be tricks, packing; ***Shrew*** 5.1.118: Here's packing ... to deceive us; ***Lear*** 3.1.26: snuffs and packings of the Dukes.

PANURGO, n. Nickname for a miser or usurer, perhaps derived from Rabelais' Panurge or independently from the Greek, for willing to undertake anything for a profit. Cf. panurgy: knavery. *[**Case*** 4.7.148: the old panurgo.

PAPER, n. and adj. Representative currency or a contract involving a monetary transaction. *Paper pellets* are IOUs. *[**TofA*** 1.2.242: in paper; ***Debts*** 1.1.54-56: Your land gone, and your credit not worth a token, I You grew the common borrower; no man scap'd / Your paper pellets.

PARCEL-BAWD, n. One who acts as pimp in a small-time way or only part- time, who takes on "parcels" of work. Skeat suggests "partially" a bawd. *[**MforM*** 2.1.63.

PARCHMENT, n. Synecdoche for financial contracts—bonds and wills— with the implication that something committed to paper is irrevocably binding; with a pun on an assurance as another kind of bond. /**2Hen.6** 4.2.79-81: a lamentable thing . . . that parchment, being scribbled o'er, should undo a man; ***JC*** 3.2.128-29: a parchment with the seal of Caesar, / . . . 'tis his will; ***BBush*** 4.1.63: I'll no parchments; ***Rich.2*** 2.1.64:

rotten parchment bonds; ***Debts*** 1.2.78-79: Like virgin parchment, capable of any / Inscription; 5.1.184; ***Ham.*** 5.1.114-17: Is not parchment made of sheepskins? / —. . . of calves'-skins too. / —They are sheep and calves which seek out assurance in that.

PATENT, n. and adj. A license, or an article conferring power or authenticating a person or situation, also used to grant a monopoly. Also public or accessible, in the original sense of open. See ***Monopoly. [Rich.2*** 2.1.202: letters-patents; ***Hen.8*** 3.2.250; ***Oth.*** 4.1.197-98: give her patent to offend; ***Well*** 4.5.66: a patent for his sauciness; ***MND*** 1.1.80: virgin patent ["maidenhead" (Partridge)].

PAUL-PENCE. See ***Pence***.

PAWN, n. and v. To risk, to stake, in the hope of some profit. To pay. Thus also the thing risked, an item offered as security for a loan or other venture. A pledge or surety. Applied metaphorically to love, sex, life, honor, *etc*. ***[Lear*** 1.1.155: My life I never held but as [a] pawn: 1.2.86: pawn down my life; ***TofA*** 3.5.80-81: I'll pawn my victories /. . . upon his good returns; ***Corio.*** 3.1.15: he would pawn his fortunes; ***WTale*** 2.3.166: I'll pawn the little blood which I have left; 4.4.808: in pawn; ***John*** 5.2.141: like pawns lock'd up in chests; ***2Gents.*** 1.3.47: her oath for love, her honor's pawn; ***CofE*** 5.1.390: These ducats pawn I for my father here; ***Rich.2*** 2.1.293: broking pawn; ***2Hen.6*** 5.1.113: They'll pawn their swords [for] my enfranchisement; ***3Hen.6*** 3.3.116: I pawn my credit and mine honor; 4.2.9: pawn'd an open hand in sign of love; ***Rich.3*** 4.2.89: your honor and your faith is pawn'd; ***DCourt.*** 2.1.191-92: this pawne, where dost dwell?; ***Killed*** 5.1.106: for thy more assurance, here's a pawn; ***2Hen.4*** 2.1.141: fain to pawn both my plate and the tapestry; ***MWives*** 2.2.6: lay my countenance to pawn; 3.1.110: lay their swords to pawn.

PAX, n. A certain type of English silver coin from the issues of Harold II and William I, about nineteen millimeters in diameter, carrying as an inscription the letters "PAX" or "PAXS" in the interstices of the cross on the obverse. Also perhaps slang for any coin with a cross stamped upon it, as a variant of pyx, a container for the Eucharist, usually marked with a cross. In the Middle Ages Trials of the Pyx were held in which a jury of independent judges would test the purity of coins. It obviously puns on pax as peace, with a hidden pun on piece, also a coin. *[**Hen.5*** 3.6.40: he hath stol'n a pax, and hanged must a' be; 3.6.44-45: Exeter hath given the doom of death / For pax of little price.

PAY (A FINE), v. To buy or employ; to trick; to beat physically or to punish, from the denotation to recompense, to mete out a due reward; to receive sexual favors; to fulfill, as the contract of life. To *pay a debt* is, metaphorically, intercourse between husband and wife (Ross). See ***Present Money.*** *[**CofE*** 2.2.75; ***AYLI*** 1.1.160; ***2Hen.6*** 4.7.122: pay to me her maidenhead; ***NHo*** 5.1.511; ***Fatal*** 4.1.148; ***OldF***. 3.1.108-09: he payes downe-right blowes; ***DCourt.*** 5.3.97: I will looke to your wives paiment; ***R&J*** 1.1.238: I'll pay that doctrine, or else die in debt; ***Temp.*** 3.2.131: He that dies pays all debts; 5.1.70-71: I will pay thy graces / Home both in word and deed.

PELF, n. Generally money, riches, or property, but as a derivation of pilfer, implies that the treasure is ill-gotten booty. Used disparagingly. *[**JofM*** 5.5.18; ***Case*** 2.1.30; ***TofA*** 1.2.62: I crave no pelf; ***Per.*** 2 Gower 35: All perishen of man, of pelf; ***Heir*** 113.

PENCE, n. Plural of penny. In the plays two or three pence are trifling amounts, which will buy a piece of fruit or, punningly, a prostitute's services as well as a goose. Stowe reports that in 1552 Holland cheese cost twopence a pound (45); five pence or eighteen pence is a typical tavern bill; sixpence buys a fish for dinner and indicates a royal reward in pension to workmen; sixpence spent on wine, saved instead, would accrue to £20 12s. at one's death; a bawd's fee is also sixpence. Ten pence as one's total worth is paltry; twelve pence is a tip or a peace offering; the hangman at Tyburn earns thirteen-pence halfpenny to pay for his supper; eighteen pence is a standard average price for admittance to a play, although *BFair* catalogues the range from sixpence to half a crown,; and forty pence constitutes a trivial wager. From 1560 to 1630 craftsmen earned around 12d. per day and laborers 8d. (Clarkson). Stowe reports on some unusually high Lenten prices in 1563: "heryngis was sold for ij a penye when they was best cheape ethar whit or red, Essyxe chesse for vj d. ye li. baryll [,] buttar for vij and viij d. ye li., a bad stockefyshe for vj d. or viij d." (122). ***Peter-pence*** and ***Paul-pence*** were annual taxes paid to the Pope until 1533 under

Henry VIII: probably a penny for all land or cattle worth 30d. in each household. ***Smoke-pence*** is probably a similar tax levied on every chimney in a house. A ***dandiprat*** is "a small coin worth 3 halfpence, first coined by Henry VII." A ***Jane*** and a ***Julio*** are small silver Italian coins current for a few pence (Skeat). The saying ***Farewell, forty pence*** comes from the proverb "Farewell, forty pence! Jack Noble is dead," indicating that a person has just spent a half-noble (40d.), depleting the whole noble (Hazlitt). Halfpence were notorious for being badly coined, and a gilded twopence could pass for a half-crown (Coursen, 123). See ***Appendix C.*** *[**Maid*** 3.3.106; ***12N.*** 1.5.80-81: he will not pass his word for twopence; 4.1.30-31: I would not be in some of your coats for twopence; ***2Hen.4*** 4.3.51: gilt twopences; ***Hen.8*** 2.3.36: a threepence bow'd would hire me; ***MforM*** 2.1.92-93: a fruit-dish, a dish of some threepence; ***2Gents.*** 2.5.9: one shot of five pence; ***MTerm*** 1.1.302-3: six-pence British; ***Vex.*** 115: this salmon . . . cost but sixpence; ***NHo*** 1.2.43; 4.3.178-79: three Geese nine pence; euery Goose three pence; ***MND*** 4.2.21: sixpence a day; ***JofM*** 4.4.36-37: What gentry can be in a poor Turk of ten pence; ***Beware*** 3.3.69- 70: I have seen almost / As tall as she sold in the fair for ten pence; ***Hen.5*** 4.8.63-64: there is twelvepence for you; ***WHo*** 2.1.45: three Elizabeth twelue-pences; ***HWhore2*** 5.2.167-68: the hangman's thirteen-pence halfpenny ordinary; ***MWives*** 2.2.14; ***Scorn.*** 440: can see a play / For eighteen- pence; ***BFair*** Ind. 115-17: It shall be lawful for any man to judge his six pen'orth, his twelve pen'orth, so to his eighteen pence, two shillings, half a crown; ***Faust.*** 4.6.6: eighteen pence on the score; ***Hen. 8*** 2.3.89: Is it bitter? Forty pence, no; ***EMen*** 526: Farewell, fortypence; ***3Lad.*** 254: I care not whom I serve—the devil, so I may get pence; 271: smoke-pence, Peter-pence, and Paul-pence; ***AYLI*** 3.2.353-56: they were all like one another as halfpence are, every one fault seeming monstrous till his fellow-fault came to match it.

PENNILESS-BENCH, n. *Sitting on penniless-bench* is a metaphor for going broke. See Tilley, P187. *[**Madam*** 4.1.43-44: he shall not / Sit long on penniless-bench.—There spoke an angel.

PENNY, n. An English silver coin, by 1601 copper, which superseded the Anglo-Saxon penny. There are twelve pence to the shilling, two hundred and forty to the pound (under the old system of reckoning). Most pennies have a portrait of the sovereign on the obverse and a cross with pellets in the interstices on the reverse. A pattern for a copper penny of 1601 reads "THE PLEDGE OF / A PENNY." About eighteen millimeters in diameter. In the plays a penny is a small sum, as in one poor pennyworth. It occurs as well in other derogatory combinations that define the low character or paltry value of the person or thing described. Sixpence is often mentioned as a small sum: a barber's fee, a payment to a minstrel for singing a song, a cheap fee for a prostitute (the usual price seems to be 12d.), the price of a small pie or pastry. A better penny seems to stand for the best part of a bargain, a larger profit, or wealth that is easily acquired (see Tilley, P189). *[**Scorn.*** 429: God's penny; 438: penny-custards; ***Wit*** 652: penny-rooms; ***Case*** 4.2.67: a packing penny; ***EHo*** 5.2.63: Twopenny Ward; ***Debts*** 3.2.44: twopenny chops; ***Hater*** Pro. 7: two-penny-gallery-men; ***WHo*** 2.1.51: foure-peny-pen-men; 3.3.15: would spend but three pence on his ordinarie; 4.2.193: ten-penny-infidell; 5.4.249-50: sixe-penny Sinfulnesse; ***1Hen.4*** 1.3.91; 2.1.74: long-staff sixpenny strikers; 3.3.104: some eightpenny matter; 3.3.159: one poor pennyworth; ***OldF.*** 2.2.99: sixe penie pies; ***HWhore2*** 5.2.171: sixpenny mutton pasty; ***Ado*** 2.1.40; ***12N.*** 2.3.31; ***2Hen.4*** 1.2.25; ***Madam*** 3.1.34: sixpenny truckers; ***Magn.*** Ind. 34: sixe- penny Mechanicks; ***Ram.*** 317: a twelve penny . . . laundress; ***MadW.*** 3.3.18: twelve-penny panderism; 5.2.33-34: two-penny room; ***Wily*** 225: a better penny; ***Prod.*** 3.1.58; ***MWives*** 1.1.60-61: a petter penny [in Welsh accent].

Elizabethan sixpence.

PENNYFATHER, n. Nickname for a miser or usurer, perhaps because he is the father of profit, its unnatural progenitor. See Tilly, P216. *[Wily 247.*

PENNYWORTH, n. A small amount of anything. A bargain, a profit, an advantage, or sufficient return for one's trouble. Cheap. Sometimes, more than one bargained for. *[**EHo*** 5.1.92; ***HWhore2*** 3.3.51; ***Ado*** 2.3.42; ***LLL*** 3.1.102: your pennyworth is good; ***MofV*** 1.2.71: poor pennyworth; ***R&J*** 4.5.4; ***WTale*** 4.4.635-36; ***2Hen.6*** 1.1.222: Pirates may make cheap pennyworths of their pillage; ***Gall.*** 204: one poor pennyworth; ***1Hen.4*** 2.4.23: pennyworth of sugar; ***BBush*** 5.2.225: good pennyworths.

PERISHED, adj. Financially ruined. *[**Scorn**.* 428.

PETER-PENCE. See ***Pence.***

PFUND. See ***Pound.***

PHILIP RYAL. See ***Royal.***

PICKT-HATCH, n. "An area of London noted for its brothels" (Riverside). *[**MWives*** 2.2.18-19.

PICTURE, n. Slang for a coin, from the portrait of the sovereign that it often bore. *[**HWhore2*** 3.2.39-40: Must have cash and pictures; ***WTale*** 4.4.603: whose purse was best in picture; ***BFair*** 3.5.68-69: to pick the pictures out of your pockets; ***MofV*** 2.7.11: The one of them contains my picture.

PIECE, n. Any coin or piece of money. Perhaps sometimes specifically the double sovereign, worth 22s. by 1660. With a pun on a woman who can be bought with money: a piece of flesh. The Biblical piece of silver is probably a *tetradrachm*; a piece of eight is the Spanish silver eight ***real*** coin, current in England in the seventeenth century for 4s. 6d. See ***Offering.*** *[**OldF.*** 1.1.301: ten pieces of bright gold; ***Oth.*** 3.1.24: piece of gold; ***Ass*** 3.3.83: a hundred pieces; ***MforM*** 2.1.270: some piece of money; ***Temp.*** 2.2.29-30: a piece of silver; ***TofA*** 3.6.21: [borrow] a thousand pieces; ***Ham.*** 2.2.427-28: a piece of uncurrent gold; ***Per.*** 4.2.43: I have gone through for this piece; 4.2.51-52: a thousand pieces; ***Cym.*** 5.4.25: take pieces for the figure's sake; 5.5.183; Pieces of gold; ***Corio.*** 3.3.32: the poorest piece; ***BBush*** 2.1.170: One small piece of money; ***Magn.*** 5.7.43:Three hundred thousand peeces; ***Debts*** 1.1.171; 2.3.115: There's a piece for my late blows [with an adnominatio on peace]; ***Madam*** 4.3.14: For a piece an hour; ***BFair*** 4.4.174: Can you lend me a piece, a Jacobus.

PIG, n. Slang for sixpence. With a pun on pork. See ***Swine.*** *[**BBush*** 3.1.123- 24: Fill till't be sixpence, / And there's my pig; ***CofE*** 2.1.66: 'The pig,' quoth I, 'is burn'd': 'My gold!' quoth he.

PILL, v. To rob or steal, from to pillage (French ***piller).*** To extort. *[**TofA*** 4.1.12: pill by law; ***Rich.2*** 2.1.246: The commons hath he pill'd with grievous taxes; ***Rich.3*** 1.3.158: that which you have pill'd from me.

PINCH, v. To steal, with a pun on to tweak, thus with sexual connotations. One humorous Renaissance tale tells of a tradesman of the Exchange who allowed his wife to attend the theater, but warned her to watch her purse. When she returned home empty-handed, her husband demanded an explanation: " 'Wife, (quoth he,) did I not give you warning of it? . . . Where did you put it?' 'Under my petticoat, between that and my smock.' 'What, (quoth he,) did you feel no body's hand there?' 'Yes, (quoth she,) I felt one's hand there, but I did not think he had come for that'" (*Harleian,* 89). *[**WTale*** 4.4.609-10: You might have pinch'd a placket.

PISTOLE, n. A Spanish gold coin minted first in 1537, a double *escudo,* worth 16s. 11d. See ***Appendix B***. *[**HWhore1*** 4.2.3-4: they are sound pistoles, and without flaw.

PISTOLET, n. A lesser ***pistole,*** current in England in 1560 for 5s. 10d., down from its previous value of 6s. 2d. Also an *ecu pistolet,* a gold coin of Geneva first issued in 1562. Sometimes with a pun on pistol or little bullets. *[**Volp.*** 2.2.267: double pistolet; ***NHo*** 2.1.247: He pai'd that shot, and then shot pistolets into my pockets.

PITCH AND PAY, v. To insist on a cash transaction. *[**Hen.5*** 2.3.49-50: the [word] is "Pitch and pay"; / Trust none.

PLATE, n. Any silver coin, from the Spanish *plata.* Also pieces of precious metal or table furnishings made from gold or silver, as representations of wealth. *[**JofM*** 2.3.101: three hundred plates; ***DCourt.*** 1.1.13; ***A&C*** 5.2.91- 92: realms and islands were / As plates dropp'd from his pocket; ***Shrew*** 2.1.347:

richly furnished with plate and gold; ***Cym.*** 1.6.189: plate of rare device; ***Volp.*** 1.1.78: bring me presents, send me plate, coin, jewels; ***Prod.*** 2.4.167: Plate, mony, Iewels; ***TofA*** 3.2.21: money, plate, jewels; ***Rich.2*** 2.1.210: His plate, his goods, his money, and his lands; ***EMen*** 557: all I have, / My money, plate, wealth, jewels, daughter; ***NHo*** 2.1.257-58: has thy father any plate in's house.—Enough to set vp a Goldsmithes shop; ***WHo*** 1.1.175-76: all your plate and most part of your Iewels are at pawne.

PLEDGE OF VALUE. See ***Token***.

PLOW, n. and adj. Slang for an amount of money, a tax, from plough alms, a tax paid to the church for lands under cultivation or for the number of plows owned, and from plough silver, a reparation paid by a tenant to a landlord if the tenant did not plough and reap crops from the rented land. *[**Hen.5*** 4.8.13-14: I will give treason his payment into plows.

PLUM, n. Slang for £100,000, from racetrack jargon (Postlethwayt). Used generally to mean money, coins, large sums, with a pun on plum as a fruit and as a boon, a real benefit. *[**2Hen.6*** 2.1.99: thou lov'dst plums well, that wouldst venture so.

PLUTO, n. Perhaps an error for Plutus; Pluto, however, was god of the underworld and sometimes, by extension, called God of Wealth, guardian of the metals in the earth. *[**T&C*** 3.3.197: Pluto's gold; ***JC*** 4.3.102: Dearer than Pluto's mine, richer than gold.

PLUTUS, n. A Roman allegorical figure of wealth, used to indicate the god of gold. *[**TofA*** 1.1.276; ***Well*** 5.3.101; ***Madam*** 3.3.108: All deities serve Plutus.

PLY, v. To work diligently, from to apply. By extension, to bend a woman to one's will: to woo, to win in marriage; with sexual connotations. *[**3Hen.6*** 3.2.50: He plies her hard; ***AYLI*** 3.5.76: Shepherd, ply her hard; ***Oth.*** 4.1.106: Ply Desdemona well.

POLL-DENNERY, n. Financial trickery, extortion. Skeat suggests pole- pennery, "extortion of pence." *[**Wily*** 229: to scrape for more rent, is poll- dennery.

POND. *See **Pound.***

PORTAGE, n. Originally, the act of carrying. A tax levied on merchandise brought in by ship, or the merchandise itself, an individual's portion of the cargo. [***Per.*** 3.1.35: Thy loss is more than can thy portage quit.

PORTAGUE, n. The Portuguese gold *crusado,* ranging in value from £3 5s. to £4 10s. Generally, any Portuguese coin. [***JofM*** 1.2.245.

PORTCULLIS, n. Portcullis money was coined by Elizabeth in 1600-1601 for the East India Company. The coins carried the device of a large portcullis on the reverse and were of crown, half-crown, shilling, and sixpence denominations. Henry VIII had coined a portcullis groat and farthing (Wriothesley), but these coins were rarely in circulation and indeed are thought to be patterns rather than actual tender. Some "better" testons worth 4 ½d. circulating in 1560 carried the device of a portcullis. [***EMOH*** 3.6.189-90: I had not so much as the least portcullice of coine before.

Portcullis money, Elizabethan.

PORTION, n. A dowry, inheritance, allowance, or economic destiny, with an implied meaning of wealth in possession. Proverbially, "Virtue and a Trade are the best portion for children" (Herbert). [***WHo*** 1.1.72; *Lear* 1.1.242; ***WTale*** 4.4.385-86: I give my daughter to him, and will make / Her portion equal his; ***AYLI*** 1.1.38: What prodigal portion have I spent?; ***Hen.8*** 3.2.107-8: What piles of wealth hath he accumulated / To his own portion; ***MforM*** 3.1.221-22: the portion and sinew of her fortune, her marriage-dowry; ***Shrew*** 2.1.359: All things answerable to this portion; ***Magn.*** 1.3.3-4: keepes the portion, / Still in his hands.

PORTMANTU, n. A suitcase; probably an error or malapropism, acyron, for *portague.* [***Case*** 5.3.36, 38: her's a crusado for thee. . . .—their's a portmantu for thee.

POSSE, n. *In posse* indicates the possibility of attainment or ownership, as opposed to *in esse,* an actual holding. See possible pun at ***Pig***. [***Scorn***. 438: pigs in posse.

POSSESS, v. To own, to have, to hold; thus, by extension of economics into the matters of love and sex, to have intercourse with. [***R&J*** 3.2.26-28: O, I have bought the mansion of a love, / But not possess'd it, and though I am sold, / Nor yet enjoy'd; 5.1.10: how sweet is love itself possess'd; ***AYLI*** 4.1.143-44: tell me how long you would have her after you have possess'd her.

POSSIBILITIES, n. Chances for a good inheritance; the potential to be wealthy. [***MWives*** 1.1.64.

POUND, n. The pound sterling, English money of account, originally equal to a pound weight of silver, from which two hundred and forty pennies of approximately equal weight were coined. Also equal to twenty shillings. Equivalent to ***libra, livre, lira, pond,*** and ***pfund,*** according to the system instigated by Charlemagne (Munro). In the Renaissance no single coin consistently represented an English pound value, but the sovereign was revalued in 1561 to equal 20s. In the plays £5 and £10 suppers are extravagant; £5 a week will also buy one a mistress, for exclusive use. "A score of good ewes may be worth ten pounds" (***2Hen.4*** 3.2.50-51). The price of a fancy riding suit is £20, which is also disparagingly mentioned as the salary for writing a play. One could buy a knighthood from the king for £30; £40 is the price of an extremely extravagant supper, a virgin's sexual favors, or a .small cottage; £50 is the price of a ring. "A man of fourscore pound a year" (***MforM*** 2.1.123) is a lowly gentleman. A *knave of a hundred pound* indicates a false gentleman, a pretender to nobility, while £300 a year is a good income, as well as the cost of running an estate for a year, and £700 is an admirable middle-class inheritance. Things worth £500 and £1000 are very expensive, and £2000 constitutes an extremely large dowry. As a substantial amount beyond the reach of most *dramatis personae*, £1000 is often mentioned as a wager in a wish—"I would give a thousand pound I could run as fast as thou canst" (***1Hen.4*** 2.4.147-48)—while £6000 will buy an estate. In addition to indicating the value of an individual, the term pound also appears in a three-level pun: an amount/an enclosure/to beat. [***Volp.*** 4.1.111: one pound sterling; ***Madam*** 2.1.111: ten-pound suppers; 3.1.82-

83: an Irish lord offer' d her / Five pound a week; ***Debts*** 1.1.60: Some forty pounds or so, bought a small cottage; 2.3.29, 31-32: twenty pounds . . . / 'twill serve to buy you / A riding suit; 4.2.86: five-pound suppers; ***Case*** 1.1.100-101: they'le giue me twenty pound a play; ***EHo*** 4.1.222-23: thirty pound knights; ***Wit*** 655: a supper of forty pounds; ***Lear*** 2.2.16; ***MWives*** 1.1.50-51; 3.3.123-24; 3.4.33; ***1Hen.4*** 2.4.61; ***Maid*** 2.1.154; 2.1.215; 2.2.14; 4.4.61-63: I shall receive two thousand pound in Gold, / And a sweet Mayden-head / Worth fourtie; ***2Hen.6*** 3.3.13; ***2Gents.*** 1.1.104-08; ***Scorn.*** 422, 429, 452; ***NHo*** 3.2.102: a thousand pound to a penny.

PRACTICE, n. and v. To trick, especially financially or sexually. To attempt a marriage based on wealth. To use for one's own profit. To cheat or steal for a living. *[MofV* 3.4.77-78: **A** thousand raw tricks ... *I* Which I will practice; ***R&J*** 3.5.209: practice stratagems; ***Debts*** 5.1.230: devilish practices you used to cozen; ***Shrew*** 3.2.251: Shall sweet Bianca practice how to bride it?; ***MforM*** 5.1.123: This needs must be a practice; ***12N.*** 5.1.352: This practice hath most shrewdly pass'd upon thee; ***AYLI*** 1.1.150: will practice against thee; ***John*** 4.1.20: My uncle practices more harm to me; ***BFair*** 1.2.74: mere piece of practice; ***2Hen.4*** 2.1.114-16: You have . . . practic'd upon the easy-yielding spirit of this woman, and made her serve your uses both in purse and in person; ***Hen.5*** 2.2.99: Wouldst thou have practic'd on me, for thy use?; ***Oth.*** 1.2.73: thou hast practic'd on her with foul charms; ***2Gents***. 4.1.45-47: Myself was from Verona banished / For practicing to steal away a lady, / [An] heir; ***BBush*** 5.2.231: Higgen must practise ... to eat; ***2.Hen.6*** 2.1.167: practic'd dangerously against your state; ***Well*** 2.1.106: the dearest issue of his practice; ***Hen.8*** 1.1.203-4: I shall perish / Under device and practice; ***Corio.*** 4.1.32-33: caught / With cautelous baits and practice; ***Ham***. 5.2.317-18: The foul practice / Hath turn'd itself on me; ***Lear*** 2.1.73: suggestion, plot, and damned practice; 5.3.152.

PRESENT MONEY, PAY, STORE, OR SUM, n. Cash on hand; coins available and ready to be spent; ready cash. With a pun on present (to show, to give). See ***On the present***. *[**JofM*** 2.3.6; 3.2.276; ***CofE*** 4.1.34; ***Hen.5*** 2.1.107; ***MofV*** 1.1.179; 1.3.53; 3.2.273; ***Fatal*** 1.2.340; 5.1.12-13: present moneys, or/ Assurance; ***MTerm*** 2.3.213; 3.4.114: present money, or present imprisonment [with a further equivocation on present as immediate].

PRESS, v. In aphaeresis, to (im)press, i.e, conscript, soldiers, with a pun on coin-making: to stamp men in one's own mold by paying them money. Contrasted to the king, who has the only legal right to coin (extended puns on crown/pay/angel). *[**Rich.2*** 3.2.58-61: For every man that Bullingbrook hath press'd / To lift shrewd steel against our golden crown, / God for his Richard hath in heavenly pay / A glorious angel.

PRESS-MONEY, n. Money given to impressed soldiers as earnest pay, a proof of their enlistment. Also money paid in advance or a loan to the sovereign. Wriothesley reports one of the latter in 1542: "This yeare was a prest demanded by the Kinge of his Lordes spirituall and temporall and the Commons" (1:136). *[**Lear*** 4.6.87.

PRICE, n. Also prise. Worth, value, cost, esteem, used in many combinations. *Of price* means of value; *in idle price* means of trifling esteem or worth; a *poor price* refers to something of small value or estimation. A *common price* indicates a prostitute. Something obtained *at an easy price* is inexpensive. To *make what price they will* means to control the market, while *at our own price* indicates what the buyer can afford. *Her price is fall'n* means that her esteem is diminished, and *I know my price* indicates a confident fellow who knows his own value. Falstaff lists the following food prices on his grocery list: a capon, 2s. 2d.; sauce, 4d.; sack, two gallons, 5s. 8d.; anchoves and sack after supper, 2s. 6d.; bread, ob. (*1Hen.4* 2.4.535-39). *[**OldE*** 5.2.291: Vertue is of price; ***EMen*** *411:* an angel of more price; ***2Hen.4*** 5.3.96: happy news of price; ***MforM*** 1.3.9; ***Well*** 4.3.276; 5.3.61: Make trivial price of serious things; 5.3.190; ***TAnd.*** 3.1.198; ***Ado*** 3.3.114-15; ***Corio.*** 1.1.10-11; ***Lear*** 1.1.197; ***Oth.*** 1.1.11; ***R&J*** 4.1.27; ***12N*** 1.1.13: low price; 3.4.230: at any price; ***T&C*** 2.2.81-82: a pearl, / Whose price hath launched above a thousand ships; 2.3.133-34: if he overhold his price so much, / We'll none of him; ***DCourt.*** 3.1.67-68: husbands are like lotts in the lottery: you may drawe forty blankes before you find one that has any prise in him.

PRISE. See ***Price, Prize.***

PRIVY SEAL NOTE, n. A coerced loan to the government; a sealed warrant for the collection of a certain sum from an individual. According to Wriothesley, an IOU: "every man havinge a privie seale for his warrant to be payd againe in two years" on a press loan to the King (1:136). *[Ass* 3.3.36.

PRIZE, n. and v. To esteem, to value; to evaluate, to rate, to appraise, to reckon a worth in price or reputation; to haggle. With sexual undertones, indicating a combination of value and desire; a treasure of wealth and sexual favors. *[**Ado*** 4.1.218: what we have we prize not to the worth; ***12N.*** 2.4.81-82: my love . . . / Prizes not . . . lands; ***WTale*** 3.2.42: For life, I prize it; 3.2.110: I prize it not a straw; ***TofA*** 5.1.181; ***LLL*** 5.2.224: Prise you yourselves; what buys your company?; ***Lear*** 1.1.70: prize me at her worth; ***A&C*** 5.2.183-84: Caesar's no merchant, to make prize with you / Of things that merchants sold; ***T&C*** 1.2.289: Men prize the thing ungain'd more than it is; ***Rich.3*** 3.7.187: Made prize and purchase of his wanton eye; ***OldF.*** 3.1.220: I prize this Iewell at a hundred Markes; ***MWives*** 2.2.137: She is my prize.

PROFIT, n. and v. Originally, progress or an advancement. Any advantage or benefit: income, interest, well-being, good fortune, the natural increase that follows copulation. Used suspiciously or pejoratively of merchandising, pecuniary gain through commerce. Proverbially, "Honour and profit lie not in one sack" (Herbert). *[**AYLI*** 2.4.98; ***2Hen.6*** 1.1.204: the profit of the land; ***3Hen.6*** 2.5.55: 111 blows the wind that profits nobody; ***Oth.*** 2.3.9-10: The purchase made, the fruits are to ensue; / That profit's yet to come 'tween me and you; ***LLL*** 4.2.75-76: their daughters profit very greatly under you; ***Faust.*** 1.1.54: what a world of profit and delight; ***MofV*** 3.3.30: the trade and profit of the city.

PROMISE. See ***Golden promise.***

PROMOTER, n. One who solicits investors in an enterprise like a joint-stock company. Because there were so many false promoters and swindlers, it is a term of opprobrium. According to Hugh Latimer in "Sermon IV," an informant. *[**MadW.*** 3.2.105: a running [scab], your promoter; ***Maid*** 2.1.122: corruption of Promoters.

PROPERTY, n. A wife married for money rather than for love. See ***Cattels.*** *[**MWives*** 3.4.10: I should love thee but as a property.

PROTEST, v. "To fix the liability for the payment of a dishonoured bill; *spec*. a formal declaration in writing, usually by a notary public, that a bill has been duly presented and payment or acceptance refused" *(OED). [**Madam*** 1.3.38: protest you.

PURCHASE, n. Income or earnings, especially from land; loot or booty (metaphorically extended from the hunt); attainment or acquisition, especially by disreputable means; a gain (by robbery); by extension, marriage. Le Comte suggests "prey." In a special use, the amount paid for a piece of land, stated in terms of the length of the payment period. Proverbially, "He that learns a trade, hath a purchase made" (Herbert). *[**Hen.5*** 3.2.41-42: They will steal any thing, and call it purchase [earnings]; ***1Hen.4*** 2.1.91-92: Thou shalt have a share in our purchase [booty]; 3.3.40: there's no purchase in money [gain]; ***HWhore2*** 4.1.288-89: the purchase is rich; the plot to get it easy; ***Rich.3*** 3.7.187: prize and purchase of his wanton eye; ***Drum*** 192: purchase of your love [attainment]; ***Volp.*** 1.1.30-31: I glory / More in the cunning purchase of my wealth; ***1Tamb*** 2.5.92: I judge the purchase more important; ***12N***. 4.1.23: fourteen years' purchase; ***MadW.*** 2.4.66; 3.2.88: This purchase came unlook'd for; ***Beware*** 1.1.12: the most unvalued'st purchase; ***Oth.*** 2.3.9-10: The purchasc made, the fruits are to ensue; / That profit's yet to come 'tween me and you; ***BFair*** 2.4.43-44: All the purses and purchase I give you to-day by conveyance; 2.5.226-27; ***BBush*** 5.2.63: his crown's purchase.

PURCHASE, v. To obtain; to earn through merit or labor; to redeem; to win, as in wooing; to gain by wealth. *[**CofE*** 2.2.62; ***AYLI*** 3.2.342; ***LLL*** 5.2.59; ***Temp.*** 4.1.14: Worthily purchas'd, take my daughter; ***A&C*** 1.4.13-14: hereditary / Rather than purchas'd; ***R&J*** 3.1.193: purchase out abuses; ***Bond.*** 1.1.2*;**2Hen.6*** 1.1.223: and purchase friends; ***BBush*** 3.1.151: to purchase money; ***MWives*** 2.2.205: purchas'd at an infinite rate; ***MforM*** 1.2.46-50:1 have purchas'd as many diseases under her roof as come to—. . . three thousand dolors a year; ***2Hen.4*** 4.5.199.

PURSE, n. Originally, perhaps, a leather bag. Literally, of course, a pouch for keeping money, papers, and other valuables. Sometimes a metaphor for a large sum, a great deal of money, or a payment. Control of the purse indicates power and domination in certain relationships, *e.g.,* marriage. Often the purse is equated to the brain or the wit, and its contents—coins—are equated to words as the medium of intellectual exchange. Since purses were often hung from the belt, a purse is also metaphorically the scrotum. Because women sometimes hung purses between their under- and outer-garments, a purse also is related to their sexual parts. The purse often is personified as the keeper of wealth, and the term appears in many combinations: *cold purses* are empty, and *hot ones*, full and free in spending. *Sickness of the purse* indicates poverty, as do *consumption of the purse* (with a pun on spending/consuming), the *leanness of his purse,* and *deepest winter* in the purse. *At my purse* means at my own cost, as *upon your purse* means at your expense. A *slow purse* is tight or empty, while *free purses* are liberal, just like wits with words. A *miser's purse* never opens, and seldom does his wit. *Festival purses* are full of coins, as is *a purse . . . best in picture.* A *halfpenny purse* is small, insignificant; one with a *halfpenny purse of wit* has a tiny brain; and a *tassel of a prodigal's purse* is an insignificant decoration on an empty, useless object. To *serve your uses both in purse and in person* not only employs an amusing paronomasia, but also implies the connection between money and sexual activity. Proverbially, "Usurer's purses and women's plackets are never satisfied" (Tilley, U31), and "A heavy purse makes a light heart" (Tilley, P655). Appears in a paronomasia on purse/ purchase. *[**Lear*** 3.1.45: open this purse; ***AYLI*** 2.4.13-14: no money in your purse; ***T&C*** 4.5.6; 5.1.32; ***MWives*** 1.3.52-53: the rule of her husband's purse; 1.3.68: She bears the purse; 2.2.132; 3.5.146; ***Rich.2*** 2.2.129-30: their love / Lies in their purses; ***Ham..*** 5.2.130-31: His purse is empty already: all's golden words are spent; ***Cym..*** 4.2.113: Cloten was a fool, an empty purse; 5.4.163-65: purse and brain both empty; the brain being the heavier for being too light, the purse too light, being drawn of heaviness; ***WTale*** 4.3.118-19: your purse is not hot enough to purchase your spice; 4.4.610-11: 'twas nothing to geld a codpiece of a purse; 4.4.614-15; 4.4.617-18:1 had not left a purse alive; ***1Hen.4*** 1.2.127: fat purses; 2.4.323; ***Shrew*** 4.3.171: Our purses shall be proud; ***Vex.*** 179: sickness of the purse; *2Hen.4* 1.2.236-37; 2.1.115-16; ***2Hen.6*** 1.1.112; ***TofA*** 3.4.14; 4.2.12: Like empty purses pick'd; ***EHo*** 4.2.298; ***Cym.***. 1.6.135; ***2Gents.*** 1.1.26; ***1Hen.6*** 1.3.64; ***LLL*** 5.1.74; ***Gall.*** 288: make a purse; ***MofV*** 1.1.138: My purse, my person, my extremest means; ***Prod.*** 2.1.111:

Fat, faire, and louely, both in purse and person; 4.2.9: a good purse; 5.1.71-72: Ile not let a sixepennie- purse escape me; ***OldF***. 2.2.331-32; ***MTerm*** 1.1.126: Ile swell thy purse with angels; 1.1.236-38: He bee kinde to women, that which I gather i'th day, He put into their purses at night; ***BFair*** 2.4.43: purses and purchase.

PURSE, v. To put away coins in a safe place, to bank them; to steal purses for a living. Metaphorically applied to love. *[**MofV*** 1.3.174: purse the ducats; ***JofM*** 1.1.6: I have pursed their paltry silverlings; ***Scorn.*** 419: I'll purse; ***A&C*** 2.2.186-87: she purs'd up his heart.

PURSENET, n. A bag for catching fish or rabbits, with a pun on purse. Figuratively, to be tricked or caught out. *[**WHo*** 2.3.35; 5.1.158: setting pursenets to conycatch vs; ***OldF.*** 1.2.77-78: gold ... is like a Conie taken napping in a Pursenet.

PURSY, adj. Fat and breathless, out of condition, with a pun on swollen, heavy with wealth. Also lack of exercise (of purse and person), causing pursiness. In his sermon "The Gallant's Burden," Thomas Adams remarks, "gluttony [makes a man] so pursy that he cannot go." *[**Debts*** 2.3.62; ***Magn***.. 3.5.31-32: It is a Pursinesse, a kind of Stoppage, / Or tumor o' the Purse, for want of exercise; ***TofA*** 5.4.12: pursy insolence shall break his wind; ***Ham..*** 3.4.153: the fatness of these pursy times.

PUT TO, v. Various meanings in combination form: *put to use* means lent at interest, but here, also a pun on allowed to copulate and thus increase "naturally"; *I put you to / The use of your own virtues* means to trust to one, here with a pun on the pecuniary "trust," expect a debt in return; also with a pun on the sexual meaning of use of virtues, to gain money by prostitution; *land . . . put to their books* is borrowed upon, mortgaged. *[**12N.*** 3.1.50; ***Well*** 5.1.15-16; ***TofA*** 1.2.200.

PUT UP, v. To pocket or put away, usually coins or money, sometimes with an implication of theft. *[**Volp.*** 1.3.58-59: take provoking gold . . . / And put it up; ***TofA*** 4.3.108: Put up thy gold; ***HWhoreI1*** 2.1.181-82: put up the money.

Q

Q. See ***Cardecue, Cue***.

QUALITY, n. Ability; profession, trade, or skill; character, moral values, social status. *[Hen.5* 3.6.137: What is thy name? I know thy quality; ***Ham.***. 2.2.346-47: Will they pursue the quality no longer than they can sing?; ***MWives*** 5.5.40: Attend your office and your quality; ***12N.*** 3.1.63: The quality of persons; ***Lear*** 5.3.119-20: What are you? / Your name, your quality?; ***2Hen.4*** 4.1.87: Concurring both in name and quality; ***BFair*** 1.5.167.

QUART D'ECU. See ***Cardecue.***

QUESTION. See ***In question.***

QUESTUARY. See ***Gainer***.

QUINTAL. See ***Kentall***.

QUIT, v. Aphaeresis for to (ac)quit, to be rid of, in the sense of to release from debt or obligation by paying the sum or fulfilling the obligation; to reward or recompense; to requite, to avenge. See ***Acquittance, Quittance.*** *[CofE* 1.1.22: to quit the penalty; ***MofV*** 4.1.381: To quit the fine; ***MforM*** 5.1.411: Like doth quit like, and *Measure* still *for Measure;* ***Rich.3*** 4.4,20- 21: Plantagenet doth quit Plantagenet, / Edward for Edward pays a dying debt; ***12N.*** 5.1.320: Your master quits you; ***Ham..*** 5.2.67-68: is't not perfect conscience / To quit him with this arm?; ***Cym..*** 5.4.166: you shall now be quit; ***Per.*** 3.1.35: Thy loss is more than can thy portage quit; ***WHo*** 4.2.115- l6: to quit / Thy losse of such a Iewel; ***2Hen.4*** 3.2.238: he that dies this year is quit for the next; ***TAnd.*** 1.1.141: To quit the bloody wrongs upon her foes; ***Madam*** 4.1.28-29: bring money with thee / To quit old scores; ***R&J*** 2.4.192: I'll quit thy pains; ***Faust.*** 4.3.13: Faustus' death shall quit my infamy.

QUITTANCE, n. A document certifying full repayment of a debt; thus both a release from obligation and a requital, extended generally to mean a renunciation or payment in kind, retaliation. Sometimes a reward. Proverbially, "Forbearance (Omittance, Sufferance) is no quittance" (Tilley, F584). See ***Acquittance, Quit***. *[MWives* 1.1.10: bill, warrant, quittance; ***TofA*** 1.1.279-80: a return exceeding / All use of quittance; ***AYLI*** 3.5.133: omittance is no quittance; ***Hen.5*** 2.2.34: quittance of desert and merit;1***1Hen.6*** 2.1.14: to quittance their deceit; ***Debts*** 5.1.100.

R

RACK, v. Probably from the Dutch *rekken,* to draw out; to stretch (usually one's credit) beyond its normal limits and thus to inflict financial pain, as if the debtor were upon an instrument of torture. Also with the implication of to impoverish. Le Comte suggests "wreck, destruction." *[**MofV*** 1.1.180-81: my credit . . . / Shall be rack'd; ***Ado*** 4.1.220: we rack the value; ***2Hen.6*** 1.3.128-29: The commons hast thou rack'd, the clergy's bags / Are lank and lean with thy extortions; ***Trick*** 1.1.43-44: all your lands / Thrice rack'd; ***Debts*** 5.1.99: I'll rack thy soul for't.

RAG, n. Slang for a farthing, a minuscule sum of money. See Tilley, R6.1. *[**CofE*** 4.4.86: not a rag of money.

RAISE, v. To liquidate funds, to produce ready money, to get cash by pawn or loan; to improve the financial status of someone; to propagate and rear. *[**MofV*** 1.1.179: raise a present sum; 1.3.55: raise up the gross; ***JC*** 4.3.71: I can raise no money; ***TofA*** 4.3.9: Raise me this beggar; ***Hen.5*** 5.2.348-49: raise up / Issue to me; ***Vex.*** 101: twice have I rais'd / His decayed fortunes to a fair estate.

RATE, n. Price, value, estimation, status, or reputation. Often refers to interest, usually expressed as a percentage, *e.g.,* ten in the hundred. Sometimes in reference to a mercantile love transaction: *at an infinite rate* indicates a metaphorical extreme interest, suffering that is not worth paying for the merchandise (a woman). Occurs in many combinations. *[**CofE*** 1.1.23: at the highest rate; 4.4.14: at the rate; ***Bond.*** 1.3.80: at any rate; ***MWives*** 2.2.205; ***Temp.*** 1.2.92: popular rate; 2.1.110: in my rate; ***MforM*** 2.2.150: whose rate are either rich or poor; ***MND*** 3.1.154: a spirit of no common rate; ***MofV*** 1.1.127: a noble rate; 1.3.45: the rate of usance; ***Well*** 5.3.91: at her live's rate; 5.3.217: Subdu'd me to her rate; ***Hen.8*** 1.1.99: a superfluous rate; ***Corio.*** 1.1.189: corn at their own rates; ***JofM*** 1.2.187: valued at indifferent rate; ***1Hen.6*** 3.2.43: buy again at such a rate; ***NHo*** 2.1.164: at such an excessiue rate; ***DCourt.*** 2.1.106: at a cheape rate; ***BBush*** 2.3.85: her rate's at more than you are worth; ***Magn.*** 1.1.43-45: You doe mistake / . . . at what rate I reckon your assistance.

RATE, v. To evaluate in terms of worth or esteem, including intrinsic value; to calculate or estimate the price of. Occurs in an aphaeresis on (be)rate. *[**TofA*** 1.1.168; ***2Hen.4*** 1.3.44: rate the cost; ***MofV*** 2.7.26: rated by thy estimation; ***Cym..*** 1.4.77: I prais'd her as I rated her.

READY COIN OR MONEY, n. Cash on hand in liquid form ready to be spent or invested. Also called *Legum pone* because "The first great pay-day of the year was March 25, on which day of the month the *Legum pone* is the first portion of the 119th Psalm read at Mattins, so that these words were easily associated with the idea of payment and ready money" (Skeat). A proverb says, "A Cutpurse is a sure trade, for he has ready money when his work is done" (Tilley, C943). Also "Ready Money will away" and "Ready Money is a ready medicine" (M1091, M1092). See ***Present money***. *[**EHo*** 2.2.342; ***MforM*** 4.3.7; ***Faust.*** 5.1.4: two thousand ducats ready coined; ***Prod.*** 3.2.168: For one groat readie downe, heele pay a shilling; ***NHo*** 4.2.9: Shee gelded my purse of fifty pounds in ready money; ***MTerm*** 2.3.229; ***Vex.*** 146; ***Volp.*** 3.7.143-44: He would have sold his part of Paradise / For ready money.

REAR, n. Arrears. Literally, behind in time of payment of a debt, duty, or obligation, with a pun on the general idea of "behind." *[**EHo*** 1.1.81: in the rear.

RECKON, v. To count or tally a sum; to make an evaluation; to render an accounting; with an equivocation on to scan poetry. *[**TofA*** 3.4.56: I have no more to reckon, he to spend; ***Well*** 5.3.90-91: she reckon'd it / At her live's rate; ***Mac.*** 5.9.26-27: We shall not spend a large expense of time / Before we reckon; ***Magn.*** 1.1.45: at what rate I reckon your assistance; ***Trick*** 2.2.62: Let my out-monies be reckon'd; ***Ham.*** 2.2.120-21:1 have not art to reckon my groans; ***A&C*** 1.1.15: There's beggary in the love that can be reckon'd.

RECKONING, n. A bill or items on a bill; metaphorically, the Last Judgment; arithmetic; a total; reputation; a sexual assignation. A *man of reckoning* is a steward. *[**1Hen.4*** 2.4.100-101: his eloquence the parcel of a reckoning; 3.2.152: tear the reckoning from his heart; 3.3.158: tavern-reckonings; ***AYLI*** 3.3.15: a great reckoning in a little room; 3.4.32: the confirmer of false reckonings [a lover and a tapster]; ***MforM*** 5.1.46: to th' end of reck'ning; ***Cym..***

5.4.157: A heavy reckoning [death]; ***Ham..*** 1.5.78- 79: No reck'ning made, but sent to my account / With all my imperfections on my head; ***LLL*** 1.2.40-41: I am ill at reck'ning, it fitteth the spirit of a tapster; 5.2.496-97: get your living by reck'ning; ***2Hen.4*** 1.2.170-71: his quick wit wasted in giving reckonings; ***1Hen.4*** 1.2.49: call'd her to a reckoning; 5.1.135: A trim reckoning; ***R&J*** 1.2.4: of honourable reckoning; 1.2.32-33: mine, being one, / May stand in number, though in reck'ning none; ***Scorn.*** 427: discharge thine office, / And cast up a reckoning; 435: man of reckoning; ***Prod.*** 2.1.33-36: he is [a] man of reckoning . . . / he hath the nobles, / The golden ruddockes he; ***Drum*** 204: as the Travailer knocketh with his Hostes for a reckning, even so do I call to thee.

RECOGNIZANCE, n. A token, pledge, or surety for a certain promised performance, usually a legal bond for debt. A recognition of such a bond through the property given as surety, to be forfeited upon nonperformance. *[**Oth.*** 5.2.214: that recognizance and pledge of love; ***Ham.*** 5.1.104-5: his statutes, his recognizances, his fines.

RECOVERY, n. A legal process for the transfer of property, especially of an entailed estate. See ***Fine.*** *[**Ham..*** 5.1.106: [a land-buyer's] recoveries; ***MWives*** 4.2.211; ***CofE*** 2.2.72-74.

RECULLISANCE, n. Error for ***Recognizance.*** *[**MTerm*** 3.4.248.

RELEASE, n. Full repayment of a debt; a written quittance as receipt for the payment. Also a legal deed for conveying property. *[**Fatal*** 2.2.237-38: Pay'em those summes upon the table, take / Their full releases.

REMERCE. See ***Amerce***.

RENDER, v. Originally, to give back. To offer in return, to give, especially in the sense of a tax or payment. Metaphorically extended to include women and the marriage bargain. *[**1Hen.4*** 3.2.150: render . . . up; ***Ado*** 4.1.29: render her again; 4.1.333: render me a dear account; ***T&C*** 4.1.38-39: there to render him ... the fair Cressid.

REPRIEVE, n. An extended date for repayment of a debt, thus an escape from debtors' prison. *[**MWives*** 2.2.7.

RESTORATIVE, n., **RESTORED,** adj. Something healthful that renews a man, here punningly applied to financial fortunes, with reference to the alleged medicinal properties of gold. Cf. Le Comte's definitions, "return to a state of grace," and "make amends for." See ***Aurum.*** *[**Wit*** 636; ***Rich.2*** 4.1.88-89: restor'd again / To all his lands and signories; ***Per.*** 3.2.45: your creatures, who by you have been restored.

RETORT, v. To repay a debt. *[**MWives*** 2.2.1: I will retort the sum.

REVENUE, n. Generally income, implying quantity or wealth. More specifically, the public coffers as the total wealth of the land, and rents received from lands under private ownership. By extension, "love- making, sexual intercourse; *rents* = either copulation or, more probably, semen-expenditure paid as rent by a man to the woman legally his" (Partridge). *[**Lear*** 1.1.137; 1.2.53: half his revenue; ***T&C*** 2.2.206: the wide world's revenue; 2.3.29: in great revenue; ***Ed.2*** 1.4.307: could my crown's revenue bring him back; 1.4.406: He wears a lord's revenue on his back; ***2Hen.6*** 1.3.80: She bears a duke's revenues on her back; ***MND*** 1.1.6: a young man's revenue; 1.1.158: of great revenue; ***Temp.*** 1.2.98: what my revenue yielded; ***AYLI***I 1.1.101-2: lands and revenues enrich the new Duke; 3.2.377-78: a younger brother's revenue [a small beard]; 5.2.11; ***WTale*** 4.3.27; ***John*** 3.1.169; *Rich.2* 1.4.46; 2.1.226: in title, not in revenues; ***Rich.3*** 3.7.158: the ripe revenue and due of his birth; ***Ham.*** 3.2.58; ***A&C*** 3.6.30; ***Cym.*** 2.3.143.

RIALTO, n. The street or section in Venice where the Exchange was located; a gathering place for merchants and money-men. Also the first public bank of Venice, established in 1587, the *Banco della Piazza di Rialto,* which was simply a depository for the safekeeping of coins. It met its expenses by duties on imports and lent no money. *[**Volp.*** 3.5.28; ***MofV*** 3.1.1: on the Rialto.

RIDDUCK. *See **Ruddock.***.

RIFLE, v. Raffle; to gamble or throw dice for a predetermined stake, here a woman; to prostitute. *[**BBofA*** 1.2.49-51: strike up a drum, set up a tent, call people together, put crowns apiece. Let's rifle for her; ***NHo*** 5.1.315: rifle her at a Tauerne.

RIOT, n., v., and adj. A prodigal expense, extravagant reveling, excess; also dissipation, wantonness. *[**Debts*** 1.1.26-27: Am I not he / Whose riots fed and cloth'd thee?; ***2Hen.4*** 5.5.62: The tutor and the feeder of my riots; ***TofA*** 2.2.1-3: senseless of expense ... his flow of riot; 2.2.159: riotous feeders; ***A&C*** 1.3.29: Riotous madness; ***Ed.2*** 1.4.404: riot it with the treasure of the realm; ***MWives*** 3.4.8; ***Staple*** 3.4.37-38: Now the public riot / Prostitutes all; ***Prod.*** 1.1.282; ***OldF.*** 5.2.211: their ryots made them poore; ***Fatal*** 1.2.156-57: May all your wives prove whores, your factors theeves, / And while you live, your ryotous heires undoe you.

ROSE, n. Slang for a three-farthing piece from the reign of Elizabeth, marked with a rose behind the portrait of the Queen. The penny lacked the rose but was otherwise a very similar coin in appearance. *[**Scorn.*** 436: washing out the roses in three farthings, / To make 'em pence; ***John*** 1.1.142-43: in mine ear I durst not stick a rose / Lest men should say, "Look where three-farthings goes!"

Rose 3-farthing, Elizabethan.

ROYAL, n. and adj. Also ryal. A Spanish silver ***real*** (piece of eight) current in England in 1626 for 5s. Also the gold rose noble of Edward IV, coined in 1465, valued at 10s., in contrast to the regular noble worth 6s. 8d.; thus forty pence or ten groats was their difference in value. Stow[e] reports that the "riall" was proclaimed worth 11s. 3d. in 1525 (2), but in 1562 Elizabeth devalued the fine gold royal from 15s. to 10s. *(TRP).* See ***Appendix E.*** A ryal of Elizabeth's coinage shows the Queen superimposed over a ship with a rose beneath her; the reverse has the sun with a flower motif. About thirty-five millimeters in diameter. A *spur-ryal* or spur-royal of James I worth 15s. shows a crowned lion holding a scepter, with the sun, crowned flowers, lions rampant, and *fleurs-de-lis* on the reverse. About thirty-three millimeters in diameter. A *Philip ryal* may have been the *brabant* or *real d'or* of Philip II of Spain or a silver version from Philip III of Aragon. The term appears in puns on the coin's value and a man's social status or character, as well as in punning reference to a face royal, i.e., clean-shaven, but also the portrait of the sovereign on the coin. *[**1Hen.4*** 1.2.140-41: thou cam'st not of the blood royal, if thou darest not stand for ten shillings; 2.4.290-91: Give him as much as will make him a royal man; ***Rich.2*** 5.5.67-68: Hail, royal prince!—Thanks, noble peer! / The cheapest of us is ten groats too dear; ***Rich.3*** 1.3.123-24: A liberal rewarder of his friends; / To royalize his blood I spent mine own; ***NHo*** 2.1.245: Philip ryalls; ***MadW.*** 2.6.102: some hundred pounds in fair spur-royals; ***Scorn.*** 417: nine spur-royals; ***2Hen.4*** 1.2.24-26: He may keep it still at a face royal, for a barber shall never earn sixpence out of it; ***Trick*** 3.1.153: a brace of royals.

Gold ryal, James I.

Silver ryal, Philip III of Aragon.

ROYAL EXCHANGE. See ***Old Exchange***.

RUBBISH. See ***Golden rubbish.***

RUDDOCK, n. Also ridduck. Slang for a gold coin, in reference to its reddish color. Similarly, white money is silver and black money billon or another alloy. Puns on ruddock or raddock, the robin. (A charitable bill is a beneficent will as well as the beak of a kind bird, who brings moss to cover the grave.) *[**Prod**.* 2.1.36: golden ruddockes; ***Cym.**.* 4.2.224-25: The raddock would, / With charitable bill.

RYAL. See ***Royal***.

S

ST. NICHOLAS, n. The patron saint of thieves; therefore, St. Nicholas's clerks are highwaymen, robbers. See Tilley, S54. St. Nicholas Lane in London ran perpendicular to Lombard Street, the financial district (Stowe). *[**1Hen.4*** 2.1.61.

SALE. See ***House of sale, Whole sale***.

SALUTE, n. and v. The *salut d'or* originally coined by Charles VI of France in 1380, later reissued by Henry V of England for France in 1422. The *salut d'or* was modeled after the Italian *saluto d'oro* coined in the thirteenth century. According to Stowe's *Chronicles,* the *Salus* was worth 22s. 8d. Although there is no explicit reference to this coin in the plays, Shakespeare alludes to it quibblingly as the gift of money offered with a greeting for friendly or mercenary purposes. *[**CofE*** 4.3.1-4: There's not a man I meet but doth salute me. . . . Some tender money to me; ***John*** 2.1.590: his fair angels would salute my palm; ***A&C*** 3.12.11: Lord of his fortunes he salutes thee.

Gold salute, Henry VI.

SATISFACTION, n., **SATISFY,** v. Financial repayment, legal remedy, or revenge on a debt or for its default; fulfillment of a marriage contract or a sexual promise. *[**Fatal*** 5.1.22; ***DCourt.*** 3.1.177; ***Madam*** 4.2.93-94: satisfaction / To the utmost scruple; ***BBush*** 1.3.77-78: unable / To make you satisfaction; ***Mo/V*** 4.1.415-16: He is well paid that is well satisfied, / And I, delivering you, am satisfied; ***R&J*** 2.2.126-27: What satisfaction canst thou have tonight? / —Th' exchange of thy love's faithful vow; ***MforM*** 3.1.263: give him promise of satisfaction [sexual fulfillment]; ***CofE*** 4.1.5: make present satisfaction [pay]; ***2Hen.4*** Ep.21: good conscience will make any possible satisfaction; ***Oth.*** 4.2.199-200: assure yourself I will seek satisfaction of you [repayment]; ***AYLI*** 5.2.115: satisfy you, if ever I satisfied man [sexually],

SCORE, n. and v. A tally used to keep track of a customer's debt, especially at a tavern, also metaphorically applied to sexual economics and the contract of life. Technically, a stick worn at the belt (the tally) was scored, i.e., notched, to indicate amounts owed on a bill. Thus, *on the score* means to be in debt. Appears in an adianoeta with score, to make marks on a person, to beat. See ***Tally***. *[**Faust.*** 4.6.6: I am eighteen pence on the score; ***Shrew*** Ind.2.23: fourteen pence on the score for sheer ale; ***DCourt.*** 3.3.19: full many fine men goe upon my score; ***1Hen.4*** 2.4.27-28: Score a pint of bastard in the Halfmoon; 5.3.30-31: Though I could scape shot-free at London, 1 fear the shot here, here's no scoring but upon the pate; ***Well*** 4.3.224: After he scores, he never pays the score; 5.3.56-57: That thou didst love her, strikes some scores away / From the great compt; ***2Hen.4*** 2.1.24: he's an infinitive thing upon my score; ***2Hen.6*** 4.2.73: all shall eat and drink on my score; 4.7.34-35: no other books but the score and the tally; ***Mac.*** 5.9.18: They say he parted well [died], and paid his score.

SCOT, n. An individual's share of the cost of a certain entertainment; also a local tax to finance usually the sheriff or bailiff. With a pun on a man from Scotland (see Tilley, S157). See ***Lot.*** *[**3Lad.*** 348: For now we neither pay Church-money, subsidies, fifteens, scot nor lot; ***1Hen.4*** 1.3.214: By God, he shall not have a Scot of them [Scottish prisoners]; 5.4.113-14: That hot termagent Scot had paid me scot and lot too.

SCOURSE, v. Also scorse, skoase. To barter or trade, perhaps with an aphaeresis on (di)scourse, to converse with the intent of business, to haggle. *[**BFair*** 3.4.30: Will you scourse with him?

SCRIBS, n. Nickname for a miser or usurer, perhaps because he keeps written records (scribbles) of his money. Scribes, or scriveners, often acted as brokers and wrote up economic bonds. *[**MadW.*** 3.3.139: Guard me from bonny scribs and bony scribes.

SCRIVENER, n. An amanuensis; a writer of contracts and bonds; a notary; an investment broker, who would take funds on consignment from his clients and, for a commission, about 1 percent, a brokage fee, invest them with other of his customers. Some scriveners also made short-term loans at interest. Because of their many money-making ruses, scriveners were, according to Stubbes in *Anatomie of Abuses,* "the Instrument wherby the Deuell worketh the frame of this wicked woorke of Usurie." Proverbially, "An Usurer is one that puts his money to the unnatural act of generation, and the scrivener is his bawd" (Tilley, U28). *[**Shrew*** 4.4.59; ***NHo*** 2.1. 140- 42: here was a scrivener but even now, to put my father in minde of a bond, that wilbe forfit this night if the mony be not payd; ***MadW.*** 3.1.36: the scrivener binds folks; ***MTerm*** 2.3.257; 4.1.99: keepe his hand from a queane, and a Scrivener; ***WHo*** 3.2.95-96: Wilt thou take my bond Sergeant? Wheres a Scriuener; 4.1.120: The Scrivener is but new gon vp to take her bond; ***Madam*** 1.2.53: Nor ever yet paid brokage to his [usurer's] scrivener.

SCRUPLE, n. Originally, a small pebble. An extremely small unit of weight, one twenty-fourth of an ounce. Used generally as a minuscule amount of anything, perhaps with a pun on scruple as a moral doubt or dilemma. *[**MforM*** 1.1.37: the smallest scruple; ***Ado*** 5.1.93: what they weigh, even to the utmost scruple; ***MofV*** 4.1.330: one poor scruple; ***Well*** 2.3.221-22: I will not bate thee a scruple; ***Fatal*** 1.2.225: to take away one scruple; ***12N.*** 3.4.78-79: no dram of a scruple, no scruple of a scruple.

SCUTE. See ***Ecu.***

Gold escudo (scute), Philip II of Spain.

SEAL, n., v., and adj. To make or agree to a financial contract, referring to the legal status such bonds attained in the Renaissance, usually requiring the stamp of a notary for validation. Metaphorically, kissing or copulation, to seal a contract of love. Joined or fulfilled, as in matrimony. See ***Cancel. [Ed.2*** 5.4.51: I seal, I cancel, I do what I will; ***MofV*** 1.2.82-83: seal'd under for another; 1.3.144-45: seal me there / Your single bond; 1.3.152: I'll seal to such a bond; 2.6.6: seal love's bonds new made; ***WHo*** 1.2.3-4: Are the bonds seald?; ***CofE*** 1.1.9: seal'd his rigorous statutes with their bloods; ***BFair*** Ind.200-201: you have . . . put to your seals already; ***Vex.*** 146: one-half in ready cash, the other seal'd for six months; ***2Hen.6*** 4.2.82-83: I did but seal once to a thing, and I was never mine own man since; ***R&J*** *4.*1.56: this hand ... to Romeo's seal'd; 5.3.114-15: seal with a righteous kiss / A dateless bargain to engrossing death!; ***1Hen.4*** 3.1.79-80: indentures tripartite **...** *I* sealed interchangeably; ***Shrew*** 3.2.122-23: my bride, / And seal the title with a lovely kiss!; ***John*** 2.1.19-20: Upon thy cheek lay I this zealous kiss / As seal to this indenture of my love; ***T&C*** 3.2.197: Go to, a [love] bargain made, seal it, seal it; ***Ham..*** 4.7.1: Now must your conscience my acquittance seal; ***Per.*** 2.5.85: your hands and lips must seal it; ***MforM*** 4.1.6: Seals of love [kisses], but seal'd in vain; ***MND*** 1.1.84: The sealing-day betwixt my love and me; ***2Gents***. 1.3.49: seal our happiness [oath of love]; 2.2.8: seal the bargain with a holy kiss.

SECTOUR. See ***Executor***.

SECURITY. See ***Surety***.

SELL, v. and adj. Originally, to give or deliver. Also, in medieval Latin, *soldum,* pay or remuneration (Skeat). Metaphorically applied to a woman, referring to one who is married, in love, or spoken for, or to one who merchandises her body, indicating an increased nexus between love and the world of marketing and finance. *[**R&J*** 3.2.26-28: 0,1 have bought the mansion of a love, / But not possess'd it, and though I am sold, / Not yet enjoy'd; ***Oth.*** 4.1.94: by selling her desires; ***MWives*** 5.5.233: Money buys lands, and wives are sold by fate; ***AYLI*** 3.5.60: Sell when you can, you are not for all markets.

SEQUIN. See ***Cecchine.***

SERVICE. See ***Golden service.***

SHARE-PENNY, n. Or shear-penny. Slang term for a miser or usurer, perhaps because he lends (shares) his money or because he clips or otherwise tries to shear the most value out of his coins. *[**Wily*** 228.

SHAVE, v. and adj. Originally, to scrape. To clip, cut, or trim edges from coins in order to make an illicit profit on the metal thus procured. Generally, to trick out of money. The term allows for a series of complex puns: to shave beards, as a barber does; since priests have shaved crowns (clipped coins), it also refers to corruption among the ordained; one can also make profit (red gold = blood) from financial tricks of the priests (shaved crowns in both senses). Also to trick out of sexual or marital profit, to take one's virginity. See ***Trim***. *[**JofM*** 2.3.112:1 can cut and shave; ***2Hen.6*** 2.1.50: I'll shave your crown for this; ***Faust.*** 3.2.27: Lest Faustus make your shaven crowns to bleed; ***DCourt.*** 2.1.203; 2.3.88-89:Trim'd, O wife, I am shav'd, did you take hence the money?; 2.3.116-17; ***BBush*** 5.1.47-48: pray God you be not shaven! / 'Twill spoil your marriage, mistress.

SHEKEL, n. Originally, to weigh. A silver coin of the Jews worth four *drachmae* or four *denarii,* first minted in 143 B.C. A general term for any coin. The form *sides* may indicate an intentional catachretic paronomasia for testicles. Cf. ***Ducat, Tester***. See ***Silverling.*** *[**MforM*** 2.2.149: fond sides of the tested gold.

SHELL, n. Slang for money in general; any coin, perhaps from the new English knowledge in the Renaissance of tribes in Africa and the Orient who used shells for money. *[**HWhore2*** 3.2.110-11: Borrow some shells of him.

SHIFT, v. To make a living, here, by uncertain, expedient, fraudulent means; to plan and plot; to steal. *[**MWives*** 1.3.34:

I must shift; ***CofE*** 3.2.182: a man here needs not live by shifts.

SHILLING, n. Originally, perhaps, a piece cut off. An English silver coin first struck in 1504 (before that, a money of account), with the value of 12d. There are twenty shillings in a pound (by the old system of reckoning). Most show the ruler's portrait on the obverse; the coins vary in diameter from twenty-eight millimeters to thirty-three millimeters (considered quite large, larger than an angel, a ducat, or a noble, about the size of a royal or a half-crown). In the plays 1s. buys an expensive seat in the theater; 2s. is the cost of a meal or a trip to the brothel; *2s. Innes a court men* are cheap but have pretensions to grandeur; 8s. is the price of Holland cloth per ell; 10s. allows for a pun on the coin royal; and 40s. will buy an inexpensive horse. A harper or Irish *harp* shilling carried the device of a harp on the reverse and was current for 9d. (Skeat). See ***Shove-groat.*** ***[Bond.*** To Reader 13-14: you have disburs'd a shilling, / To see this worthy STORY; ***Hen.8*** Pro. 12-13: [playgoers] may see away their shilling / Richly in two short hours; ***Scorn.*** 440: feast myself / With my two shillings; ***MadW.*** 3.3.137: scorn two-shilling brothel; ***DCourt.*** 2.2.29; ***1Hen.4*** 1.2.141; 3.3.71-72; ***2Hen.6*** 4.7.22-23; ***Madam*** 2.2.181: a nag of forty shillings; ***MWives*** 1.1.156-57; ***2Hen.4*** 2.4.192-93: a shove-groat shilling; 3.2.221-22: four Harry ten shillings in French crowns; ***Prod.*** 5.1.92: a brasse shilling; ***Hater*** 121: take his money from him, lest he swallow a shilling, and kill himself.

Elizabethan shilling.

SHORES. *See* ***Golden shores.***

SHOT, n. An individual's portion of a bill at a tavern or at an entertainment; a fee, a tavern bill; occurs in puns on bullet, entertainment, and final reckoning. See ***Scot.*** *[**2Gents.*** 2.5.6: till some certain shot be paid; 2.5.9: for one shot of five pence; ***Cym.***.5.4.156: the dish pays the shot; ***3Hen.6*** 1.4.29:1 am your butt, and I abide your shot; ***1Hen.4*** 5.3.31; ***NHo*** 2.1.245- 47: did thy father pay the shot?—He pai'd that shot, and then shot pistolets into my pockets.

SHOT-CLOG, n. A gull who is welcome company only because he pays the entire bill: his own and that of everyone else. *[**EHo*** 1.1.183-84: thou common shot-clog, gull of all companies; ***EMOH*** 5.9.47; ***Staple*** 4.1.47.

SHOT-FREE, adj. A free meal, drink, or entertainment, with many levels of puns. Besides a bill, shot is also bullets and death, the final reckoning. Shot-free implies scot-free, meaning safe or unpunished; free from taxation; and immune from fighting the Scots. Shakespeare seems conscious of all these meanings here. *[**1Hen.4*** 5.3.30-31: I could scape shot-free at London, I fear the shot here.

SHOT-SHARK, n. One who seeks, chases after the shot, thus a cashier, a collector of the reckoning, usually in a tavern. *[**EMOH*** 5.4.1.

SHOVE-GROAT, n. A shilling of the coinage of Edward VI. Because these coins were large and broad, they were valuable as counters or players in the game of shovel-board (shuffleboard). *[**2Hen.4*** 2.4.192-93: Like a shove-groat shilling.

Silver shove-groat shilling, Edward VI..

SHOVEL-BOARD, n. Another name for the shove-groat shilling. *[MWives* 1.1.156-57: Two Edward shovel-boards, that cost me two shilling and two pence apiece.

SHOWER. See ***Golden drops, Golden showers***.

SHRUNK. See ***Custom-shrunk.***

SICLE. See ***Shekel.***

SIGNORY, n. Territory over which one has dominion and authority, perhaps also income; property, land. *[**2Hen.4*** 4.1.109; ***Rich.2*** 3.1.22: you have fed upon my signories; 4.1.88-89: restor'd again / To all his lands and sig- nories.

SILVER, n. A general term for money, with a pun on music, extended from the chink of coins shaken together. Proverbially, "Music has a silver sound" (Tilley, M1319.1). *[**R&J*** 4.5.134-35: musicians sound for silver; ***MTerm*** 3.1.279-80: good jests are worth silver.

SILVERLING, n. Another name for a *shekel.* Generally any silver coin of small value. (Interesting in that when Barabas rejects the importance of these coins, he also in a sense throws off his heritage and becomes representative of the modern mercantilist.) *[JofM* 1.1.6.

SIQUIS, n. A bill of advertisement, beginning "If anyone. . . ." *[EMOH* 2.6.194.

SIT, v. To have as regular expenses. *[MWives* 1.3.8: I sit at ten pounds a week.

SKOASE. See ***Scourse***.

SLIP, n. Slang for a counterfeit coin. One from the Renaissance in the Numismatic Society Collection would probably not fool the wary, for it is made of an extremely black metal, with a cartoon of Henry VIII on the obverse and a simple crowned rose, a common device, on the reverse. This coin has crude lines, a lack of detail, no inscription, and wrong proportions in the styling of the device. Counterfeit coins are equated punningly with false words, escape, and loss. See ***Counterfeit.*** *[MadW*. 5.1.67; ***MofV*** 3.1.11: slips of prolixity; ***R&J*** 2.4.46-48: What counterfeit did I give you?—The slip, sir, the slip; ***T&C*** 2.3.25-27: If I could 'a' rememb'red a gilt counterfeit, thou [wouldst] not have slipp'd out of my contemplation.

SMOKE-PENCE. See ***Pence.***

SOL, n. A *sou.* A Renaissance French coin first of silver and later of copper, corresponding to the shilling. Perhaps also the Italian *soldino,* a small silver coin (fifteen millimeters in diameter) from the fourteenth century, with a wolf face on the obverse, called in England a galley-halfpenny. Also gold in alchemy and the sun, with a pun on Son (Christ). See ***Appendix B.*** *[**Volp.*** 4.5.97.

SOLIDARE, n. The *solidus,* a gold coin minted *by* Constantine around A.D. 312 312, worth about twenty-five *denarii.* The Greek name for this coin was *nomisma.* It was the model for the shilling and later was called a *bezant.* *[**TofA*** 3.1.43.

SOU. See ***Sol.***

SOVEREIGN, n. and adj. An English gold coin worth 20s. first issued in 1489. Also a double ryal. It was variously revalued at 22s. (1526), 20s. (1543), 30s. (1551), and 20s. (1561). Elizabeth distinguishes in value two kinds of sovereigns: fine gold (20s.) and crown gold (13s.4d.) *(TRP).* One from Elizabeth's coinage shows the Queen crowned, with a globe in hand, on the obverse. About forty-four millimeters in diameter. After James I took the throne, this coin was called a unite and some issues laurels, "on account of the laureated head on the obverse" (Frey). Because of its pun potential, one would expect Shakespeare to have used this term as often as royal and noble. However, only one possible pun on sovereign occurs; and if it is intended as a pun, it is anachronistic, since the coin was not issued until the reign of Henry VII. See ***Appendix E.*** *[**WHo*** 1.2.11: you shall haue it all in new soueraignes; ***1Hen.4*** 3.2.152, 161: I will tear the reckoning from his heart. . . .—Thou shalt have charge and sovereign trust herein; ***EMOH*** 5.10.30.

Elizabethan gold sovereign.

Gold unite, James I.

SOW. See ***Swine***.

SPAN-COUNTER. See ***Compter***.

SPANGLE, n. Slang for a coin. *[**OldF**.* 3.1.340: Spangles of pure gold.

SPARING, n. Thrift, frugality, "natural" economy. *[**R&J*** 1.1.218: in that sparing [makes] huge waste.

SPECIALTY, n. A bill, bond, or contract or the particular items therein agreed. Sometimes in reference to the marriage contract and property settlements involved in the match. *[**LLL*** 2.1.163-64: the packet is not come / Where that and other specialties are bound; ***Shrew*** 2.1.126: Let specialties be therefore drawn between us.

SPENDTHRIFT, n. A prodigal, with the equation of coins and words and sex. To spend may be to have orgasm (Ross). *[**Temp.*** 2.1.24: what a spendthrift is he of his tongue; ***Beware*** 1.3.54; ***HWhoreI*** 3.3.53: Spendthrifts of soul and body.

SPUR, A spur-royal; a coin in general. Possible puns on a device worn on the boot to goad a horse and on profits as spurs (coins/incentives). See ***Royal.*** *[**MadW.*** 2.6.102: spur-royals; 3.2.78-80: I have not spurs for nothing, I see.—No, . . . they cost you an angel; ***WTale*** 1.2.74-76: Our praises are our wages. You may ride's / With one soft kiss a thousand furlongs ere / With spur we heat an acre; ***Lear*** 2.1.75-76: the profits of my death / Were very pregnant and potential spurs; ***Scorn***. 417: nine spur-royals.

Gold spur royal, James I.

STAMP, n. and v. A coin, from the word (impress) and portrait (seal) of the ruler that, aside from intrinsic value, give a coin its worth and currency. Also a plan or device and anything produced, *e.g.,* children (counterfeits, therefore, are bastards). Often used in a pun with the sexual currency of a woman, a prostitute, *of the stamp.* The *last stamp* is the most recent mintage; a *base stamp* is a counterfeit or debased coin, as are *stamps that are forbid. To stamp* is to make good, to seal, to attest to the value of. *Your stamp will go current* means your plan will succeed. See ***Gold, Golden stamp. [NHo*** 1.2.81-83: Siluer is the Kings stampe, man Gods stampe, and a woman is mans stampe, wee are not currant till wee passe from one man to another; ***MWives*** 3.4.16: stamps in gold; ***Mac.*** 4.3.153: a golden stamp; ***WTale*** 4.4.725: stamped coin; ***MadW.*** 1.1.85-86: tricks ... of the last stamp; 3.1.109; ***Beware*** 4.2.37; 5.1.14; ***MforM*** 2.4.45-46: do coin heaven's image / In stamps that are forbid; ***Ado*** 1.2.6-8: Are they good? / —As the [event] stamps them, but they have a good cover; they show well outward; ***MojV*** 2.7.56-57: A coin that bears the figure of an angel / Stamp'd in gold; 2.9.39: stamp of merit; ***Hen.8*** 3.2.12: The stamp of nobleness; 3.2.325: Your holy hat to be stamp'd on the King's coin; ***1Hen.4*** *4*.1.4-5: not a soldier of this season's stamp / Should go so general current; ***Rich.3*** 1.3.255: Your fire-new stamp of honor is scarce current; ***Cym..*** 5.4.24: 'Tween man and man they weigh not every stamp; ***Ham..*** 3.4.168: use almost can change the stamp of nature; ***Oth..*** 2.1.243: can stamp and counterfeit advantages; ***Staple*** 4.2.102-04: The stamp and strength of all imperial lines, /. . . shines / In her [Lady

Pecunia's] sweet face!; ***HWhore1*** 5.2.515: The cuckold's stamp goes current in all nations.

STAND, v. To haggle; a temporary pause in concluding a bargain. *[**Faust**.* 4.5.21: I will not stand with thee.

STAPLE, n. Originally, a place to stop. Generally a marketplace. Also a monopoly, and a place for storing merchandise, or the goods themselves. *[**Wit*** 655: An thou wert all the staple; ***Staple*** title et passim.

STATE, n. Aphaeresis for ***Estate***.

STATUTE, n. Any law; a bond stipulating that a creditor may attach certain property of a debtor upon non-payment. Metaphorically, one's lease on life. *[**CofE*** 1.1.9: rigorous statutes; ***3Hen.6*** 5.4.79: His statutes cancell'd, and his treasure spent; ***Ham.***. 5.1.104-5: with his statutes, his recognizances, his fines, his double vouchers; ***Debts*** 1.1.50: foolish mortgages, statutes, and bonds; 5.1.129: [by] mortgage or by statute.

STERLING, adj. Originally, perhaps, a "coin with a star," from the Old English *steorling,* referring to the Norman penny. Genuine, valid, current, high quality money, in reference to the English sterling penny and pound (of) sterling. Also in an analogy with words as coins, sterling words being sound and believable like sterling coins. *[**2Hen.4*** 2.1.120: sterling money; ***Volp.***. 4.1.111: one pound sterling; ***Rich.2*** 4.1.264: if my word be sterling yet in England; ***Ham.*** 1.3.106-7: you have ta'en these tenders for true pay, / Which are not sterling; ***BBush*** 1.3.74: three thousand sterling.

STIVER, n. Also *stuiver.* A billon or copper coin of the Low Countries, minted in the sixteenth century (Frey), worth about five pennies, current in England for 1d. Also called *patard, vierlander, plaque, griffon,* and *briquet* (Munro). Generally, a coin of little value. An *orkyn* is "a quarter of a stiver . . . two doits" (Skeat). See ***Appendix B***. *[**BBush*** 1.3.81: you shall have your money to a stiver.

STORE, n. In reference to money: saved wealth; liquid assets; personal savings; any amount or supply, implying sufficiency or abundance; one's total possessions; and capital. With a pun on beauty or chastity as a woman's assets. See ***Present money***. *[**Ram.*** 276: take; there's my store; ***12N.*** 3.3.45-46: your store ... is not for idle markets; ***MofV*** 1.3.53: my present store; ***CofE*** 3.1.34: store [of wenches]; ***3Hen.6*** 2.5.57: some store of crowns; ***2Hen.6*** 3.1.115: many a pound of mine own proper store; ***Corio.*** 1.9.32-33: we have ta'en . . . good store of all / The treasure; ***1Hen.4*** 2.2.89: I would your store were here; ***R&J*** 1.1.216: when she dies, with beauty dies her store; ***Staple*** 5.6.26: The use of things is all, and not the store; ***Madam*** 4.2.133: All human happiness consists in store.

STRETCH. See ***Rack***.

STRONG, adj. Economically, in great number; wealthy; expensive; valuable. *[Per.* 3.1.52: strong in custom; ***Rich.2*** 3.2.35: grows strong and great in substance; ***1Hen.4*** 5.1.37-38: you were in place and in account / Nothing so strong; ***R&J*** 3.1.190: I'll amerce you with so strong a fine.

STUFF, n. Originally, provisions. Merchandise, store, or furnishings, especially moveables. Metaphorically, a wife, a prostitute (as merchandise), and "semen" (Partridge) as store. With a pun on Bordeaux merchandise as wine. ***[MTerm*** 5.3.124; ***Hen.8*** 3.2.126: Rich stuffs, and ornaments of household; ***Shrew*** 3.2.230-31: she is my house, / My household stuff; ***Per.*** 4.2.18: The stuff we have [whores]; ***TofA*** 4.3.271-74: Thy father . . . put stuff / To some she-beggar and compounded thee / Poor rogue hereditary; ***2Hen.4*** 2.4.63-64: a whole merchant's venture of Burdeaux stuff in him.

STUIVER. See ***Stiver***.

SUBSIDY, n. Originally, help or assistance. Financial aid for the sovereign, raised by the Parliament by specially taxing the citizens "upon urgent occasions" (Postlethwayt). Two basic subsidies were on commodities and on lands and other property: the first imposed duties on importing and exporting certain items like wool and wine (first only upon aliens, but later upon all traders) and was eventually called tonnage and poundage; the second exacted, from about 1350 on, 4s. per pound of the total value of one's land and 2s. 8d. per pound of value of other property. A man *in the subsidy* would be on the subsidy list, i.e., liable to pay extra tax and thus probably well-off financially. Wriothesley tells how, in 1536, "at assise for the Kinges subsidie kept in Lyncolneshire, the people made an insurrection" (1:56), and Stowe reports of the year 1563, "On Estar evyne ye Parliament brake upe and gave to y^{e}

quene a subsedie, and that was of everie man beynge valuewyd worth iij *li.* on goods, or lands, or otharwys, and so uppewarde, ij *s.* viij *d.* of y[e] *li.,* besyds they gave her ij fyfftens" (122). See ***Fifteens.*** *[**3Lad.*** 348: For now we neither pay Church-money, subsidies, fifteens, scot nor lot; ***2Hen.6*** 4.7.22-23: pay one and twenty fifteens, and one shilling to the pound, the last subsidy; ***3Hen.6*** 4.8.45: Nor much oppress'd them with great subsidies; ***Scorn.*** 429: am I hoist into the subsidy; ***NHo*** 2.2.63-64: do you want any money? or if you be in debt, I am a hundreth pound ith' Subsidie; ***WHo*** 3.2.103: remember which of his friends is in the Subsidy; ***BBush*** 2.1.161-62: When the subsidy's increased, / We are not a penny sess'd.

SUBSTANCE, n. Originally, "essential nature, essence" *(OED).* The total of one's wealth; income plus property; implying a large amount or value. *[**CofE*** 1.1.23-24: Thy substance ... *I* Cannot amount unto a hundred marks; ***2Gents***. 4.1.15: You take the sum and substance that I have; ***Hen.8*** 1.2.58: the sixt part of his substance; 3.2.326: innumerable substance; ***MWives*** 1.3.37: he is of substance good; 3.2.75; ***JofM*** 1.2.86: half of my substance is a city's wealth; ***Rich.2*** 3.2.35: strong and great in substance.

SUFFICIENT, adj. Having enough, able, adequate to the task; thus, financially capable—solvent or economically responsible (and not exclusive to Shylock's lexicon). See ***Good.*** *[**MofV*** 1.3.17; ***EHo*** 4.2.78: my sufficient son; ***MTerm*** 3.4.61-62: I think you sufficient enough for seaven hundred pound; ***1Hen.6*** 5.5.92; ***Gall.*** 222: sufficient pawn; ***2Gents.*** 5.4.74- 75: if hearty sorrow / Be a sufficient ransom; ***DCourt.*** 3.2.3: Your bill had ben sufficient y'are a good man.

SUM, n. and v. An amount or total, implying great wealth or large numbers. Also a price or a payment, or the total of a debt owed. *To sum* is to calculate a total. Occurs in a pun with "some." See ***Present money.*** *[**2Gents.*** 4.1.15: sum and substance; ***MWives*** 3.4.16: sums in sealed bags; ***LLL*** 2.1.130: the one half of an entire sum; ***MofV*** 1.1.179: a present sum; ***Well*** 4.3.179: sums of gold; ***TofA*** 1.2.232-33: I doubt whether their legs be worth the sums / That are given for 'em; 3.4.49: sums and bills; ***R&J*** 2.6.34: I cannot sum up sum of half my wealth; ***2Hen.4*** 2.1.72-73: For what sum?—It is for more than some, my lord, it is for all.

SUNK, adj. Financially ruined, with a pun on drowned at sea, for merchandise lost at sea was often the cause of bankruptcy for merchants or investors. *[**Scorn.*** 428.

SUPERFLUITY, SUPERFLUX, n. Overabundance, more than is necessary, a spare or a store; excess wealth. According to medieval religious laws governing riches, one was obliged to share the superflux with the poor. St. Augustine and St. Ambrose softened earlier total disdain for money by giving in their writings a more sympathetic view of wealth that was earned and stored up, but then distributed in alms to the truly needy. Moreover, St. Aquinas formulated four rules for the proper use of wealth, three of which were liberality, preparation (for an occasion of generosity), and munificence. Everyman is partially redeemed by his determination to give away half of his substance in alms (11. 699-700), and a popular Renaissance tale related the story of Piers Toller the Usurer, who, though he simply threw a loaf of bread at a beggar in anger, was redeemed in the eyes of God for this charitable act. In the moral interlude *Liberalitie and Prodigalitie* (1602), the right use of wealth is illustrated by the dispersal of accumulated wealth to the needy and deserving. As stated in a maxim in *Vex.* 102, *"*Some are made poor, / That rich men by giving may increase their store*"* (*cf.* Herbert: "Giving much to the poor, doth enrich a man's store" and Latimer: "the rich man is but God's officer, God's treasurer: he ought to distribute"). This precept contributes to the plot in several plays, being the motivating factor for a great charitable deed—Gresham's building of the Exchange in *If you know not me, 2,* and Brewen's desire to build a *Domus Dei* in *Vex.* Stow[e] reports of August, 1552, "began to gooe forwarde y[e] great provysyon for y[e] poore, towards y[e] whiche every man was tributorie & gave a certayn wykelye" (26). Robert Sanderson, in his sermon "Ad Populum" of 1621, warns that alms are to be given only to the truly needy, not to the idle, who should be stocked or whipped; in "Sermon XVIII" of 1623, Donne reiterates the necessity of giving: "thou owest them [the poor] a debt of alms, though not restitution: though thou have nothing in thy hands which was theirs, yet thou hast something which should be theirs; nothing perchance which thou hast taken from them, but something certainly which thou hast received from God for them." *[**2Hen.4*** 2.2.17- 18: one for superfluity, and another for use; ***Corio.*** 1.1.17: If they would yield us but the superfluity; 1.1.225-26: means to vent / Our musty superfluity; ***Lear*** 3.4.35: thou mayst shake the superflux to them; ***Hen.8*** 1.1.99.

SUPPOSITION, n. Assumed or expected rather than actual, present wealth: a return expected on an investment. *[**MofV*** 1.3.15: means in supposition.

SURETY, n. and v. Also security. A pawn—a material object or person of some value to the debtor—kept by the creditor as a security or assurance that he will receive payment. Usually all, including the surety, is stipulated in a formal contract of obligation. Also a person who assumes financial responsibility for another's debts. Proverbially, "He that will be surety, shall pay" (Herbert). *[**T&C*** 5.2.60: give me some token for the surety of it; ***1Hen.4*** 3.1.251: givest such sarcenet surety for thy oaths; 4.3.108-9: let there be impawn'd / Some surety; ***Well*** 5.3.297: he shall surety me; ***2Hen.6*** 5.1.116: shall be surety for their traitor father; ***Corio.*** 3.1.177: We'll surety him; ***Temp.*** 1.2.476: I'll be his surety.

SWINE, n. Also sow. Perhaps a punning extension of pig, slang for sixpence. This pun is particularly apt when Barabas curses the Christians who have confiscated his wealth, i.e., taken his coins for their own extravagant purposes, as *swine-eating Christians.* Thus he invokes the entire traditional opposition of Gentiles and Jews in regard to financial ethics. A *sow-gelder* is quibblingly one who robs purses. See ***Pig.*** *[**JofM*** 2.3.7; ***Drum*** 199: yoke themselves to swine; ***John*** 5.2.141-42: To lie like pawns lock'd up in chests and trunks, / To hug with swine; ***BBush*** 3.1.59-60: groats apiece!—There, sweet sow-gelder.

T

TAKE-UP, v. To buy a large amount of a commodity, usually with the intent of selling it at a profit; to borrow money by means of a bill of credit, to undertake a debt. *[**BFair*** Ind. 214: take up a commodity; ***2Hen.6*** 4.7.127: take up commodities upon our bills; ***EMOH*** 4.7.68; ***BBush*** 3.2.77: Taken up of merchants to supply my traffics.

TALENT, n. An ancient Greek weight and money of account, equal to six thousand *drachmae* or about £240. Also an ancient Hebrew money of account. The silver talent equaled three thousand silver *shekels,* or about £400; the gold talent equaled ten thousand gold *shekels,* or about £6000. Ross suggests "illicit appetite" as a metaphorical extension. Also a possible pun on "natural abilities": fools in the drama are often (unjustly, it seems) wealthy and thus rich in talents (coins) rather than intelligence. *[**TofA*** 1.1.95, ***Bond.*** 1.3.198; ***12N***. 1.5.15: those that are fools, let them use their talents.

TALLY, n. A square stick worn on the belt of a tapster, scored on one side with notches to indicate the amount of the bill. When the stick was split lengthwise, both creditor and debtor retained a record of the debt that could not be altered. In cacemphaton, an indecent reference to the penis. See ***Score.*** *[**Vex***. 138: I have carried the tallies at my girdle . . . for I did ever love to deal honestly in the nick; ***2Hen.6*** 4.7.34-35: our forefathers had no other books but the score and the tally.

TELL, v. To count, with a double pun in aphaeresis on (re)count, *e.g.,* say (tell). *[**Lear*** 2.4.54-55: as many dolors for thy daughters as thou canst tell in a year; ***LLL*** 2.1.17: tell my worth; ***MTerm*** 2.1.82: tell out two or three hundred pound; ***Maid*** 5.3.11: tell a hundred pound out for the Gentleman.

TEMPLE, n. A figurative expression for one's purse, a sacred temple of angels (coins). *[**OldF.*** 1.2.176-77: Wee the wags haue gold, Father; but I thinke there's not one angell more wagging in this sacred Temple; ***TofA*** 5.1.47-48: What a god's gold / That he is worshipp'd in a baser temple.

TENDER, n. and v. Legally, to offer, usually payment, in fulfillment of a contract. Generally, to offer, exchange, or pay. An offer of marriage. Also to value or esteem, to care for lovingly; and to show forth or reveal, with a pun on to offer, "to give birth to a bastard" (Partridge). Also puns on young, inexperienced. *[**WHo*** 1.2.14; ***BBofA*** 1.4.176: no penny tender'd; ***Lear*** 1.1.195: Nor will you tender less; ***CofE*** 4.3.4: Some tender money to me; ***Ado*** 2.3.177-78: If she should make tender of her love; ***MND*** 3.2.87: for his tender; ***CofE*** 5.1.132: He shall not die, so much we tender him; ***12N.*** 5.1.126: whom ... I tender dearly; ***R&J*** 3.1.71-72: which name I tender / As dearly as my own; ***MWives*** 1.1.208, 221: a tender, a kind of tender . . . concerning your marriage; ***Rich.3*** 4.4.405: I tender not thy beauteous princely daughter; ***Temp.*** 2.1.269-70: how does your content / Tender your own good fortune; 4.1.5:1 tender to thy hand; ***Ham..*** 1.3.106- 09: you have ta'en these tenders for true pay, / . . . Tender yourself more dearly, / Or ... / you'll tender me a fool; ***Rich.2*** 2.3.41-42: 1 tender you my service /. . . being tender.

TENTH, n. A tithe, in reference to certain financial transactions: similar to fifteens, a tenth was a 10 percent tax imposed on the citizens in times of the ruler's financial need, assessed upon the values of owned land and possessions. Stow[e] remarks that in *1555,* "the qwen did remyt the first frute of x^{ths}" *(46).* A tenth also refers to the practice of certain unscrupulous moneylenders, who would accept a tenth of the total loan as full repayment so that their bankrupt debtors could regain financial independence on a stake lent by the broker, upon which he could then expect a healthy return in interest. See ***Fifteens.*** *[**1Hen.6** 5.5.96:* Among the people gather up a tenth; ***Cym..*** *5.4.19-20:* of their broken debtors take . . ../ a tenth, letting them thrive again.

TEN TO ONE, n. Generally used as a figure of speech to indicate good odds or a sure bet, usually applied in a wager made in jest. *[**Shrew*** 5.2.62; ***2Hen.4*** 1.1.182; ***1Hen.6*** 5.4.157; ***2Hen.6*** 2.1.4; ***3Hen.6*** 5.1.46; ***Hen.8*** Ep. 1; ***BBush*** 2.3.69.

TENURE, Originally, to hold. Legally, a title to a tenement held by the occupant; the conditions of his right to hold and occupy the property. Thus, generally, any legal title or document setting forth certain conditions. *[**Ham.*** 5.1.100: [a lawyer's] tenures; ***MofV*** 4.1.235: paid according to the tenure.

TESTAMENT, n. A will, originally disposing of only personal property after death; also the naming of an executor for the will. Metaphorically, any binding contract, as of love. *[**AYLI*** 1.1.74: a lottery my father left me by testament; 2.1.47: thou mak'st a testament as worldlings do; ***Well*** 5.3.197: conferr'd by testament to th' sequent issue; ***Hen.5*** 4.6.27: seal'd a testament of . . . love; ***TofA*** 5.1.28: performance is a kind of will or testament.

TESTED GOLD. See ***Gold.***

TESTER, TESTON, TESTRIL, n. Also testoon, testone, testern. Strictly speaking, any coin bearing a head or portrait of the ruler (cf. French *tete*). Also a silver coin of 1504 and later, worth 12d., about thirty-two millimeters in diameter, the first

English coin to bear the face of the king. All testers were called in to the mint in 1548 because they were debased, but they continued in circulation. In 1560 Elizabeth proclaimed especially base those testons stamped with a lion, rose, harp, greyhound, or *fleur-de-lis* and lowered their value to 2 ¼d.; better testons worth 4 ½d.. were marked with a portcullis *(TRP)*. See ***Appendix E.*** This coin value was replaced by the shilling after 1560. Holiinshed refers also to the sixpence as a testoon, and a proverb maintains that "He that loses his wife and sixpence has lost a tester" (Tilley, W360). In the plays a tester is a usual small gratuity and the wage to a minstrel for singing a song. Sometimes punningly synonymous with a cross, sometimes with an implied pun on testicles (money and sex, money as lucre), and a strange form from a Devonshire clothier with a heavy rustic accent—perhaps combining forlorn with testy or indicating poverty, "testorne," although Wriothesley also uses this form to refer to the tester. ***[Maid*** 1.1.79; ***Vex.*** 125; ***MWives*** 1.3.87; ***2Hen.4*** 3.2.276-77; ***2Gents.*** 1.1.144-45: you have testern'd me; ***Faust.*** 3.3.36-37; ***HWhorel*** 2.1.107; ***EHo*** 1.1.159-60: Wipe thy bum with testones; ***12N.*** 2.3.33; ***Scorn.*** 420: a cross? There's a tester; ***Gall.*** 210: a testern ... to a servant; ***Prod.*** 2.4.51-52: for I see thou art somewhat testorne; holde thee, theres vortie shillings.

Teston du dauphine, Henry II of France.

THALER. *See* ***Dolor.***.

THISTLE. *See* ***Crown.***

THRIFT, n. and adj. Originally, prosperity. Economy, in Aristotle's sense of good allocation of funds, household management. Also profit or financial success as a result of sanctioned industry, in opposition to interest, which is chrematistic and requires no labor. By extension and in adnominatio, household management in the sense of courtship and opposed to large waist (waste). French thrift is superficially having only one servant rather than a retinue, but it is also economy in the sense of copulation resulting in profit or increase (pregnancy). To be thriftless is to be prodigal and nonproductive. *[Ham..* 1.2.180-81: Thrift, thrift, Horatio, the funeral bak'd- meats / Did coldly furnish forth the marriage tables; ***MofV*** 1.1.175: I have a mind presages me such thrift; 1.3.50-51: my well-won thrift, / Which he calls interest; 1.3.90: thrift is blessing, if men steal it not; ***MWives*** 1.3.43:1 am about thrift; 1.3.84: French thrift; ***Rich.2*** 5.3.69: As thriftless sons their scraping fathers' gold; ***Magn.*** 1.6.33-34: has reduc'd his thrifte, / To certaine principles.

TIME. See ***Golden time.***

TOKEN, n. Originally, a symbol. Also pledge of value. A piece of metal or other material (*e.g.,* leather) issued as a coin by both cities and private parties to supplement the standard coinage, which lacked small units of value. Tokens were often issued as change from shopkeepers and were a type of representative currency. Often counterfeited, the tokens became nearly worthless, as sometimes even the issuer, doubting their authenticity, refused to accept them. Sometimes synonymous with farthing. See ***Harrington. [HWhore1*** 1.4.30: tavern token; ***WHo*** 2.2.176; ***Debts*** 1.1.54: your credit not worth a token; ***Staple*** 5.4.33-34: There's thy penny, / Four tokens for thee; ***Madam*** 4.3.32: I will be satisfied to a token; ***BFair*** 2.4.5: cost you but a token a week.

TOLL, TOLLAGE, n. and v. A charge for entering a fair with goods to sell and for setting up a stall in which to display the goods. Perhaps with a pun on to toll as to attract or entice. Figuratively extended to include the "buying" of a spouse. Also a tax for any transaction completed at a fair or for transporting goods or passing on certain roadways or into certain buildings. Tollage is the requirement of the tax, and to toll is to collect the tax. *[**Vex.*** I11: at the second hand you'll have a fee too; you sell in the church . . . you must have tollage; ***Well*** 5.3.148-49: I will buy me a son-in- law in a fair, and toll for this; ***John*** 3.1.153-54: no Italian priest / Shall tithe or toll in our dominions.

TONGUE. See ***Golden tongue.***

TOSSEL, n. A tassel, an insignificant decoration (on a purse, which is empty, not fulfilling a purpose, and is thus similarly insignificant). *[**T&C*** 5.1.32: tossel of a prodigal's purse.

TOUCH, v. A complex metaphorical term. Originally, to hit or strike. To approach for money or payment; to pay close to the requested amount. From a touchstone, which reveals the true nature of metals, to try or to test one's intentions, value, "mettle." With a pun on vein as ore and blood (to touch for blood-letting). Also to arrest, and to try (bring to trial) as a punning extension of to test. Sometimes with sexual connotations. See ***Golden stamp, Try***. *[**TofA*** 1.1.14: if he will touch the estimate; 3.3.6: They have all been touch'd and found base metal; 4.3.389: O thou touch of hearts; ***Rich.3*** 4.2.8-9: now do I play the touch, / To try if thou be current gold indeed; ***John*** 3.1.99-101: a counterfeit /. . . which being touch'd and tried, / Proves valueless; ***MforM*** 2.2.70: Ay, touch him; there's the vein; ***AYLI*** 2.7.94: You touch'd my vein at first; ***Lear*** 4.6.83: they cannot touch me for [coining], I am the King himself; ***Oth.*** 3.3.81: I mean to touch your love indeed.

TOUCHSTONE, n. A stone (basanite) used to test the purity of gold and silver. "Tried gold was a symbol of fidelity" (Riverside). Any test of true mettle. Proverbially, "As the Touchstone tries gold, so gold tries men" (Tilley, T448). *[**AYLI**:* character = Touchstone; ***Per.*** 2.2.37: Holding out gold that's by the touchstone tried.

TRADE, n. and v. Originally, a course or track. Business, vocation, commerce, a productive enterprise. With a hidden pun on a religious vocation. Disparagingly, merchandising, as opposed to moneylending, which involves no labor. By extension, courtship as the business of marriage, the buying and selling of spouses; or using a woman sexually and economically. The *hold-door trade* is pandering; *good trading* is a cheap and active market; and to be *trade-fallen* is to be unemployed. *[**Ham.**.* 3.2.334: Have you any further trade with us?; ***MofV*** 3.3.30: the trade and profit of the city; ***Per.*** 4.2.38-39: Neither is our profession any trade, it's no calling; ***JofM*** 1.1.35: the vulgar trade; ***12N.*** 3.1.74-75: My niece is desirous you should enter, if your trade be to her; ***A&C*** *2.5.2:*

us that trade in love; ***T&C*** 5.10.51; ***1Hen.4*** 2.4.365; 4.2.29; ***MWives*** 1.3.68-72.

TRADER, n. A participant in the merchandising of sex; a pander, or one who frequents a brothel. *[**T&C*** 5.10.37.

TRAFFIC, n. and v. In general, a trade or a business. Specifically, merchants and their merchandise, and travels undertaken for commerce. Often used pejoratively or extended to include stealing as one's "business." Also "sexual commerce; (sexual) intercourse" (Partridge), or the woman herself, a prostitute. See ***Golden traffic.*** *[**TofA*** 1.1.237, 239; ***CofE*** 1.1.15: to admit no traffic; ***1Hen.6*** 5.3.164: in traffic of a king; ***WTale*** 4.3.23: my traffic is sheets; ***Shrew*** 1.1.12: A merchant of great traffic through the world; ***R&J*** Pro. 12: the two hours' traffic of our stage [with a play on literal traffic, comings and goings]; ***Temp.*** 2.1.149-50: no kind of traffic / Would I admit; ***EMen*** 506: the men / Of Amsterdam have lately made a law, / That none but Dutch . . . may traffic there; ***BBush*** 3.2.77: to supply my traffics.

TRAFFICKER, n. Pejoratively, a merchant. *[**MofV*** 1.1.12: Do overpeer the petty traffickers.

TRASH, n. A contemptuous term for money. See ***Dross, Dunghill-muck.*** *[**JC*** 4.3.72-74: I had rather coin my heart / And drop my blood for drachmaes than to wring / From the hard hands of peasants their vile trash.

TREASURE, n. Wealth, a prize, or something valued or coveted, expressed in a variety of ways: when applied to a woman, chastity, virginity, beauty, bodily charms, sexual innocence still unlocked; a man's progeny, heirs; metaphorically, words, as the treasure of the brain, analogous to coins. See ***Fairies' treasure, Untreasured.*** *[**Rich.2*** 1.1.177-78: Thc purcst treasure mortal times afford / Is spotless reputation; ***Shrew*** 2.1.32: she is your treasure; ***Cym.***. 2.2.42: I have pick'd the lock and ta'en the treasure of her honor; ***MforM*** 2.4.96: the treasures of your body; ***WTale*** 5.1.54: taken treasure from her lips; ***Corio.*** 3.3.115: treasure of my loins; ***2Gents.*** 2.4.43-44: you have an exchequer of words and ... no other treasure; ***Killed*** 4.2.115: Frankford's richest treasure [Mrs. Anne Frankford],

TREASURY, n. A place where wealth is stored; a purse, merchandise. Metaphorically, a woman, a woman's sexual charms and value. *[JofM* 4.3.3; ***WTale*** 4.4.350; ***Heir*** 131; ***TAnd.*** 2.1.130-31: serve your lust... *I* And revel in Lavinia's treasury.

TRENCHER-FRIEND, n. One who professes friendship and celebrates such love only when it is at the host's expense. The opposite of a ***Shot-clog.*** See Tilley, T515. *[TofA* 3.6.96.

TRIBUTE, n. and adj. Also truage. A tax paid in homage as recognition of affection or submission. Metaphorically, a marriage portion or the woman herself. *[**2Hen.4*** 3.2.308: the Turk's tribute; ***1Hen.6*** 5.4.130: pay him tribute and submit; ***2Hen.6*** 4.7.121; ***JofM*** 1.2.41: ten years' tribute; 1.2.68: tribute money; 3.5.10; 5.1.71-72: goods . . . were sold / For tribute money; ***Temp.*** 1.2.113: annual tribute; 1.2.124: homage, and I know not how much tribute; 2.1.293: free thee from the tribute which thou payest; ***Shrew*** 5.2.152-54: Craves no other tribute at thy hands / But love . . . / Too little payment for so great a debt; ***MofV*** 3.2.56: the virgin tribute paid by howling Troy; 4.1.422-23: Take some remembrance of us as a tribute, / Not as fee; ***Ham.***. 3.1.170: the demand of our neglected tribute; ***Cym..*** 2.4.20: any penny tribute; 3.1.8: granted Rome a tribute; 3.1.34: no more tribute to be paid; 3.1.47-48: Romans did extort / This tribute.

TRIED GOLD. See ***Gold.***

TRIM, v. Originally, to strengthen or comfort. In the sixteenth century, ironically, to abuse physically, usually with sexual or economic motives: to trick, rob, or rape. By extension, a horrible four-layer pun, on trimming a beard and trimming a coin (i.e., committing economic fraud, taking unfair profit or advantage), with equivocations on trim as neat and fine; as proper and in order; and as a clipping. See ***Shave.*** *[**TAnd.*** 5.1.93-96: cut her hands, and trimm'd her as thou sawest. / —O detestable villain, call'st thou that trimming? / —Why, she was wash'd, and cut, and trimm'd, and 'twas / Trim sport for them which had the doing of it; ***DCourt.*** 2.3.88-89: Trimd, O wife, I am shav'd, did you take hence the money?; 2.3.116-17.

TRUAGE. See ***Tribute.***

TRUCK, v., **TRUCKER,** n. One who transports and barters merchandise for profit, used pejoratively for a small-time merchant of dubious morals. To barter. See ***Trafficker.***

[Madam 3.1.34: sixpenny truckers; ***BFair*** 2.6.23-24: You were best truck with him.

TRUE GOLD. See ***Gold.***

TRUE-PENNY, n. Nickname for a dependable, steadfast person, indicating faith in the inviolable value of the currency. *[**Ham.*** 1.5.150.

TRUST, n. and v., **TRUSTER**, n. *On* or *of trust* is on credit; *to put in trust* is to depend on someone for economic support; a *truster* is a creditor, one who trusted (i.e., relied upon without material evidence) a debtor to repay an obligation. With a pun on trussed. *[**Ram.*** 272; ***MofV*** 1.1.183-85: Go presently inquire ... / Where money is . . . / To have it of my trust; ***Lear*** 1.4.14: put me in trust; ***Per.*** 1.3.12: left in trust with me; ***TofA*** 4.1.8-10: Bankrupts . . . / cut your trusters' throats; ***Gall.*** 268: It cost me three pounds this morning upon trust.—Nay, I think you had it upon trust, for no man that has any shame in him would take money for it; ***EHo*** 5.1.65- 66: she will not trust us another meal; ***Trick*** 4.2.72-73.

TRY, v. and adj. Originally, to cull out. To test the purity of the metal of a coin; by extension, to test in the sense of discover, and to find out a woman's worth in terms of chastity or virginity, a friend's worth in terms of the strength of his "mettle," or his economic commitment. Tilley (G284) cites that "Gold is tried in the fire." See ***Touch***. *[**Killed*** 4.2.2: To try two seeming angels [coins/a wife and a friend]; ***John*** 3.1.99-101: a counterfeit . . . which being touch'd and tried, / Proves valueless; ***MofV*** 1.1.180: Try what my credit can in Venice do; 2.7.53: tried gold; ***CofE*** 1.1.152-53: Try all the friends thou hast in Ephesus; / Beg thou, or borrow; ***Rich.3*** 4.2.8-9: now do I play the touch, / To try if thou be current gold indeed; ***Drum*** 191: as pure as the gold that hath bene seven times tryed in the fire; ***BBush*** 3.3.2: To try these people.

U

UNCLEW, v. To ruin economically. *[**TofA*** 1.1.168.

UNCOINED, adj. Metal in pure form, not current for exchange. Also, not vulnerable to debasement or fluctuation in value. *[**Hen.5*** 5.2.153-54: a fellow of plain and uncoin'd constancy.

UNCURRENT, adj. Worthless, unacceptable as exchange, not legal tender, *e.g.,* words rather than coins. Also a coin that is in some way rendered worthless, by clipping, cracking, washing, *etc.* *[**12N.*** 3.3.16: uncurrent: pay; ***Ham..*** 2.2.427-28: your voice, like a piece of uncurrent gold, be not crack'd.

UNDERVALUED, adj. Inferior in worth; a comparative term. *[**MofV*** 1.1.165: 2.7.53: ten times undervalued to tried gold.

UNDO, v., **UNDONE**, adj. Ruined economically (or sexually). To lose money, to become bankrupt, to forfeit payment on a contract, to lose status or land or title, to lose virginity (a loss of value equated to losing money). Opposite of ***Make.*** *[**Madam*** 2.1.29; ***MofV*** 3.1.124: Antonio is certainly undone; ***2Hen.4*** 2.1.23:1 am undone by his going; ***AYLI*** 5.4.46: I have undone three tailors; ***Mac.*** 5.5.49: wish th' estate o' th' world were now undone; ***TofA*** 4.3.481: his undone lord; ***Hen.8*** 3.2.210: This paper has undone me. 'Tis th' accompt; ***LLL*** 5.2.425: seek not to undo us; ***Well*** 5.3.145-46: a seducer flourishes, and a poor maid is undone; ***Drum*** 218. ***WHo*** 1.1.188, 190: Your prodigality, your diceing . . . hath vndone vs. ***Fatal*** 1.2.156: your ryotous heires undoe you; ***NHo*** 5.1.29: Nothing hath vndone my wife, but too much riding.

UNPAY, v. To redeem or rescind a wrong by paying with a right action *[**2Hen.4*** 2.1.118-19: Pay her the debt you owe her, and unpay the villainy, you have done.

UNSPEAKABLE, adj. Certainly in the usual sense of too good (or too bad for utterance, but also (and in Shakespeare the primary denotation) too large to enumerate, too valuable to assess with words, and sometimes with a pun on both meanings. *[**WTale*** 1.1.34: an unspeakable comfort; 4.2.40: an unspeakable estate; ***TAnd.*** 1.1.256: unspeakable deserts 5.3.126: wrongs unspeakable; ***CofE*** 1.1.32: to speak my griefs unspeakable.

UNTHRIFT, n. A prodigal; a spendthrift. *[**Rich.2*** 2.3.121-22: given away / To upstart unthrifts; ***TofA*** 4.3.311.

UNTREASURED, adj. Empty of riches, here applied to the intrinsic value of a beautiful woman. *[**AYLI*** 2.2.7: they found the bed untreasur'd of their mistress.

UNVALUED, adj. Priceless, of value so great that it cannot be assessed. "Invaluable" (Le Comte). *[**Rich.3*** 1.4.27: unvalued jewels; ***Beware*** 1.1.12: the most unvalued'st purchase.

USE, n. A rich word for economic puns: interest on money, sometimes applied to the exchange of love; profit in general, with implications of sexual profit; employment, sometimes indicating servitude; custom or habit; treatment (of an object) and wear from such treatment. Often several meanings are implied simultaneously. *In use* is money given in trust or for the beneficiary to invest, i.e., use. *Put to use* is money lent, allowed to propagate, with a pun on nature's activities. Money *to my use* is for my employment, to spend; and *to serve your use* implies sexual profit, "sexual enjoyment" (Partridge). Proverbially, "Better is the Use of riches than the possessing of them" (Tilley, U20). *[**Temp.*** 2.1.154: use of metal; ***MforM*** 1.1.39-40: the glory of a creditor, *I* Both thanks and use; ***Ado*** 2.1.279-80:1 gave him use for it, a double heart for his single one; ***2Gents.*** 2.4.68: Made use and fair advantage of his days; ***Lear*** 1.4.130-31: Can you make no use of nothing; ***Oth.*** *2*.1.129-30: fairness and wit, / The one's for use, the other useth it; ***Temp.*** 2.1.152: use of service; ***Ham..*** 1.2.133-34: How [weary] . . . and unprofitable / Seem to me all the uses of this world!; 3.4.168: use almost can change the stamp of nature; ***MforM*** 1.4.62: to give fear to use; ***TofA*** 1.1.280: use of quittance; ***Mac.*** 1.3.137: Against the use of nature; ***MofV*** 4.1.383: the other half in use; ***A&C*** 1.3.43-44: my full heart / Remains in use with you; ***12N.*** 3.1.50: being kept together, and put to use; ***2Hen.6*** 3.1.113: any groat I hoarded to my use; ***Hen.5*** 2.2.99: practic'd on me, for thy use; ***2Hen.4*** 2.1.115-16: made her serve your uses both in purse and in person; ***R&J*** 1.5.47: Beauty too rich for use; 3.3.123-24: like a usurer abound'st in all, / And usest none in that true use; 3.5.225: and you no use of him; ***Drum*** 184: To exile ones fortunes from their native use; ***OldF.*** 5.2.275-76: He made no vse of me, but like a miser, / Lockt vp his wealth; ***WHo*** 4.1.125-26: a good honest wench, that liues wholy to his vse; ***MadW.*** 4.5.91-92: What, so coy, so strict? Come, come.—Pray change your opinion, sir; I am not for that use; ***DCourt.*** 1.2.133: Beauti's for use; 2.1.83: A creature of a publique use; ***Killed*** 3.1.28: Where's my three hundred pounds, beside the use?

USE, v. Generally, to employ for profit; thus, sleep with a woman, pander her, take her virginity, or rape her; to manage or to treat, with sexual implications; to take interest; to practice or have a custom; often several meanings simultaneously. With a pun in aphaeresis on (ab)use. *[**Bond.*** 3.3.121: use her; ***Temp.*** 4.1.36: I must use you; 5.1.71-72: Most cruelly / Didst thou . . . use me; ***2Gents.*** 5.3.14: use a woman lawlessly; ***MWives** 2.2.273-74:* I will use her as the key of the cuckoldly rogue's coffer; 3.3.202: you use me well; ***MforM*** 2.1.42-43: use their abuses in common houses; ***CofE*** 3.2.6: for her wealth's sake use her with more kindness; ***Per.*** 4.6.141-42: use her at thy pleasure; ***TAnd.*** 5.2.194: worse than Philomel you us'd my daughter; ***Lear*** 4.6.162: Thou hotly lusts to use her; ***3Hen.6*** 3.2.124: Edward will use women honorably; ***2Hen.4*** 5.1.30-32: I will use him well: a friend i' the court is better than a penny in purse. Use his men well; ***R&J*** 3.3.123-24: like a usurer abound'st in all, / And usest none in that true use; ***MofV*** 1.3.70:1 do never use it; ***Staple*** 2.5.19-22, 24-25: You dare not use your money, and I have none.—Not use my money, cogging Jack? Who uses it / At better rates, lets it for more i'the hundred / Than I do, sirrah? . . . —Sir, I meant / You durst not to enjoy it; ***Prod.*** 5.1.189-92: Did you vse her vell?—Vse her? there's neuer a gentle-woman in *England* could be better vsed then I did her; ***WHo*** 2.2.54-55: vse her like a woman my Lord; 4.2.54: Beautie (like gold) being vs'd becomes more bright.

USURER, n. Literally, of course, one who lends money for interest. Extended into a general term of economic contempt for a social pariah, one who exploits others, one who works against Nature and natural economics, one who is greedy and hoards his money. The classic usurer story from the Renaissance relates how a usurer attempting to commit suicide is cut down by a benevolent passer-by. The usurer then charges his savior for the price of a new rope. Proverbially, "To speak of a Usurer at the table, mars the wine" (Herbert). *[**Lear*** 4.6.162: The usurer hangs the cozener; ***Ado*** 2.1.189-90: like an usurer's chain; ***WTale*** 4.4.262-64: a usurer's wife was brought to bed of twenty money-bags; ***R&J*** 3.3.123-24: like a usurer, abound'st in all, / And usest none in that true use; ***TofA*** 2.2.60: usurers' men, bawds between gold and want!; ***MadW**.* 3.2.104: a sore scab, your usurer; ***Maid*** 1.2.102-3: Doe you thinke 1'le trust him? As a Usurer / With forfeited Lordships.

USURER'S, USURING KINDNESS, n. The practice of discounting a debt and then renewing it at higher interest in hopes of an even greater profit. Generally, any seemingly generous activity done solely for mercenary reasons. See ***Bate***. [***TofA*** 4.3.509.

USURY, n. Lending money at interest, at any rate. Generally, profit, and by extension, copulation, Nature's usury. Used primarily as a term of ugliness and contempt, probably because of an enduring sense of the unnaturalness of monetary propagation combined with the extortionate practices of many moneylenders, Jews and Christians alike. However, one proverb maintains that "There is no Merchandise but usury" (Tilley, M879). Stowe relates the confession of Master Rychard Allington esquere in 1561, in which, after God has in a vision commanded him to repay every penny of usury that he has exacted in his life, Allington says, "I dyd condeme my conscyence for sufferynge me to commite suche abominable usery and other most detestable synnes agaynst my hevenly Father" (120), which seems more accurately to represent the consensus. See ***Hundred, Interest,*** and ***Appendix A.*** [***Corio.*** 1.1.81-82: make edicts for usury, to support usurers; ***1Tamb***. 2.5.43: ransom them with fame and usury; ***MforM*** 3.2.5-6: of two usuries the merriest was put down, and the worser allow'd by order of law; ***TofA*** 3.5.98-99: banish usury, / That makes the Senate ugly; ***Cym.*** 3.3.45: the city's usuries; ***NHo*** 3.1.87-88: venery is like vsery that it may be allowed tho it be not lawfull.

V

VAIL, n. and v. A profit. Also a gratuity, gift, or perquisite. To vail is to lower, to incline: thus a pun on two senses of vail, to incline one's stomach (i.e., sexual organs) to one's husband because pregnancy is the only profit (vail/boot) of marriage. [***EHo*** 2.2.6-7: the young outlaw hoards the stolen vails of his occupation; ***Per.*** 2.1.150-51: certain condolements, certain vails; ***Shrew*** 5.2.176: Then vail your stomachs, for it is no boot.

VALIANT, adj. Of value; thus worth or income. *[**Trick*** 1.1.73: four hundred a year valiant.

VALUE, n. Importance or worth, but also price, indicating an acceptance of exchange valuation as the standard of worth. *[**MforM*** 1.5.55: matters of needful value; ***Ado*** 4.1.220: We rack the value; ***MofV*** 4.1.366: Thou hast not left the value of a cord.

VENDIBLE, adj. In demand, saleable; applied to virginity and women (marriageable, for sale on the marriage market). *[**Vex.*** 153; ***Well*** 1.1.154-55: Off with't [virginity] while 'tis vendible; ***MofV*** 1.1.112: a maid not vendible.

VENICE GOLD. See ***Gold.***

VENT, v. To sell; to value or evaluate. *[**Maid*** 4.1.242; ***BBush*** 2.3.91.

VILLAIN, n. In its original sense, a bondman. *[**CofE*** 1.2.19.

VIRGINIAN GOLD. See ***Gold.***

VOUCHER, n. In economics, "A written document or note, or other material evidence, serving to attest the correctness of accounts or monetary transactions, to prove the delivery of goods or valuables" *(OED);* a receipt. In law, double-vouchers are "documents guaranteeing title to real estate, signed by two persons" (Riverside). *[**Ham.*** 5.1.105: double-vouchers; 5.1.108-9: Will [his] vouchers vouch him no more of his purchases?

W

WALLET, n. A beggar's bag, or a pouch for keeping money and other provisions, usually worn on the back. A proverb maintains, "In the kingdom of a cheater, the wallet is carried before" (Herbert). *[**T&C*** 3.3.145-46: Time hath ... a wallet at his back, / Wherein he puts alms for oblivion.

WARE, n. and v. Originally, "object of care" *(OED).* "To spend money" (Skeat). Merchandise, a material embodiment of wealth. By extension, a woman, for her intrinsic and exchange value. With an adnominatio on "where."

Proverbially, "Pleasing ware is half sold" and "111 ware is never cheap" (Herbert). *[**WTale*** 4.4.321-23: Come to the pedlar, / Money's a meddler, / That doth utter all men's ware-a; ***JofM*** 1.1.33: This is the ware wherein consists my wealth; *Beware* 2.2.33: old ware; ***DCourt.***. 1.2.34-35: the Baud above all, her shop has the best ware.

WARRANT, n. and v., **WARRANTIZE,** n. Originally, a protection or authorization, a place of safety. Beginning in the fifteenth century, an assurance or guarantee of responsibility. Later, a document of a license for power in enforcing legal and debt matters; in special usage, "A writing which authorizes one person to pay or deliver, and to another to receive, a sum of money" *(OED).* Used generally as a figure of speech implying certainty: "I warrant you." *[**MforM*** 1.4.74: a warrant for's execution; 5.4.459: a special warrant for the deed; ***Ado*** 4.1.166: with experimental seal doth warrant; ***John*** 3.1.184: there's law and warrant; ***Per.*** 4.2.58: warrant of her virginity; ***Lear*** 3.1.18: upon the warrant of my note; ***Rich.3*** 3.7.33: nothing spake in warrant; ***1Hen.6*** 1.3.13: I'll be your warrantize; 5.5.46: his wealth doth warrant a liberal dower; ***2Gents.*** 2.4.102: his worth is warrant for his welcome; ***MWives*** 1.1.10: bill, warrant, quittance; 4.2.207: the warrant of womanhood; ***BFair*** 4.1.27: warrant of warrants; 4.1.137-38: Have you a warrant? An you have a warrant, show it.

WASH, v. Literally to cleanse or remove. Numismatically, "To sweat (gold or silver coin) by the application of acids" *(OED).* To alter and counterfeit coins by applying a thin veneer of metal resembling gold or silver after the precious metals have been leeched out of the coin and replaced by baser materials. Generally, to cheat, to abuse. See ***Laundress.*** *[**Scorn.*** 436: for washing out the roses ın three farthıngs, / To make 'em pence; ***12N.*** 3.2.25- 26: The double gilt of this opportunity you let time wash off; ***TAnd.*** 5.1.95: Why, she was wash'd, and cut, and trimm'd; ***MWives*** 1.2.4-5: his laundry—his washer and his wringer.

WASTE, n. and v. Originally, to ravage. To spend great sums of money, especially if frivolously; in contrast, not to use, in accordance with medieval rules governing riches, the wealth with which one is entrusted, including bodily wealth. Thus, ironic to the original sense, chastity and virginity are wastes. To empty or exhaust one's purse (or one's wit); to lay waste, i.e., spoil or plunder the wealth of another. To spend more than one takes in. Sometimes with an adnominatio on waist, with a double paronomasia on expense (great waste)/expanse (great waist). *[**MofV*** 1.1.157: made waste; 2.5.50-51: help us to waste / His borrowed purse; ***JC*** 4.3.200: waste his means; ***Oth.*** 4.2.185-86:1 have wasted myself out of my means; ***Lear*** 2.1.100: th' expense and waste of his revenues; ***A&C*** 4.1.16: they have earn'd the waste; ***R&J*** 1.1.224: huge waste [chastity]; ***MWives*** 1.3.42-43: I am now about no waste; I am about thrift; 4.2.211-12: he will never ... in the way of waste, attempt us again; ***2Hen.4*** 1.2.140-41: Your means are very slender, and your waste is great; 1.2.170-71: his quick wit wasted in giving reckonings.

WAVES. See ***Golden waves***.

WEALTH. See ***Common-wealth***.

WHITE AND BLACK. See ***Black and white***.

WHITE MONEY, n. Silver coins, as opposed to black money (billon) and red money (gold). An *asper* is a Turkish silver coin worth about two farthings, from the word for white money (Skeat). See ***Bianco, Ruddock***. *[**HWhore2*** 3.1.61; ***Maid*** 5.2.21; ***EMOH*** 4.7.46.

WHOLE SALE, n. Merchandise sold in gross lots rather than by individual items; the opposite of retail. Appears in a cacemphaton on hole sale, i.e., prostitution, the merchandising of sexual value. *[**WHo*** 2.1.53-54: we that edifie in priuate, and traffick by whole sale; ***MTerm*** 4.2.13-15: is not hole-sale the chiefest marchandize? doe you thinke some Merchants could keepe their wives so brave but for their hole-sale?; ***Ram.*** 273-74: we annual younger brothers / Must go to't by wholesale; ***DCourt.*** 1.2.36, 38: shee sels divine vertues as virginitie . . . like a great marchant by whole sale, *wa, ha, ho.*

WILL, n. A document apportioning goods and property at one's death; in an economically misunderstood pun on desire, wish. Also, of course, "sexual passion" (Ross). *[**MWives*** 3.4.56, 57-58: What is your will? /. . . —I ne'er made my will yet. ... I am not a sickly creature; ***MofV*** 1.2.24-25: so is the will of a living daughter curb'd by the will of a dead father; ***AYLI*** 1.1.2-3: bequeath'd me by will but poor a thousand crowns; ***12N.*** 1.5.246-47: inventoried, and . . . labell'd to my will;

John 1.1.109; 1.1.130; 2.1.192; ***Rich.2*** 3.2.148; ***2Hen.4*** 4.1.172; ***JC*** 3.2.135 passim; ***Per.*** 1.1.47.

WORDS. See ***Golden words.***

WORK, n. and v. In addition to the usual denotations of productive activity or occupation, the sexual connotations of working as copulating, usually expressed as *to work with* or *to go to work with.* According to Partridge, "To embark upon a love-bout with (a woman)"; *half-workers* are part-time prostitutes, necessary collaborators for propagation, or "women [who] are not content with one man but must forever have a second sexual intimate"; and *stair-work* is "'Dirty work' on the staircases; casual copulation." *[**Oth.*** 2.1.115: go to bed to work; ***MforM*** 5.1.278: I will go darkly to work with her; ***MofV*** 1.3.82: the work of generation; ***Cym.*** 2.5.1-2: women / Must be half-workers; ***WTale*** 3.3.74-75: stair-work, some trunk-work, some behind-door-work; ***EMen*** 540: We'll work our lands out of Pisaro's daughters, / And cancel all our bonds in their great bellies.

WORTH, n. and adj. Value, but applied to persons, virtue, reputation (intrinsic worth), and to women, virginity, which is valuable, in demand. Also the sum of one's material possessions. *[**MofV*** 1.1.167; ***MforM*** 5.1.244: against his worth and credit; ***MND*** 2.1.219: the rich worth of your virginity; ***Well*** 1.1.154: [virginity] the longer kept, the less worth; ***LLL*** 2.1.17: tell my worth [speak/count]; ***Drum*** 224: sulley his bright worth.

Y

YOUNGER, n. and adj. Also younker. A younger brother, thus a gentleman without the prospect of inheritance and therefore a bad marriage-match and one who perhaps tries to earn a living by trickery or by wit. *[**MofV*** 2.6.14; ***Heir*** 105; ***Scorn***. 427: Take heed of young smooth varlets, younger brothers; ***Maid*** 2.1.93: I am a younger Brother, and have nothing; ***Ram***. 273; ***Prod.*** 5.1.76-77: a poore Gentle-man, a yonger brother; ***Drum*** 188: a hatefull fault, he is a younger brother . . . —o intollerable; ***AYLI*** 1.1.53-54: elder brother, you are too young in this; 3.2.377

Z

ZECCHINO. See ***Cecchine***.

Gold zecchino d'oro, Mantua, 1612-1626.

Appendix A

Usury and the Right Use of Wealth:

A Study in Renaissance Sources and Applications

Charging usury had been forbidden from time immemorial. Although today usury is defined as lending money at exorbitant rates, in the Middle Ages it had a much wider application, including any profit derived from material goods or money without introducing the factor of human labor. The *OED* shows the earliest uses of the term to be simply "lending money at interest" or any "gain made by lending money." One would be making profit from another's "use" of money or goods, which was a violation of both natural law and the concept of commutative justice.

Medieval economic theory had a long history of reinterpretation and clarification. Basically its tenets were those set forth by Aristotle in his *Politics* and *Nichomachean Ethics,* scholastically summarized some nine hundred years later by St. Thomas Aquinas in the *Summa Theologica.* First, the primary definition of money is teleological: it was invented for the purpose of exchange. Thus it must be considered a barren medium, and to foster its breeding or growth would be an unnatural act. This identity contributes to one of the basic arguments against usury. Second, commutative justice must be observed in any transaction, which means that both parties involved should feel satisfied with their exchange: they "must necessarily gain by it in the sense that they must prefer their economic situations after the act to the economic situations in which they found themselves before the act—or else they would not have any motive to perform it."[29] On these two bases, generally, charging any fee for a loan of money or goods, unless one could prove damages incurred, was usury.

Two kinds of damages in loans were commonly recognized and almost invariably awarded a legal charge of retribution, that is, a loss (interest) rather than a gain (usury).[30] These were *damnum*

---

[29]Joseph A. Schumpeter, *History of Economic Analysis* (New York: Oxford Univ. Press, 1954), 61. See also Aristotle, *Politics,* bk. 1, ch. 9, and *Aquinas Ethicus,* translated by Joseph Rickaby, 2d ed. (London: Bums and Oates, 1896), 2:91

[30]Sidney Homer, *A History of Interest Rates* (New Brunswick: Rutgers Univ. Press. 1963), 73.

emergens (loss arising) and *lucrum cessans* (outgoing profit). The first was an actual loss suffered through having made the loan, *e.g.*, lack of sufficient food to serve one's family, while the latter was a lost opportunity for profit in another arena during the time the money was in the hands of the borrower. The relationship between lender and debtor might also help to define the legality of interest. A lender could justifiably, some argued, expect payment beyond his principal if the borrower was his enemy, a vassal, or an unjust possessor.[31] The first of these is the oldest exception to the taking of use, based on the Biblical text from Deuteronomy 23:19-20: "You shall not lend upon interest to your brother, interest on money, interest on victuals, interest on anything that is lent for interest. To a foreigner you may lend upon interest" (RSV).

As Benjamin Nelson demonstrates, the historical problem lay in interpreting who was one's brother and who a foreigner or stranger. The ancient Hebrews read the law literally and forbade the taking of usury within the clan. The medieval Church, following the Church fathers and early theologians, was bothered by the permission of usury on any occasion and thus attempted to disallow the Deuteronomic brother/other distinction.[32] To assert that there was a unified stance on usury, however, would be in error. Clement of Alexandria (150-215) recommended prohibition of usury only between brothers, and Cyprian (200-258) asserted that the taking of usury should be forbidden for the clergy. Thus the Council of Elvira in 305 decreed against clerical usury, but their edict was almost universally applied (O'Brien, 168-71). St. Basil (329-79), St. Jerome (340-420), and St. Ambrose (340-97) were perhaps the first to take on the text itself, Basil denouncing usury as a sin against community charity and Jerome declaring that the New Testament universalized humanity to the extent that all were brothers and the Deuteronomic distinction negated. Ambrose's interpretation differed slightly, defining as others only the enemies of God's chosen. The text, however, remained problematic and required constant scrutiny. Rabanus Maurus (784-856) clarified the passage to his satisfaction by reading it as an econo-spiritual metaphor: "To take usury for the loan of 'metallic money' is entirely forbidden; to

---

[31]George O'Brien, *An Essay on Medieval Economic Teaching* (1920; rpt. New York: Augustus Kelley, 1967), 184-86; and John T. Noonan, Jr., *The Scholastic Analysis of Usury* (Cambridge: Harvard Univ. Press, 1957), 101-03.

[32]*The Idea of Usury,* 2d ed. (Chicago: Univ. of Chicago Press, 1969), xx-xxii, 3-5.

ask usury for the offering of 'spiritual' sustenance is legitimate," and indeed the canonists as well would distinguish between spiritual and corporal usury, allowing and condoning the former.[33]

In the twelfth century Ambrose was reinterpreted as sanctioning interest, Christians taking usury from Moslems, Jews taking usury from Christians. By the thirteenth century many Christian usurers actually cited Deuteronomy in defense of their actions (Nelson, 6-7). But the Second Lateran Council (1139), fearing that the permission of usury would encourage other sins, reiterated that all usury was illegal and prohibited usurers from Christian burial. Both Alexander III (d. 1181) and Innocent III (d. 1216) concurred, following Aristotle's reasoning: usury was selling something that either did not exist or did not belong to man, *i.e.,* use or time. Money could not self-propagate as could other commodities, say ewes or rams *(pecunia pecuniam non parere potest);* it "was invented chiefly for the purpose of exchange; and consequently the proper and principal use of money is consumption" (O'Brien, 176). However, according to O'Brien, "as late as the first half of the thirteenth century there was no serious discussion of usury by the theologians. William of Paris [d. 1270], Alexander of Hales [1175-1245], and Albertus Magnus [1206-80] simply pronounced it sinful" (176). Peter Lombard argued with a different logic but to the same effect: usury was a form of theft and thus both un-Christian and illegal. Aquinas confirmed this stance in that he believed we should consider all men our brothers (Nelson, 9).

At this point theological interpretation was augmented by the "golden age of canonical studies." The canonists assumed the task of annotating the *Corpus Juris Canonici* and Gratian's *Decretum* of 1140, which summarized all the Church law from the fourth, fifth, and sixth centuries. Gratian's statement on usury was standard: "To demand or receive or even to lend expecting to receive something above the capital is to be guilty of usury; usury may exist on money or anything else; one who receives usury is guilty of rapine and just as culpable as a thief; the prohibition against usury holds for laymen as well as clerics but, when guilty, the latter will be more severely punished" (McLaughlin, 82).

The main problem of the canonists dealt not with the brother/other context, but with a possible or apparent conflict

---

[33]T. P. McLaughlin, "The Teaching of the Canonists on Usury," *Mediaeval Studies* 1 (1939):98.

between canon law and the *Corpus Juris Civilis* of Justinian. Did civil law forbid usury, and if so, which system took precedence, civil or canon? While the civil law did not directly state a position on usury, it allowed interest as a way of avoiding rapine, as a sort of lesser evil. The famous civilian commentator Azzo in the early thirteenth century denied the legality of usury but allowed for interest as consistent with the laws of God and the Church. This interest was retribution for delay in payment or damages resulting from the loan.

Comments like those of canonist Raymond of Penafort (b. 1175) were in agreement with the civilian position (or *vice versa*), but it really did not matter, since he had decided that no civil law violating natural law may be considered binding, and that a temporal law cannot supersede God's law in any case. Hostiensis also agreed with Azzo, denouncing usury but enumerating fully thirteen exceptions when an additional charge could be accepted, placing them in Latin verse form so that they could be easily remembered: in fiefs, as surety for clerics, as revenue from a pledge, in ecclesiastical benefices, in revenues from land over time, as a weapon against enemies of the Church, in future sales, in delayed payment, in penalty for nonperformance, in rescission of contract, in a gift from the debtor, in a contract of hire, and in compensation for labor (McLaughlin, 84-125). Canonist Antoninus of Florence (1389-1459) maintained further (following Aristotle) that money was barren and could not reproduce—unless man applied work to it, in which case, some argued, the income is not from the money, but rather from the labor of man (O'Brien, 181).

In the early fourteenth century Dante vividly summarized contemporary attitudes toward usurers by their portrayal in the *Inferno.* He assigns them to the bottom of the seventh circle, three steps lower than the merely prodigal or avaricious. Other economic abusers, those who actually alter money, are placed even lower, in the tenth pouch of the eighth circle. Usurers are condemned here as committing a violence against God: perverting both nature and art, intruding where man should not presume to tread. Dante pays special attention to clergy who sin economically, those of *"mal dare e mal tener"* (to give and to take painfully, Canto VII, l. 58). He pinpoints the common hypocrisy surrounding the practice of usury by showing us Reginaldo Scrovegni, whose family tried to negate his usury through good works, and Giovanni Buiamonte dei

Becchi, who was ironically an honored Florentine in Dante's own lifetime, as well as an infamous usurious banker.[34]

Aquinas generally set the tone and theory for all theological analysis of usury of the fourteenth and fifteenth centuries, yet the later theologians offered a more flexible view of the legality of usury and the nature of money. Although he still maintained that man cannot sell (and make a monetary profit from) time, which belongs to God alone, theologian Johannes Nider (1380-1438) did admit to a few kinds of allowable interest: for penalties, delay of payment, and in leasing out goods for display or ornament, goods that would not be consumed in such a transaction. Even engrossing was allowable (he writes from the point of view of merchants), providing that the result was "useful to the commonwealth." Agreeing with Aristotle that the chief purpose of money is exchange, Nider nonetheless follows Duns Scotus in arguing that the primary criteria for evaluating profit from money in damages and penalties are the intent or purpose of such payments (*i.e.,* not fraudulent) and the satisfaction or benefit of both parties in the arrangement (*i.e.,* commutative justice).

According to Nider's logic, the profit accrues from the commodity nature of money: "money can itself be farmed out like a horse or something else farmable for its usefulness. When ownership is retained and money is lawfully farmed out to another, and in consequence there is a contract for farming out or hiring out the money, this is not to be considered an act of lending or the giving of a loan."[35] Much theological analysis is based on this kind of semantic subtlety and redefinition, and Nider's insistence on the legality and contractuality of the arrangement is also typical of the late medieval attitude of the common law toward cases involving usury, as we shall see.

In addition to this new theological flexibility, from time to time special conditions arose that, in all common sense, required a custodial fee on loans. From about 1460, for instance, the Franciscans had run "benevolent banks" so that the poor could borrow capital without paying large interest rates to moneylenders, sometimes 20 to 50 percent. By 1509 eighty-seven of these *monti dipieta* had been established, with papal authority. Their

---

[34]Translated by Allen Mandelbaum (New York: Bantam, 1982), 348.

[35]*On the Contracts of Merchants,* translated by Charles H. Reeves, edited by Ronald B. Shuman (Norman: Univ. of Oklahoma Press, 1966), 53-63.

management necessitated, however, a "small charge," and this the Dominicans promptly termed usury. In 1515, finally, the Fifth Lateran Council in a decree called *De reformatione Montium pietatis,* allowed "a small percentage of interest on loans, sufficient to defray expenses, . . . but there was to be no profit in the transaction."[36] In the sixteenth century new terminology was also tried to expedite lending without spiritual ramifications: *damnus et interesse* (damages and interest) to replace usury.

Francisco Suarez (1548-1617), said to be the last of the scholastic theologians yet writing in the Renaissance, analyzed usury in his consideration of the nature and limits of natural law in *De legibus* of 1612. Although he adheres closely to Aquinas, Suarez also "objects" to and modifies the precedents, recognizing that the prohibition of usury is not always reasonably accessible to all. Usury, he concludes, is contrary to natural law and thus (following Gratian) *malum in se* (evil in itself). Civil and canon law, even if they allow usury, carry no authority in this regard, for no human power, even the Pope, can oppose natural law, which is unchangeable. However, consistent with the opinions of Nider, Suarez agrees that there are variations in some transactions that require "relaxations of natural law": usury may be accepted, for instance, if it is offered as a gift.[37]

As O'Brien argues, "though there were branches of commercial law which were, in the main, independent of the canonist doctrine, there were none that were opposed to it" (23). English Common Law actually took no formal stand on usury and instead focused on the contractual nature of provisions for default on loans. Indeed, according to the jurist Glanvill, "private agreements are not usually protected in the court of our lord the King."[38] Common Law principles were, however, consistent with both the Roman civil law and the canon law, as evidenced in Maine's complaint of their archaism: "the entire form and a third of the contents were directly borrowed from the Corpus Juris" (Fifoot, 218). If a debtor offered a

---

[36]Richard J. Schoeck, "The Fifth Lateran Council: its partial successes and its larger failures," in *Reform and Authority in the Medieval and Reformation Church,* edited by Guy Fitch Lytle (Washington, D.C.: Catholic Univ. of America Press, 1981), 110; Nelson, 19-24

[37]In *Classics of International Law,* translated by Gwladys L. Williams *et al.* (New York: Oceana, 1964), 2:271-75.

[38]C. H. S. Fifoot, *History and Sources of the Common Law* (New York: Greenwood, 1970), 218-36.

pledge of faith as security on a loan and then defaulted, the lender actually had recourse only in the ecclesiastical courts, for "spiritual satisfaction." Common Law did allow fixed rent charges, which were sometimes called usurious, and it provided for collection of both principal and interest on a debt if the proper legal procedures were followed. The debt must have been legally entered in the royal record, and a sealed, written agreement of terms must be presented as evidence. Since the days of Richard I Jews had used this method to collect on their moneylending contracts; the Statute of Acton Burnell under Edward I provided for attachment of possessions if repayment of a loan was delayed, but Jews were specifically exempted from this provision.[39]

Jews and the taking of interest became closely identified for several historical reasons. Thus this group was subjected to even more severe prosecution than other offenders under both the religious and the secular law. In a document called "The Disposition of Debts Due to Jews" (1290), Edward I proclaims that formerly "we ordained and decreed that no Jew thenceforth should lend anything at usury to any Christian on lands, rents or other things, but that they should live by their commerce and labour." But since that proclamation, the Jews had "maliciously" devised an even worse kind of usury, courtesy. Since Edward does not feel the need to explain the new mechanism, economists today are in some confusion about precisely what courtesy was. It appears to be an informal obligation, extra-contractual, which exacted a gift or a fee (thus, a courtesy) for the loan of money. An early *OED* definition supports this interpretation: "by favour or indulgence . . . as distinguished from inherent or legal right." Since the "interest" payment was not contractual, it was beyond the law in both enforcement and punishment. For this offense the Jews were subsequently expelled from the realm of England as traitors, and any Christian owing any Jew a debt at the time was required to repay only the principal.[40] Of crucial importance in Edward's edict is the underlying philosophy. "Commerce and labour" as opposed to financial activities are condoned, and Christianity intrudes to a discriminatory extent: right economic behavior is equated with right religion.

---

[39] Arthur R. Hogue, *Origins of the Common Law* (Bloomington: Indiana Univ. Press, 1966), 206.

[40] *English Economic History: Select Documents,* edited by A. E. Bland, P. A. Brown, and R. H. Tawney (London: G. Bell, 1914), 51.

Although the restriction against usury was a major premise of medieval economic thought, supported by Biblical text and generally agreed upon in the abstract, it demonstrates perhaps more clearly than any other activity the collision of theory and practice that was to concern Renaissance dramatists so deeply. Not only Jews, but everyone, it seems, violated even first economic principles. Tawney reports that in the country, farmers, innkeepers, and yeomen were the most common moneylenders. Even though Jews had been exiled to help abolish usurious practices, extortionate economic dealings were carried on handily by their Christian brothers:

> A grocer who did business as a money-lender gets a country gentleman into his clutches, discounts his bills at twenty-five per cent., renews them at compound interest, and finally, having sold up the debtor, becomes lord of the manor. ... In the opening years of Elizabeth's reign, a Norfolk money-lender had on hand ... no less than thirty suits arising from usurious dealings with his neighbours, maintained a gang of bullies who intimidated witnesses, forcibly kidnapped and imprisoned an opponent with whom he had a quarrel, [and] threatened to drive the parson out of the village.[41]

We can understand the frustration and moral indignation of Edward VI and his counselors when, in 1552, faced with similar practices, they issued a summary "Byll against Usurie" to define the civil law stance, directing it toward a situation obviously out of hand:

> Forasmuche as Usurie is by the worde of God utterly prohibited, as a vyce moste odyous and detestable, as in dyvers places of the hollie Scripture it is evydent to be seen, which thing by no godly teachinges and perswations can syncke in to the hartes of dyvers gredie, uncharitable and couvetous parsons of this Realme, nor yet by anny terrible threatninges of Goddes wrathe and vengeaunce that justly hangeth over this Realme for the great and open Usurie therein dailye used and practysed they will

41 Thomas Wilson, *A Discourse upon Usury,* edited by R. H. Tawney (London: G. Bell, 1925), 22, 37, 89.

> forsake such filthie gayne and lucre, onles some temporall punishment be provyded and ordeyned in that bihalfe.[42]

In 1571 Elizabeth's Parliament reiterated "An Act against Usury" allowing a maximum of 10 percent, an act which, in 1581, she felt the need to proclaim yet "in full strength and force" and to urge "all and every her said subjects to accept of it as a law yet standing in full force."[43]

As early as 1550 Hugh Latimer, the Anglican preacher, had reported rates of 40 percent usury, and he spoke against even the maximum of 10 percent. All use is ungodly, so that if it is illegal to take 20 percent, one may not justify taking 10 percent; it is like stealing only 6d. rather than 13d. halfpence. He does condone a metaphorical usury similar to that of Rabanus Maurus, however, "God's usury," that returns a "quadruplum": those who freely give to the poor receive four times back in return.[44] In the latter half of the sixteenth century Henry Smith devoted whole sermons to the problem, basically reiterating canonist thought, declaring that usury is no more than legal thievery, cruelty, extortion, persecution, deceit, slander, revenge, oppression, and the opposite of love; it opposes the laws of charity, nations, nature, and God and the teachings of Christ; and he condemns hidden usury charges in the taking of pawns, the use of arbitrage, the inequitable exchange of services, overpricing, *etc.*, all of which he terms the "Mystery of Usury" (Welsby, 80-85). The religious doctrine required bolstering by civil authority, but expanding economic activity continued in spite of these combined efforts at moral enforcement.

While public banking in England developed only in the seventeenth century, private banking grew earlier along similar lines as in Italy. Here, however, the independent money specialist, allied to his trade or profession, replaced the large, powerful banking family. Primary dealers in money and economic matters in the sixteenth century in England were wool broggers and corn

---

[42] *Tudor Economic Documents,* edited by R. H. Tawney and Eileen Power (London: Longmans, Green, 1924), 2:142-43.

[43] *Tudor Royal Proclamations (TRP),* edited by Paul L. Hughes and James F. Larkin (New Haven: Yale Univ. Press, 1969), 2:486.

[44] In *Sermons and Society: An Anglican Anthology,* edited by Paul A. Welsby (Baltimore: Penguin, 1970), 47.

bodgers (middlemen), brokers, goldsmiths, and scriveners.[45] Broggers and bodgers filled the need of credit advances to producers on the security of the forthcoming crop of wool or corn; on the other end they sold wool on credit to clothmakers. Thus they performed the functions of a bank on a small and very specialized scale. Brokers were mostly pawnbrokers, or "retayling" brokers, reputed to be the most vicious of Renaissance moneylenders, for they borrowed money at 20 to 25 percent from usurers and then lent it at 60, 80, or even 100 percent interest to the poor. Their practice eventually became so extortionate that in 1598 the profession in London was limited to two "credible and honest" brokers.

Goldsmiths are said to have fathered English banking, but scriveners also played a large role in its development. Although goldsmiths were primarily jewelers, merely because of their proximity to precious metals they were associated with coins and money. Most had been kept busy early in the sixteenth century making plate, which became a form of hoarded wealth in many families. Hoarding was a popular medieval activity, and the dangers of theft became greater as social mobility increased. Even Richard III was a hoarder: in the sixteenth century a cleaning woman discovered by accident a false bottom in his bed left at an inn near Bosworth field. Inside was some £300 in coins and plate. As fewer people hoarded and more began investing in the new opportunities, goldsmiths were forced to expand their functions in order to retain a living. They began collecting deposits, holding them securely for their customers. However, having been appointed public judges of the fineness of coinage in 1560, goldsmiths could put this skill to profit by immediately melting down any heavy coins deposited, having them re-minted, and keeping the excess metal. When they eventually began lending money, they did so from the deposits of their other customers, thus putting the old moneylender out of business, for he was still forced to lend out of his personal capital. Goldsmithing was probably a lucrative business, for in 1566 there were one hundred and seven London goldsmiths, most living in Cheapside or on Lombard

---

[45]R. D. Richards, *The Early History of Banking in England* (London: Frank Cass, 1958), 8-19. See also Ellis T. Powell, *The Evolution of the Money Market 1385-1915* (1915; rpt. London: Frank Cass, 1966), 53-61; and Dorothy Johnson Orchard and Geoffrey May, *Money-lending in Great Britain* (New York: Russell Sage, 1933), 29-44. Some of the following material is also drawn from Lawrence Stone, *The Crisis of the Aristocracy 1558-1641* (Oxford: Clarendon, 1965), 511-37.

Street, and later concentrating around the Royal Exchange. Eventually they offered 10 to 12 percent interest on deposits and relent these deposits at 20 to 30 percent, making a tidy profit.

Scriveners have a similarly fascinating development in the world of high finance. They began, of course, simply writing up bonds, contracts, and bills obligatory, but by doing this they became acquainted with those most involved in trade and exchange. By exploiting knowledge gained in writing contracts, they became expert financial advisors. Furthermore, scriveners could put prospective buyers in touch with appropriate sellers and pocket a small commission for this service, probably ¼ to 1 percent (Stone, 537). Eventually they began taking money from prospective investors in advance, in case they discovered an appropriate opportunity in the course of daily scrivening and needed the funds immediately. A natural activity for the enterprising scrivener was then to make short-term loans with these deposits, thus earning his brokerage fee and interest in the bargain. According to Stubbes in his *Anatomie of Abuses,* such moonlighting in terms of offering expanded services was economically immoral:

> [T]he Scriuener is the Instrument wherby the Deuell worketh the frame of this wicked woorke of Usurie, hee beeing rewarded with a good fleece for his labour: For, firste he hath a certaine allowance of the Archdiuel who owes the money, for helping him to such vent for his coyne: Secondly, he hath a greate deale more usurie to himselfe, of him who borroweth the money, then he alloweth ye owner of the mony: And thirdly, he hath not the least part for making the writings betweene them.[46]

In addition to these professional lenders, Tawney speculates that anyone and everyone in the English countryside could play the usurer. Since many loans were made in wares instead of money, repayment of more than the principal was easy to mask. Country people did not necessarily borrow out of extravagance or wastefulness, as did their city cousins, but moneylending became firmly entrenched in country dealings out of necessity. As Tawney comments, "The money-lending which concerns nine-tenths of the population is spasmodic, irregular, unorganised, a series of

---

[46]Phillip Stubbes, *The Anatomie of Abuses* (London: Richard Jones, 1583), n.p. (microfilm).

individual, and sometimes surreptitious, transactions between neighbours. . . . What made the usurer indispensable was the helplessness of the farmer or tradesman without the reserves needed to carry him over a bad season, or to enable him to hold on while working up a connection" *(Discourse,* 22-30).

In the course of these new financial activities, many of them illegal or at least practiced *sub rosa,* sometimes sophisticated economic transactions required more complex mechanisms than simple barter or cash sales had developed. When dealing by credit became a current practice, credit instruments were necessary. These became especially attractive, for in the midst of a wealth of contractual paper a dealer could hide exorbitant interest, still banned in England until 1571, except for a short time in 1545, and then when legalized still restricted and regulated heavily. To facilitate the movement of funds and trade in foreign currencies, medieval traders had established the bill of exchange, but Renaissance merchants were to develop negotiable paper to the point of its becoming representative currency—another earthquake in the established terrain of values inherited from the Middle Ages.

In his essay, "Of Usury," Sir Francis Bacon summarized the current Renaissance problem of financial investment: "Two things are to be reconciled. The one, that the tooth of usury be grinded, that it bite not too much; the other, that there be left open a means to invite moneyed men to lend to the merchants, for the continuing and quickening of trade."[47] Most agreed with Bacon, conceding that usury was a necessary evil, necessary for the demands of capital investment, trade, and exploration, and evil because of its abuses against noble and poor alike. But how to reconcile the tension? Religious teaching still frowned on usury except in rare circumstances. In the early years of Elizabeth's reign, Edward VI's ban of 1552 constituted governmental policy. Interest hidden in contracts like bills of exchange or tradesmen's bills was one way to circumvent the prohibition. Other more intricate developments included rent-charges; dubious partnerships called commenda, loans on bottomry, and insurance; contracts involving three parties called a *contractus trinus;* and extensive use of *damnus emergens* and *lucrum cessans* (Orchard, 18-21).

---

[47] "Of Usury," in *The Essayes or Covnsels Civill and Morall of Francis Bacon,* edited by Walter Whorral (New York: Dutton, 1900), 178.

Thomas Gresham, factor for the crown and eventually Queen's Merchant, felt, like other merchants, the strain between precept and practice. In a letter to Elizabeth before 1571, he made a plea for some legal interest in order to further the royal business: "I wold wyshe myght be pressently set at libertye, yff it were possible, for the better accomplishinge of her highness' enterprise."[48] Eventually this last expediency moved the Queen and Parliament; in 1571 they legalized the taking of interest up to 10 percent as had the government of Henry VIII in 1545. As Stone views the measure, though, it was only partly altruistic: "It was the need to accommodate the realities of business life and the desire of the Crown to borrow on the English market" (530). While seemingly everyone either took or paid interest, hostility toward the practice remained strong even after legalization. The words of the statute itself best summarize the dichotomy in feeling:

> [Under Henry VIII] there was then made and established one good Act for the reformation of usury, by which Act the vice of usury was well repressed. . . . [The ban of Edward VI] hath not done so much good as was hoped it should, but rather the said vice of usury, and specially by way of sale of wares and shift of interest, hath much more exceedingly abounded, to the utter undoing of many gentlemen, merchants, occupiers, and other, and to the importable hurt of the commonwealth. . . . [The previous law is re-enacted.]
>
> And be it further enacted that all bonds, contracts and assurances, collateral or other, to be made for payment of any principal or money to be lent . . . upon or by which loan or doing there shall be reserved or taken above the rate of ten pounds for the hundred for one year shall be utterly void.[49]

Even with a 10 percent legal interest charge, those forced to borrow continued to compare usury to a canker on the economy. According to Stone, "It is impossible to find a single witness who thought borrowing was anything but a desperate and dangerous expedient" (539). Truly, however, "It was an evil fruit universally eaten" (Powell, 52).

---

[48]John William Burgon, *The Life and Times of Sir Thomas Gresham, Knt.* (New York: Burt Franklin, 1839 [?]), 2:343.

[49]*Elizabethan People: State and Society,* edited by Joel Hurstfield and Alan G. R. Smith (London: Edward Arnold, 1972), 67-68.

What is preserved for us of English Renaissance preaching and socio-religious analysis also confirms this dichotomy of thought. Sixteenth- and seventeenth-century Anglican preachers almost universally condemn usury and condone the free and duteous giving of alms—the latter metaphorically as the best kind of God's usury, a spiritual investment. This is made clear in the popular 1623 edition of *Certaine Sermons or Homilies appointed to be read in CHVRCHES,* where, in "Of Almes deedes," we are shown in econolingua how Christ "promiseth a Princely recompence, for a beggarly benevolence ... he will requite with double and treble. For so sayth the Wise man: Hee which sheweth mercy to the poore, doeth lay his money in banke to the Lord, for a large interest and gaine."

True usury, however, is vividly portrayed and vehemently damned, as in this late sixteenth-century sermon (XI) by Edwyn Sandys: "That biting worm of usury, that devouring wolf, hath consumed many: many it hath pulled upon their knees, and brought to beggary; many such as might have lived in great wealth, and in honour not a few. This canker hath corrupted all England. . . . Repress it by law; else the heavy hand of God hangeth over us and will strike us" (Welsby, 76). Henry Smith and others gave entire sermons over to the subject, in which usurers are shown as unnatural, bestial pariahs, abandoning human community and obligation for gold: "The usurer speaks to his gold, saying 'Thou art my confidence. . . . The world hisseth at me, but I hug and applaud my own soul, and fat my spirits in the sight of my bags'" (Thomas Adams, "The Gallant's Burden," c. 1614 [Welsby, 106]).

The connection between social welfare and proper economic theory and behavior was not ignored, especially by the eminent Richard Hooker, who, in Book I of *The Laws of Ecclesiastical Polity* sets the tone for his economic precepts. He insists on an extant natural, organic law that emphasizes the common weal over individual desires and necessitates the primacy of reason over appetite. Along with his general distrust of riches inherited almost verbatim from Augustine—"Although therefore riches be a thing which every man wisheth, yet no man of judgment can esteem it better to be rich, than wise, virtuous, and religious"—he equates temporal and spiritual governance. It is the king's obligation to enact and enforce laws for the spiritual benefit of his people. Indeed, primary laws of the realm include those devoted to regulating trade and traffic.[50] Regarding money, an attitudinal revision is necessary, for "whereas nature requireth God to be honoured with wealth, we honour for the most part wealth as God. . . . [F]or worldly goods it sufficeth frugally and honestly to use them to our own benefit, without detriment and hurt of others" (2:442).

If these ambivalences between economic precept and practice, well documented by government, art, and religion, are representative under Roman Catholic and Anglican domination, one must ask how economic attitudes were affected by the beginnings of Protestantism, a phenomenon that spans the late medieval and Renaissance periods. Tawney affirms a tight link between religion and the change in economic outlook.

Early in the sixteenth century Luther set in motion the waves of Protestantism that would eventually affect much of social equilibrium; his economic theories, however, were for the most part merely supportive of medieval doctrine. He admired the peasant who could earn a living by the sweat of his brow; he deemed the crafts honorable, for they were of service to the community; and his most detested sins were idleness and greed, for they set Christian brother against brother. Even though Luther abhorred institutions like the medieval Church, his instructions to individual men were consistent with Church teachings: "Love thy neighbor as thyself, and Do unto others as ye would have them do unto you" (Tawney, 92-99). These tenets resuscitate the neighborly theory of economic behavior. Moreover, as appraised by Max Weber, the new idea of an individual calling was instrumental in defining daily economics, for Luther saw "the valuation of the fulfillment of duty in worldly affairs as the highest form which the moral activity of the individual could assume."[51]

Calvin, the next widely to influence individual behavior in a religious context, taught a more progressive economic doctrine. He, as opposed to Luther, assumed a context of sophisticated rather than simplistic economic necessity. Condoning economic participation, Calvin nonetheless maintained strict rules governing

---

[50] 1907; rpt. London: J. M. Dent, Everyman's Library, 1963, 1:189-91.

[51] *The Protestant Ethic and the Spirit of Capitalism,* translated by Talcott Parsons (New York: Scribners, 1958), 17. I rely on Tawney's argument in *Religion and the Rise of Capitalism* (1926; rpt. Gloucester, Mass.: Peter Smith, 1962), 22-176 for the following generalizations.

one's behavior, but in general these guidelines were in better accord with the economic realities they confronted. The only danger in accumulating wealth lay in its misuse, for "self-indulgence or ostentation." For those who followed Calvin's teachings, business itself became a kind of religion, success in it requiring the Christian virtues of thrift, diligence, and sobriety. Industry was an obligation, but the rewards it brought were to be governed by discipline. Individual virtues would be rewarded by financial gain, but still the social context held: "the pious man owes to his brethren all that it is in his power to give" (Tawney, 102-18).

Later, the Puritan movement was to reach perhaps even more citizens with its "sober exaltation—an earnest, zealous, godly generation, scorning delights, punctual in labor, constant in prayer, thrifty and thriving, filled with a decent pride in themselves and their calling, assured that strenuous toil is acceptable to Heaven" (Tawney, 211). With these new religious movements economic behavior became more and more acceptable—as long as it observed certain Christian guidelines. So, for the Puritans as for medieval Catholics, wealth was fine, in moderation and if one could resist its vicious allure. Still we see in Puritanism an ambivalence: no longer suspicious of economic motives, as medieval folk had been, Puritans condoned economic activity but warned that a peril still lay in wait for those who became too devoted to the pursuit of riches. Luxury, great pleasure, and extravagance were for them the greatest evils, but poverty was no longer meritorious. The poor were abused for idleness: "distress is a proof of demerit" (Tawney, 211-67). The emphasis in Puritan thought on industry as a necessary step toward financial comfort was based primarily on the words of St. Paul, "He who will not work shall not eat." A suspicion that the poor were somehow merely reaping the profits of their inferior moral behavior crept more and more frequently into sermons and other pious tracts, so that by 1597, in *Provision for the Poore,* Henry Arthington was able to offer this categorical indictment:

> The proceeding sinnes from the poore themselves, whereby they provoke the Lord to pinch them, are these six especially:
>
> 1. First, their misspending of former times in idlenesse, when they might have wrought.
>
> 2. Secondly, their wilful wasting of their goods when they had them, in bibbing and belly-cheare.

3. Thirdly, their impacient bearing of their present want, complaining often without cause.

4. Fourthly, their dayly repining at others prosperitie, to have so much and they so little.

5. Fiftly, their banning and cursing, when they are not served as themselves desire.

6. Sixtly, their seldome repairing to their parish Churches, to heare and learne their duties better.[52]

As the new Protestant work ethic was forced to confront the paradoxical nexus between riches and religion, it conformed to a mercantilist sense of economic value. As John Wesley came to address the problem, he concluded that "religion must necessarily produce both industry and frugality, and these cannot but produce riches. ... We must exhort all Christians to gain all they can, and to save all they can; that is, in effect, to grow rich" (Weber, 159, 175).

Christopher Hill summarizes the economic effects of Protestantism as follows: "The protestant revolt melted down the iron ideological framework which held society in its ancient mould. ... In a society already becoming capitalist, protestantism facilitated the triumph of the new values. There was no inherent theological reason for the protestant emphasis on frugality, hard work, accumulation; but that emphasis was a natural consequence of the religion of the heart in a society where capitalist industry was developing."[53]

But more important than what it changed is what Protestantism retained. Even within the thriving economic milieu of trade and mercantilism and good industry and hard work, the individual and social perils of wealth were feared. Even while acquisition was condoned, moderation was stressed. And even while individual economic reward was applauded, social economic obligations were still mandatory.

---

[52]In Helen C. White, *Social Criticism in Popular Religious Literature of the Sixteenth Century* (1944; rpt. New York: Octagon, 1965), 250.

[53]"Protestantism and the Rise of Capitalism," in *Essays in the Economic and Social History of Tudor and Stuart England,* edited by F. J. Fisher (Cambridge: Univ. Press, 1961), 15-39, quotation from 36. See also Louis B. Wright, *Middle-Class Culture in Elizabethan England* (1935; rpt. Ithaca: Cornell Univ. Press, 1963), 175-92.

Throughout the sixteenth century medieval concepts of right economic behavior survived, influencing both individual and social actions. Even though changes in economic demands would modify them somewhat, and even though Protestantism would emphasize certain values that the medieval Church had not, the tenacity of medieval attitudes about wealth is clearly demonstrated. Based on Aristotle's teleological definition of money as a "barren" entity that could not breed naturally since it was invented for exchange rather than for growth or production as a commodity, combined with a recognition of natural economy primarily as household management and acquisition or chrematistics as "unnatural," the philosophy concerning wealth was only slightly altered through the ages. Perhaps these theories seemed intuitively right; perhaps they survived because they were linked so tightly to social structure and religious ethics. More amazing than their mere survival is their continuing influence in the face of massive violation, caused by the confrontation of an archaic body of doctrine with a complex and sophisticated arena of economic needs. These economic tensions between theory and practice were to become source materials for plots and problems set forth in much of Renaissance drama and were to influence lexicon and metaphor in what became manifested as what I have termed econolingua.

Appendix B
Shakespeare's Economics

The plays of Shakespeare reveal a habit of mind that links love and money in an intricate metaphorical complex in turn relating to character, theme, and structure. David Hawkes comments that "the convergence of ethics, semiotics, and finance that fascinated Shakespeare was . . . unavoidable in early modern England. It was thrust upon people in the most mundane economic transactions of their daily life."[54] John Russell Brown, among others, remarks that the metaphor of merchandise in Shakespeare typically conveys a tenor of love, despite apparent contradictions between the two activities. Other playwrights as well habitually examine the relationship between bonds of the heart and obligations of the purse. Usurers and misers, who abound in plays of this period, almost invariably become blocking figures to a love match; when a suitor wins a beautiful and virtuous wife, it is as though he has made a financial coup; material gifts and tokens of social solidarity usually reinforce this feeling of the wealth of love. Shakespeare, like his fellow playwrights, made use of the finance-love nexus and its typical characters but in a manner that differs in both kind and degree.

In contrast to Jonson, Dekker, and Middleton, Shakespeare's plots do not generally rely solely on a financial ploy, although money and economic well-being are omnipresent underlying concerns: in coins and metals rendered for services, in gifts, in loans, in material tokens of love and friendship, and in characters' desires to improve their incomes or to raise their status by marrying rich women. In addition to this underlying current of economic behavior, Shakespeare employs language to its fullest potential in carrying the impact of his financial concerns. In the realm of metaphor almost parallel spheres exist in relation to

---

[54]David Hawkes, *Shakespeare and Economic Theory* (London: Bloomsbury, 2015), 172; John Russell Brown, *Shakespeare and his Comedies* (London: Methuen, 1957), 45-46. See also Leslie A. Fiedler, *The Stranger in Shakespeare* (New York: Stein and Day, 1973), 88, for the idea that Eros and Mammon share a close dramatic link. Alexander Leggatt, in *Citizen Comedy in the Age of Shakespeare* (Toronto: Univ. of Toronto Press, 1973), 4, bases his generic distinction on this same connection: "how to get money, and how to spend it; how to get a wife, and how to keep her."

natural processes on one side and artificial economic connections on the other.[55] The two worlds share a common lexicon, each with its own type of bonds, debts, dues, accounts, estimates, increase, profit, thrift, value, and use. One realm can be used to explain the other, as in the sonnets; eventually, because of their imagistic similarity and because the latter seems to encroach upon the former, the two systems become confused, leaving man bewildered, as in *Timon of Athens*.

Shakespeare's investigation of the impact of financial transactions upon human relations, then, is more symbolic than realistic. This is apparent in characters like Shylock, whom we know as a miser not because we see him in his counting-house like Barabas or burying his gold like Jaques de Prie, but because he is stingy and usurious with his words. Words, as the currency of social and intellectual exchange, are as real and tangible to Shylock as his ducats.[56] No single image in Shakespeare portrays the link between natural and economic processes as well as the connection of usury with sexual fecundity and prostitution. Usury, according to E. C. Pettet, appears in Shakespeare as a large, inclusive metaphor for the operations of a society based on the money ethic. In the natural realm of human relations, usury parallels human propagation but becomes equivalent to prostitution, "because they are the degeneration of a human relationship into a purely mercenary one."[57] By employing such suggestive and wide-reaching tropes, Shakespeare is able to include in almost every play, regardless of its main idea, an ancillary commentary upon the conflict between the spheres of human and natural economics.

---

[55] This distinction may derive from Aristotle's separation of household economy as allocation of resources for the primary needs of life from chrematistics, or acquisition for its own sake. See *Politics*, Bk. I, ch. 9.

[56] See especially Sigurd Burckhardt, *Shakespearean Meanings* (Princeton: Princeton Univ. Press, 1968), 23, 232; and Marc Shell, *The Economy of Literature* (Baltimore: Johns Hopkins Univ. Press, 1978), 3, and his "The Wether and the Ewe: Verbal Usury in *The Merchant of Venice*," *Kenyon Review* 1, no. 4 (1979): 66, 71. When Shylock puns, he exults at his own wit in being able to commit a type of semantic usury.

[57] E. C. Pettet, "*Timon of Athens*: The Disruption of Feudal Morality," *Review of English Studies* 23 (1947): 330, 335.

I.

The sonnets display, although under the guise of more basic and usual themes like love, friendship, and immortality, the essentials of Shakespeare's economic thought; in many cases the sonnets explore in miniature similar themes, issues, and methods as the plays and may offer a key to understanding certain economic problems in the drama. First, the sonnets affirm the same human values as the plays. Beauty, propagation and fertility, friendship, and reputation—all are natural, desirable, and "associated goods." Extrinsic values like high birth, wealth, and the manifestation of wit are important only when supported by their inner equivalences of worth. Excellence of mind and spirit, for example, are "prior values" to attributes relying only on outward display.[58]

For Shakespeare the processes of nature are to be desired over social processes contrived by men. This natural/artificial dichotomy relates to intrinsic and external or exchange value as well as to the concept of double-seeing, or a discrepancy between appearance and reality. Nature herself teaches a kind of economics that instructs us in our reciprocal obligations. Sonnet IV, building on the images of I through III, sets forth the concept of the right use of nature's gifts. Our abilities and attributes are not true donations, but rather loans; the receiver is obliged to put the sum of the loan "to use" so that he can repay nature with interest upon the day of reckoning. Most often in these first sonnets that interest is viewed as the outcome of breeding or propagation: nature's "use" produces more heirs. Breeding is an investment in the future, for a child is entered on the asset side of the ledger of life's economics (see Sonnet II). Nature is thus bountiful to those who understand her system of economics, those who, themselves "free," repay her in kind.

The connection between nature's system of "natural" economics and man's contrived system of high finance is neither tenuous nor illusory. Shakespeare incessantly, almost excessively,

---

[58]Edward Hubler, *The Sense of Shakespeare's Sonnets* (Princeton: Princeton Univ. Press, 1952), 126. See also 67, 70, 88-90 on values. In Sonnet XI fertility is proposed as a reward for beauty and goodness. The interest in how to distinguish between intrinsic and exchange value was, with usury, one of the paramount concerns of late medieval and Renaissance economists. See Marion Bowley, *Studies in the History of Economic Theory Before 1870* (London: Macmillan, 1973), 64-90.

plays upon their relationship in diction and image, forcing us to realize both the similarities and crucial differences between the two overlapping spheres. As Neal Dolan remarks, economic metaphors are used so pervasively in the sonnets that we become almost numbed to their effect.[59] In Sonnet IV, for example, financial terminology comprises a persistent, extended analogy for the economic processes and principles of nature. In a surfeit of financial jargon, the poet enjoys his extended metaphor by stretching it to the limit and stressing the opportunities for equivocation on words like *use* (l. 7) and *live* (l. 8); this double-sense extends as well into the basic dichotomy of his economic viewpoint. That human relations under the aegis of nature may so aptly (although paradoxically) be expressed in terms of a man-created system of artificial relation points to their closeness in form, however their underlying intents may differ. This similarity of expression for economic systems of markedly different functions—the one a natural relationship whose activities are of the greatest good in creating and cementing society, and the other an artificial relationship that breeds an unnatural offspring of financial profit and that tends to isolate and alienate individuals—eventually contributes to problems in discerning between the two. Timon, for instance, believes that he lives in the sphere of natural connection and finds his appropriately-gauged behavior thwarted by a society operating on the "unnatural" system of financial ethics. Since much of their language and many of their actions seem similar, such confusion is not dramatically atypical.

This confusion is further adumbrated by Shakespeare's imagistic insistence on the disparity between appearance and reality, between outward show and inner worth. The ability to recognize true but hidden value is a virtue allied with the side of nature and "natural" economics. Irresponsible financial behavior more often than not expresses itself in an inwardly empty show of finery. In contrast, the greatest wealth attainable expresses itself in a congruency between inner worth and material riches and extends itself socially in bounty, hospitality, and generosity.

Directly pointing to this double-sense inherent in economics, Pompey the clown in *Measure for Measure* comments on the social encroachment of merchandising ethics into the natural

---

[59] Neal Dolan, "Shylock in Love: Economic Metaphors in Shakespeare's Sonnets," *Raritan* 22.2. (Fall 2002): 126.

processes of love: "'Twas never merry world since of two usuries the merriest was put down, and the worser allow'd by order of law . . ." (3.2.5-7). This distinction of the "two usuries" is at the core of Shakespeare's economic theory. The worser is, of course, moneylending at ten percent interest; the merrier is "the generating of offspring construed as a payment made to nature in recompense for the use of the body."[60] Although man's relationship with nature is thus primarily an economic tie—"he is the steward and not the owner of his qualities" (Hubler, 69)—their interaction is a positive force for both the individual and society. All parties profit from this bond, and legislation is unnecessary. With economic usury, however, the propagation of profit is still viewed as unnatural, as set forth in medieval church doctrine, and the relationship is not invariably equitable for all parties. The legal contract or bond, as a material embodiment of the relationship, lasts only as long as the financial indebtedness; therefore, the natural human bond of man to man is altered and subsumed by strict pecuniary necessity. J. W. Lever sees this opposition as central to many of Shakespeare's dramatic themes. The merry usury of love, including generosity, bounty, and increase of progeny, extends into all "natural" relationships of sex, society, and finance. These are typically set in opposition to the barren perversity of monetary usury, which negates the traditional bonds and values of friendship and community.[61]

Shakespeare in the sonnets demonstrates not only his concern with the function of modern economics *vis-a-vis* traditional relationships, but also a knowledge of the intricacies of high finance with an emphasis upon the many varieties of bonds that people form.[62] The famous Sonnet III, for instance, cloaks dear

---

[60]E. Pearlman, "Shakespeare, Freud, and the Two Usuries, or, Money's a Meddler," *English Literary Renaissance* 2 (1972): 217. Shell also addresses the question of natural and unnatural economics in "Verbal Usury," 65. All Shakespeare quotations are from *The Riverside Shakespeare*, gen. ed. G. Blakemore Evans (Boston: Houghton Mifflin, 1974).

[61]See J. W. Lever, "Correspondence: Shylock, Portia, and the Values of Shakespearian Comedy," *Shakespeare Quarterly* 3 (1952): 383.

[62]The Renaissance was a time of confused economic transition. While mercantilism and its ethics, defined then as "commerce," "merchandising," and "dedication to money as the sole embodiment of wealth" (*OED*), constituted more often than not one's daily activities, the traditional morality governing socio-economic transactions was anachronistic and inadequate. These moral precepts were typically derived from medieval church doctrine and the Schoolmen, passed on to the Renaissance in morality plays and moral interludes. The economically

friendship in financial robes; similarly, Sonnet LXXXVII investigates the bond of love in terms of price, obligation, and worth, making its point by means of financial diction. Contemporary Renaissance economic concerns also appear in the sonnets, usually in conjunction with the themes of love and friendship and the duties and violations of these bonds. Sonnet CXXXIV depicts a cruel love bond that, when expressed in legal and financial terms, is reminiscent of the bond of Shylock and Antonio, instigated for Bassanio's sake. Not only does the poet demonstrate his knowledge of the complex workings of debt instruments, but he also indicates poetic delight at the possibilities for equivocation with the term *bond* itself.[63] He sees it simultaneously as a natural factor of unification as in community, family, love, and friendship; as restricting ropes or shackles, *i.e.*, physical bonds; as a legal contract or obligation; and as slavery or servitude, *e.g.*, a bondman. While such equivocation allows for great linguistic sport in the sonnets, in the drama its implications become increasingly serious and minatory. Upon precisely which bonds is modern Renaissance society based?

II

Keeping in mind the principles and methods of economic metaphor in the sonnets, we can trace Shakespeare's use of these same

---

reactionary *Liberalitie and Prodigalitie*, for example, was performed before the Queen in 1603. The Renaissance witnessed a proliferation of sophisticated economic machinery, like bills of exchange, insurance, investment in mercantile and exploratory ventures, and representative currency. These developments, coupled with a distrust of the currency stimulated in part by the coinage debasements of the mid-sixteenth century in England, resulted in an economic ethical confusion caused by a divergence between economic theory and practice. Much of Renaissance drama wrestles with questions of a changing system of economic morality and human value. A bond became confusingly equivocal in actual as well as lexical terms. See Sandra Kay Fischer, "'Who steals my purse': Economics and Value in Renaissance Drama," Diss. Univ. of Oregon 1980, Ch. 1, 2.

[63]For a discussion of Shakespeare's extensive knowledge of the law and its documents, see W. Nicholas Knight, "Equity, 'The Merchant of Venice' and William Lambarde," *Shakespeare Survey* 27 (1974): 93-104. Sigurd Burckhardt, "*The Merchant of Venice*: The Gentle Bond," *English Literary History* 29 (1962): 257, notices a similar equivocation on the term "gentle," meaning at once well-born, Christian (Gentile), kind, generous, and loving. Critics notice the primacy of bonds in *The Merchant of Venice*, but not generally elsewhere. See especially Shell, "Verbal Usury," and Jan Lawson Hinely, "Bond Priorities in *The Merchant of Venice*," *Studies in English Literature* 20 (1980): 217- 39.

themes, images, and characters in the drama. Chronologically, the plays indicate a progression in Shakespeare's financial outlook, in his attitude toward the proper role of wealth. This progression is linked to and perhaps a partial cause of the resolution of each play, but the structural impact is attained primarily through language and situation. This progression, moreover, roughly coincides with changes in economic outlook found in plays by other dramatists of this period. Looking in depth at three representative plays corresponding more or less with the early, middle, and late portions of Shakespeare's playwriting career, we notice that early on, as in *The Comedy of Errors*, economic problems are easily circumvented by a contrived but nonetheless joyous comedic ending. This is also usually the case in economic plays by other authors until about 1603, when the facile ending is no longer attainable because of the truly menacing nature of many of the financial problems portrayed.[64] There are hints of this uneasiness a bit earlier in Shakespeare, in *The Merchant of Venice* for instance, with the unresolved status of Shylock, the money-man. By 1607 most economic playwrights find the situation baffling: there are no longer easy answers to the question of proper economic behavior, and many move toward a wholesale acceptance of the new system of financial ethics, but not without for a time fighting against it. This is the case in *Timon of Athens*, where the two systems collide with simultaneous tragic and less-than-tragic results. In all his investigations of economic morality, Shakespeare emphasizes the equivocal and changing nature of bonds, as the human and artificial systems of economy clash.[65]

---

[64] An "economic play" can be defined in two ways: (1) it may belong to that genre which relies on a financial ploy to motivate its plot and which uses standard, stereotypical economic characters like misers, usurers, prodigals, and "jewels" of wives and daughters as well as emphasizing the machinery of finance (*e.g.*, coins, chests, bags, wills, bills, scriveners, purses, *etc.)* to advance this plot; or (2) it may traditionally be considered part of another genre, like tragedy or domestic drama, but its basis of both character and plot motivation may lie in an economic concern, like determining the seat of human value (*Troilus and Cressida*), or discovering one's own worth in relation to wealth and its apportionment (*King Lear*), or justifying one's behavior in light of new economic language (*1 Henry IV*). All of these plays, moreover, test the traditional meaning of bond. See my "Drama in a Mercantilist World," *Mid-Hudson Language Studies* 6 (1983): 29-39 and "'He means to pay': Value and Metaphor in the Lancastrian Tetralogy," *Shakespeare Quarterly* 40, 2 (1989): 149-64.

[65] This tendency is also apparent in plays which space would not allow me to discuss here, especially *Troilus and Cressida*, *Twelfth Night*, and *King Lear*.

The Comedy of Errors (1592) builds upon a blatant financial framework.[66] Its setting is a marketplace or exchange, and its *dramatis personae* include Egeon and Balthazar the merchants, the Dromios as bondmen, Angelo the goldsmith, and two more merchants, one of whom is also the creditor of Angelo. The foundation of the plot, moreover, arises from an economic issue: Syracuse no longer allows trade with Ephesus because the Ephesian merchants have been accused of unethical transactions and banished from the state. Ephesus, angry at the treatment of its merchants, has reciprocated, and now if any alien merchant is discovered still in the city, his penalty is set legally at one thousand marks or death. The assumption here is that when economic morality errs, it can be legislated back onto track: its bonds are entirely legal and thus supposedly controllable. In defining the limits of these economic bonds, however, the legislators themselves become bound to upholding the law.

Although the Duke is moved by Egeon's tale of natural prosperity—wealth acquired through investment and a double boon of two heirs—followed by mishap, he cannot step outside the law and recognize his human bond to a man who is obviously not a criminal. The Duke is bound to the law, the sentence, and the oath rather than to mankind individually. Within these limits he can allow Egeon to free himself from the bondage of the law through the obligations owed by his friends: if he can raise the money in time, Egeon can escape the sentence. In this action among others, it is clear that the artificiality of man-made bonds (like economics and law) begins to dominate social behavior. A life may easily be bought, but mercy and common sense cannot spare it.

Leaving the fate of Egeon in suspense until Act V, with Egeon literally in the bonds (shackles) of the jailer, Shakespeare turns to his main plot, which also examines the nature of social bonds. This major action has a similar economic base, for its situations rely upon the effect of mistaken identities on financial

---

In the latter, Cordelia sets the tone which will dominate the economic themes of the play: "I love your Majesty / According to my bond, no more nor less" (1.1.92-93).

[66]For the sake of consistency and convenience I have consulted for probable dates throughout Alfred Harbage, *Annals of English Drama 975-1700*, 2nd ed., revised by. S. Schoenbaum (1940; Philadelphia: Univ. of Pennsylvania Press, 1964). Charles Haines, "Some Notes on Love and Money in *The Comedy of Errors*," in *Critical Dimensions*, ed. Mario Curreli and Alberto Martino (Cuneo, Italy: SASTE, 1978), 107-16, notes the central position of money in relation to all the incidents in the play, emphasizing its power and tyranny over human activity.

transactions, and, by extension, the trust, obligations, and relations which these transactions imply. Immediately in scene ii Antipholus of Syracuse gives his money to his Dromio for an errand of safekeeping. This trust is foremost in his mind, for when Dromio of Ephesus enters only some twenty-five lines later, Antipholus seriously and repeatedly demands a report upon his purse:

> Where have you left the money that I gave you …
> Tell me, and dally not, where is the money? …
> Where is the gold I gave in charge to thee?...
> Tell me how thou hast dispos'd thy charge . . .
> Answer me,
> In what safe place you have bestow'd my money …
> Where is the thousand marks thou hadst of me?
> (1.2.54-81 *passim)*

While this exchange ends in confusion for both interlocutors, the befuddled Dromio adds to Antipholus' anxiety about his bondman by misconstruing several of the questions put to him. Just as a bond may be equivocal (4.4.124, 5.1.290), so is a mark (as a unit of monetary measure and the scar from a lashing) (1.2.82), and being in earnest (as seriousness and a pledge to secure a deal) (1.2.24).

This confusion surrounding the bonds of servitude, friendship, and marriage in an economic context is reinforced by the predicaments of Antipholus of Ephesus and Angelo. The former, when denied recognition by his wife, gives the token of their love, the carcanet, to his courtesan instead. The latter, when pressed by his creditor for payment, looks to his friend for appropriate recompense and instead meets with skepticism and denials. Antipholus, in true merchantly fashion, will not pay until he gets the necklace; Angelo, however, has sent it to him in trust and now must sue to save his own reputation, his financial good name. The Courtesan, moreover, whose livelihood stems from the nexus between sex, money, and love, is similarly confused when she demands her ring, a token of intimacy, back from Antipholus, who, because he is of Syracuse rather than Ephesus, abuses her and denies their bond.

Social chaos grows until Act V, when we learn that unreturned purses and love tokens and the various denials of bonds all stem from the situation of mistaken identities. The free offering of ducats and diamonds at the end of the play in recognition of kinship and other social bonds restores proper identities and relationships and renews the obligations of service, friendship, and marriage previously called into question by confusing economic behavior. While this ending is structurally facile in that it relies upon a series of coincidences miraculously explained all at once, the conclusion does imply that the free exchange of goods helps to brings society together. It is denial of exchange, as in the economic situation between Syracuse and Ephesus, that divides society and confuses its natural system of bonds. Material goods must be returned to their rightful owners, but such proper economics augments social as well as individual wealth and harmony.

III

Another comedy, *The Merchant of Venice* (1596), is Shakespeare's most obvious economic play because of Shylock's role as usurer. By focusing upon the Jewishness of the usurer and his opposition to Christian generosity in mercy, however, critics have sidestepped a major intent of the play. While Shakespeare does show us the two usuries in action here, he has more in mind than merely demonstrating the worser and the merrier. Classic criticisms of this play gravitate to polar readings of Shylock: either they see him, as H. B. Charlton explains, in terms of "an outbreak of traditional Jew-baiting. . . [Shakespeare] planned a *Merchant of Venice* to let the Jew dog have it,"[67] or they exonerate him on the basis of anti-Semitism and historic persecution.

Others have viewed Shylock as central in a plot of irony that exists primarily to show "the manner in which the Christians succeed in the world by not practising their ideals of love and mercy."[68] This faction projects Shylock into the mercantilistic

---

[67] H. B. Charlton, *Shakespeare's Jew* (Manchester: Manchester Univ. Press,1934), 7. Some also contend that the character of Shylock builds consistently on traditional stage Jews, but one can certainly find exceptions, as in Wilson's *The Three Ladies of London*. Nor does Shylock seem farcically exaggerated as other stage misers. See especially Alan C. Dessen, "The Elizabethan Stage Jew and Christian Example: Gerontus, Barabas, and Shylock," *Modern Language Quarterly* 35 (1974): 231-45. Bernard Grebanier, in *The Truth about Shylock* (New York: Random House, 1962), 185, even sees in Shylock a sort of tragic greatness, feeling that his moneygrubbing nature wastes his otherwise large human potential.

[68] A. D. Moody, *Shakespeare: The Merchant of Venice* (Woodbury, N.Y.:Barron's, 1964), 10. Moody gives the most convincing, lucid, and consistent reading based on irony that I have found. Grebanier, after warning against erroneous ironic readings, contends that Shylock has maliciously and with a

future rather than characterizing him as an economic holdover from the Middle Ages: in his moneylending enterprise, obviously quite successful, and his insistence upon economic thrift and sobriety, he does not work against nature but rather improves upon her operation. The Christians, in contrast, abuse nature, trusting to her bounty without recognizing any reciprocal obligations. They are the villains of the piece in refusing to honor their bonds, their basic human obligations, forcing Shylock into his role. According to this reading, Shylock is a victim of "the Christian club" rather than a malicious, sub-human, cannibalistic, stereotypical Jew and money-grubber motivated by depravity.

Shakespeare created Shylock with enough ambiguity that he fails to fit either stereotype perfectly. He is not a monster; we glimpse his intimate past with Leah and see the product of this union, lovely Jessica.[69] On the other hand, he hates Antonio intensely, with a complex motivation resulting from their conflict over usury, Antonio's insult and public abuse of Shylock, their opposing religions, and eventually revenge and Antonio's rejection of Shylock's "friendship." While Shylock's Jewishness is important to the play, it cannot wholly account for his character and the plot. Similarly, while Shylock is moneylender *par excellence,* and Venice is the site of "evolving notions of finance," according to Stephen Orgel, eventually money comes to mean less to Shylock than the insistence upon his bond. As Robert Alter notes, Shylock is "an explosively unstable figure" whose portrayal "bursts through the conventional limits of the comic *senex* in two opposite directions": he is outsider, demon, beast, killjoy, *and* a

---

premeditated intent effected the ruin of Antonio, so that he may use the knife on him, by spreading rumors which wreck his credit abroad and at home (207).

[69]The critics differ on Jessica almost as much as on Shylock. While in one sense she represents filial ingratitude, Shakespeare equivocates on her character to such an extent that Richard Henze can label her "warm and loving" in "Which is the Merchant Here? and Which the Jew?" *Criticism* 16 (1974): 293. Grebanier, 198-201, summarizes some of the standard critical views of her character and actions. In the following discussion of Shylock, I stress his positive side that seeks human bonds because it has been most often neglected. The negative aspects of his character, obviously necessary to a reading relying on a double perspective, seem readily accessible in most critical studies. He, like his miser predecessors, is apparently single-minded and heartless in his perseverance of the flesh-bond. He seems to have a restrictive, kill-joy personality that does not understand great affection and thus generosity.

possessor of "touching humanity."[70] It becomes impossible to see Shylock in terms either totally black or white; whichever way the critic leans in his reading of the play as a whole, he eventually must recognize that "Shylock spooks in the background, an unappeased ghost" (Burckhardt, *Meanings*, 207).

Although the play itself prompts these ambiguous views of Shylock and the Christians, part of the problem in reaching a compelling critical stance has been an erring emphasis in interpretation. If we may take a cue from the two major plot actions of *The Merchant of Venice*—Antonio's legal financial obligation to Shylock and Portia's duty to fulfill her father's will in choosing a mate—rather than from the characters, it is immediately clear that the play is "about" bonds. The sonnets show Shakespeare's prior interest in the many possibilities of defining this term, as well as his concern with the effect of financial transactions on basic human relationships. Similarly, most of the characters are, from the beginning of the play, defined by their economic roles Portia is "a lady richly left" (1.1.161), Shylock is "the rich Jew" (2.2.123) Bassanio is "the prodigal Christian" (2.5.15), and Antonio is alternately "the fool that lent out money gratis" (3.3.2) and "this poor merchant" (4.1.23) Within this economic framework, Shakespeare stresses the equivocal nature of bonds, especially in a changing financial milieu. Kenneth Gross pinpoints the complexity of the bond theme by noting that all "bonds are always tangled up with something else, and their very liability to be so tangled is what gets explored so subtly."[71]

The significance of Shylock in this environment is his "otherness," not only as a moneylender, but as a Jew and a widower, and as one whose economic creed stresses a frugality and tight-handedness almost unknown in Venetian society. He is truly an alien here—and I think Shakespeare exploited in this character what he knew of the separateness of the Ghetto and the mandatory badge of the Jew/ moneylender—and can participate in society only when its members require his special services. Then the bond

---

[70]D. M. Cohen, in "The Jew and Shylock," *Shakespeare Quarterly* 31 (1980): 53-63, offers an opposing viewpoint, which I feel cannot fully illuminate the play. Stephen Orgel, "Imagining Shylock" in *Imagining Shakespeare* (London: Palgrave Macmillan, 2003), 144. Robert Alter, "Who is Shylock?" *Commentary* (1993): web.

[71]Kenneth Gross, *Shylock is Shakespeare* (Chicago: Univ. of Chicago Press, 2006), 48.

is palpable and legal, not a bond of the soul, but a bond of necessity. Stephen J. Greenblatt stresses the point of Shylock's alienation in noting that while "linguistically, psychologically, ethically, as well as religiously, he is different, . . . [a] sameness runs like a dark current through the play, intimating secret bonds that no one, not even the audience, can fully acknowledge."[72] He is, after all, a man. (And this, perhaps, is the point of Portia's often ironically-interpreted question, "Which is the merchant here? and which the Jew?" [4.1.174].) If Shylock indeed threatens this society, it is with the intent of uncovering his very sameness beneath the apparent alien exterior, of exposing the bonds upon which society is based. In this sense he too is a leaden casket that contains at least an ounce of the gold of humanity.[73]

Shakespeare exploits this essence of Shylock's otherness in his delineation of the character. Critics have at least been unanimous in understanding his alien presence: Shylock is as out of place among the Venetian Christians as Bottom among the fairies.[74] He differs in speech, in attire, in age, in religion in economics, and in values. But this difference does not automatically make him the villain, nor does he fully acquiesce to any preconceived stereotype that we can discover. Even those who subscribe to the villain theory realize that "our response to Shylock must accommodate what is good in him."[75]

In maintaining his differences, moreover, Shylock displays a real sense of personal integrity and discipline in the face of constant rejection and abuse. In this respect, many of his so-called villainous traits are illuminated differently. His house, for example, he keeps secure and isolated not because he runs it as a prison, although Jessica views it as one, but because such a refuge is essential to his dignity and way of life. Perhaps Charlton overstates the point, but he is on the right track: as an alien, Shylock can only

---

[72] Stephen J. Greenblatt, "Marlowe, Marx, and Anti-Semitism," *Critical Inquiry* 5 (1978): 295.

[73] Lever suggests something of this in the juxtaposition of laws with humanity, mercy, and kindness: the intent is to test the validity of traditional values (385).

[74] Hermann Sinsheimer, *Shylock: The History of a Character* (1947; rpt. New York: Benjamin Blom, 1963), 84. See also Graham Midgley, "*The Merchant of Venice*: A Reconsideration," *Essays in Criticism* 10 (1960): 122.

[75] Lawrence Danson, *The Harmonies of* The Merchant of Venice (New Haven: Yale Univ. Press, 1978), 138. See also Grebanier, 93.

maintain his personal integrity "by practising a disciplined imperturbability for the public hours of the day, in the strength that he secures for himself in the privacy of his own home" (17). While the Jew is a social outcast in Venice, his very presence and economic necessity bind him to society in an ambiguous manner. The play seems intent first upon examining the connection between human or "natural" and economic or "unnatural" systems of relation. Within this context Shylock again finds himself odd man out: when his economic legs are knocked out from under him, he finds enforced Christianity a weak crutch for supporting his new social stance.

The last act—from which Shylock is meaningfully excluded, but which his presence haunts, as "the man that hath no music in himself" and as "the rich Jew" granting "a special deed of gift"—most often troubles Shylock's defenders and delights his detractors. Here, ironically, we see the role Shylock plays in the drama as a whole. Among the evocative images expressed in this lovely Belmont night scene are two rather disturbing ones from Portia herself. Upon approaching her house, she and Nerissa converse:

> *Por.* That light we see is burning in my hall.
> How far that little candle throws his beams!
> So shines a good deed in a naughty world.
> *Ner.* When the moon shone, we did not see the candle. . .
> *Por.* Nothing is good, I see, without respect. ...
> The crow doth sing as sweetly as the lark
> When neither is attended; and I think
> The nightingale, if she should sing by day
> When every goose is cackling, would be thought
> No better musician than the wren.
> (5.1.89-92, 99, 102-06)

This exchange has no obvious purpose in furthering the plot, aside from reinforcing the leisurely and melodic mood that dominates here. The images, quite deliberately, I think, given to Portia, whose "wisdom" we have just witnessed, serve instead to emphasize the relativity of perspective that is necessary in understanding Shylock fully. Before realizing the impact of Portia's observations completely, we should note that bonds are the center of this last scene as well. Shakespeare attains all meanings simultaneously when Bassanio enters and introduces Antonio:

> This is the man, this is Antonio,
> To whom I am so infinitely bound.
> *Por.* You should in all sense be much bound to him,

For as I hear he was much bound for you.
(ll.134-37)

Straightening out the possession of the rings as love-tokens, moreover, is nothing less than a reiteration of the value of the human bonds that the rings represent, as well as a reminder of how easily, coincidentally, and nonvolitionally the absolute commitment of the bonds may be violated or trespassed.[76]

These final words and rituals gain significance as a whole when coupled with Portia's first philosophical observation of the play: "If to do were as easy as to know what were good to do, chapels had been churches, and poor men's cottages prince's palaces. It is a good divine that follows his own instructions; I can easier teach twenty what were good to be done, than to be one of the twenty to follow mine own teaching" (1.2.12-17). Portia's sentiments here, among the first words uttered by her character, along with her final imagistic observations indicate that the play demands understanding by a kind of double-seeing, a perspective that judges neither black nor white nor strictly by appearances, but that instead takes relativity into account. This is also the lesson taught by the caskets: one should not expect outer appearance and inner reality (or value) to be congruent.

In applying these principles to the interpretation of Shylock, then, we realize how his character explodes all stereotypes. The problem dramatically presented is that most of' the Venetians act as though Shylock were indeed the stereotypical Jew/usurer/alien, while the character itself to some extent belies those expectations.[77] Gratiano is perhaps the worst abuser here, along

---

[76]Notice how frivolously Jessica and Lorenzo have disposed of Shylock's only love-token, his turquoise ring from Leah. This act reiterates their attitude toward him as a stereotypical villain rather than as a man with needs similar to theirs. Just as they violate their human bonds to him, society also escapes its legal obligations to the outsider. The "monkey" for which Jessica trades the turquoise ring may also have an economic significance. In English race-track jargon it is slang for £500. See Albert R. Frey, *Dictionary of Numismatic Names* (New York: Barnes and Noble, 1947), 154.

[77]This reading, proposing a surface attitude toward Shylock presented by the other characters, with a substructure composed of action and metaphor that undermines the surface, is similar to an interpretation of *Macbeth* by Harry Berger, Jr., in "The Early Scenes of *Macbeth*: Preface to a New Interpretation," *English Literary History* 47 (1980): 1-31. Matthew Proser, *The Heroic Image in Five Shakespearean Tragedies* (Princeton, N.J.: Princeton Univ. Press, 1965), 92-135, uses a similar approach to *Othello*. The necessity for double-vision in *The Merchant of Venice* is adumbrated by several images early in the play: "two-headed Janus"

with Salerio and Solanio, with their halter jokes, but even Jessica allows him to be identified as "the rich Jew" rather than as her father. Lorenzo seems as small a creature as Jessica: having prodigally wasted what Jessica was able to carry away from Shylock initially (see, especially, Tubal's account in 3.1), he lusts more avariciously than the usurer after more treasure. When Portia offers him the coerced deed of gift, his greedy reply is, "you drop manna in the way / Of starved people" (5.1.293-94). Eventually the play demonstrates that ostensibly good characters can teach the apparent villain to be even worse—"The villainy you teach me, I will execute, and it shall go hard but I will better the instruction" (3.1.71-73)—and that the stereotyped villain through deeds partaking of humanity only becomes reinforced in his alien stereotype.

As the play develops, this stereotypical image that the Venetians hold of Shylock becomes a self-fulfilling prophecy. They limit him to a single role yet berate him when he plays his character of moneylender faithfully: "Shylock is accepted only because of his wealth and economic usefulness: otherwise in all the things which a man needs for happiness with his fellows, friendship, respect, social intercourse, sympathy, co-operation, he is denied and spurned" (Midgley, 130). His only real human tie is with his daughter, Jessica, and she violates this bond of bonds by deception and thievery. Before this disruption, however, Shylock makes an attempt at extending his circle of human bonds, however guardedly and tentatively, by making "a merry sport" of for once lending without interest. This is not a simple whim; as René Girard notes, Shylock "confuses financial matters with other passions." While many critics view the "merry bond" as maliciously preconceived by Shylock, a close examination of the events of the play reveals that it could not have been.[78] If we persist in seeing

---

(1.151), who is both young and old and sees the sun both rise and set; the discrepancy between the financial appearance and reality of Bassanio, who is noble but impecunious; the similarity between Portia and Brutus' Portia, who urged him to accept the truth of her dream-vision, another way of seeing; Shylock's appearance to Antonio as "a goodly apple rotten at the heart" (1.3.101); Morocco's nobility despite his foul appearance; the casket game itself; Old Gobbo's need for "other eyes" to "see" his son; and Bassanio's warning to Gratiano that the "eyes" of Belmont will judge him differently from the eyes of Venice (2.2).

[78]René Girard, *A Theatre of Envy: William Shakespeare* (Carthage Rpt., 2004), 246. See also Dessen, 232, who has Shylock vindictive throughout the play in order to comment on the behavior of the Christians; and Danson, 90. Shell, "Verbal Usury," 70, is one of the few to understand the "merry bond": "Only by

Shylock with the eyes of single vision, we err as badly as the other characters in the play.

From the beginning Shakespeare clearly exposes the mercantilistic values of the Christians. In attempting to locate the source of Antonio's melancholy, his friends—representative Venetians—link religion and money, love and money, sex and money. When describing Portia, Bassanio similarly puts her fortune first, but then moves to her inner qualities as well. In being rich, fair, and virtuous, Portia combines the best of all their values: she is like a golden casket, richly inlaid, which opens to reveal more gold. As an interesting juxtaposition in this first act, which introduces the characters to us, Shakespeare shows Portia weighing the worthiness of her suitors just as Shylock weighs the worthiness of Antonio to enter a bond different in kind. And, as Dagny Boebel notes, the portrayals of Portia and Shylock unify them as "secret sharers" of "moral outlook and of personality."[79]

Scene iii clearly indicates, despite the claims of those who want to see only a villain, that Shylock is in his own way convivial. He at least understands and appreciates a good pun (even though this may simply constitute another kind of usury to him, semantic usury) and attempts to defend his profession to closed and prejudiced ears. While Shylock admits his antipathy for the man who hinders his living, he is civilized enough not to vent his anger unrestrainedly, but rather pointedly and graciously to express his confusion to his abusers.

Shylock is befuddled by the merchant's request, since it seems to violate Antonio's most persistent economic ethic; moreover, the situation takes Shylock out of his customary role of abuse at the merchant's hands. When offered a bond instead of the usual spittle, Shylock attempts in a moment of inspiration to break out of his stereotype and into the more human bondage of society. This, his economic wealth, is perhaps his only avenue to social inclusion. Here he in fact out-Christians the Christians, even of the last act, by offering the loan as a brother. This offer, I believe, is not ironic, for it follows a catalogue of the abuses that Shylock has

---

taking no interest and substituting a corporeal penalty, then, could Shylock be or appear to be brotherly (gentile) to Antonio. This is what he does. To buy Antonio's friendship Shylock extends this kindness."

[79] Dagny M. H. Boebel, "Shylock and Portia: Secret Sharers," *CEA Critic* 53.3 (Spring/Summer 1991), 39.

endured. His attitude, as given to us in an aside, is to parry with Antonio, to "catch him once upon the hip." This phrase cannot be translated "to kill him" or "to eat his heart," as some interpolate. A wrestling term, it connotes a playful sally, a victory in one round rather than a total defeat. We have noticed Shylock's appreciation of puns, and he may be playing here on the alternative meaning of "hip" as "morbid depression of spirits; the 'blues'" (*OED*). If he can catch Antonio in low spirits, he may perhaps win a verbal if not an actual economic battle. Shylock sports with Antonio, offering him first a loan without interest—

> I would be friends with you, and have your love,
> Forget the shames that you have stain'd me with,
> Supply your present wants, and take no doit
> Of usance for my moneys, and you'll not hear me
> (1.3.138-41)—

but the game becomes more serious than either man realizes. When the Christians refuse a friendly loan and insist upon a legal bond (and it is they, not Shylock, who insist), he pulls an ancient, probably unenforceable, "merry bond" out of the air. Antonio, not Shylock, is the cormorant here, for he pounces eagerly upon the bond, thinking to have the advantage in avoiding both friendship and usance in dealing with "the Jew." As Charlton notes, the final bond evolves naturally out of the situation, and neither Shylock nor Antonio believes that it will ever come to forfeit and payment (24-25).

After the major bond of the play, strange and aberrant though it is, is sealed at the end of Act I, Act II shows an even greater variety of bonds, obviously the main subject of the drama. Portia's father, for example, binds her to the casket game from his grave; Old Gobbo, in contrast, even while alive fails to recognize his son, who in turn is in a type of bondage to Shylock. Launcelot, like Antonio, persists in characterizing his master according to the stereotype,[80] but Shylock's attitude toward his servant is revealing in that it shows him more humane than the stereotyped treatment that he receives in turn. After recognizing Launcelot's discontent,

---

[80] Particularly in his exaggerated accounts of "starvation" (which Grebanier reads seriously). Shylock maintains that Launcelot was accustomed to "gurmandize" at his table, which, given Launcelot's opportunistic character, is not improbable. More importantly, however, this discrepant view of the same situation underscores Shakespeare's theme of double-seeing.

Shylock has recommended him to Bassanio, mainly because he finds the servant of an opposing temperament to his own. Launcelot, typical of many of the shallow single-seers in this society, is motivated solely by the richness of Bassanio's livery, an external rather than intrinsic show of wealth. In dismissing Launcelot, after first finding him another job, Shylock merely seeks the best management of his house and affairs. Jessica's complaint is typical of a young girl: she finds business "tedious" rather than pleasant. But this scene does not show Shylock a devil. His actions tend to belie the stereotype instead of reinforcing it.

When Shylock attends the fateful dinner at Bassanio's, he exhibits a complex psychological relationship with the Christian mercantilist society. Still grasping at bonds, here the human bond of celebration and companionship, Shylock attends even though he knows it is only a pretense of community on the part of Bassanio. He knows not to expect much, since his usual treatment is mockery and rheum, yet he finds a spark of hope in the invitation itself. He must keep up his defenses, however, so he rationalizes to go "in hate." He has mockingly revealed such a defense mechanism earlier, when he insists on a strict business relationship with Bassanio and Antonio, who would have it both ways.

By abusing Shylock, then demanding his services not in friendship but in law, and then inviting him to dinner, they confuse him in his social function. Is he to be pariah, magnate, or consort? When they change roles on him, Shylock's usual defense is to resort vigorously to a stance with which he is familiar, to remind the Christians how they treated him yesterday. There is no other sensible dramatic reason besides the hope of community for Shylock to dine with the Christians. The stereotypical miser would attend to save on his own food bill, and Shakespeare plays on this tradition, but it cannot be Shylock's sole motive. As when he offers a loan without interest and, upon being refused in that, a ludicrous "merry bond" as a token of proffered friendship, Shylock here hopes yet again that he may be treated as a man, accepted for what he is.

His care in locking up the house before leaving is neither psychotic nor unreasonable, although perhaps obsessive. He has had a foreboding dream dealing with money, and to lose his ducats would be to lose status and livelihood. According to Charlton, "ducats are more to Shylock than mere material possessions. They are the only means by which, in an alien world, he preserves a refuge for the true life of his own spirit" (29). Perhaps identity is a better term than spirit, but the ducats are palpable symbols of Shylock's continued assurance of some role of power or at least necessity in this community. His economic values, in contrast to other financial abusers portrayed in the drama (*e.g.,* Volpone, Gripe, Jaques de Prie, Leon), are rather traditionally admirable. He is sober, thrifty, industrious, and protective, and we have certainly witnessed worse treatments of daughters (*e.g.,* Abigail, Lelia, and, including wives, Celia Corvino and Winnie Security) than Shylock's of Jessica. He merely admonishes her to care for herself and their livelihood during his absence, advice that she, in her own deceptive way, follows.

Jessica's elopement during Shylock's absence, ironically at a moment when he has ventured to expand the arena of his human bonds, is the crucial event in his realization of the extent of his alienation and the inflexible stereotype of his characterization. Some contend that Shylock is humanized in the course of the play, but 1 believe rather that he is dehumanized as he slowly realizes his isolation in lacking human bonds. [81] By presenting the discovery of Shylock's loss through the eyes of Salerio and Solanio, Shakespeare emphasizes his stereotypical treatment at Christian hands as they delight at his ruin. Shylock, in contrast, feels betrayed. He has lost his closest and most treasured bond of kinship as well as prestige and livelihood in his ducats. He emphasizes the filial relationship—"my daughter," not the ungrateful wench—while Jessica and her friends persist in calling him not her father, but "the wealthy Jew." John Gross notes similarity between Barabas' and Shylock's loss of their daughters and the money, and a similar situation in *Othello* can be instructive here. When Brabantio finds Desdemona stolen away, he demands recourse under law and is immediately gratified by an open hearing. Shylock, violated in his closest bond, similarly turns now to the only satisfying social relationship open to him, the justice of his bond with Antonio. [82]

---

[81] See Charlton, 13. Grebanier, 201, maintains that Jessica does not steal from Shylock, but merely takes her dowry, as any sensible girl would. See also Cohen, 59.

[82] John Gross, *Shylock: A Legend and its Legacy* (New York: Simon and Schuster, 1994), 21. The similarity of these two scenes is striking. Iago warns Brabantio in 1.1.80, "Look to your house, your daughter, and your bags!" while in 1.3.68 the Duke promises the enraged father "the bitter letter" from "the bloody book of law."

Proof that Shylock has not deviously plotted the result of this bond from the beginning comes when Salerio and Solanio bait him. Upon hinting that Antonio may have lost his argosies, they find Shylock morose rather than victorious as he should be if he has planned on the forfeit. He does not exclaim "Aha! it worked!" but rather "There I have another bad match" (3.1.44). His economic tenets seem to be losing on all fronts; he feels conspired against. Having already lost Jessica, now he is faced with losing his chance for economic community as well. In this scene Shylock slowly begins to realize that the only human connection left him is a bond in law. Feeling his alienation deeply, he speaks the famous "Hath not a Jew . . ." lines, attempting to probe the causes of his isolation. The key similarity here is "affections" (1. 60). By treating Shylock as the stereotype, society has ignored his human needs.[83] Realizing his complete exclusion, Shylock convinces himself in this speech to take revenge, one of the few truly human actions left him.

In speaking with Tubal immediately after this encounter, Shylock feels even more strongly the filial and financial betrayal of Jessica. As Tubal intersperses his account with news of Antonio's financial ruin, Shylock also sees the loss of his dreams of a completed transaction on the basis of friendship. Antonio has ever been a threat because of his free loan policy, which usurped business from Shylock. The usurer now feels that if he can symbolically exorcise Antonio, he may perhaps recoup his losses by increased trade and regain an identity by playing the moneylender with a vengeance. Denied the basic bonds of society, Shylock seeks refuge and consolation in the only bond left to him. In this situation Shakespeare offers a new perspective on the function of bonds in a society dominated in all phases by the money ethic.

The necessity of double-seeing, so neglected in the plot of Shylock, is now immediately underscored by the episode of Bassanio and the caskets. The discrepancy between appearance and reality extends into law, religion, beauty, and value. Inner

---

[83]The reading gains reliability when Shylock's scene is compared to a similar situation in *Richard II*. Richard, upon realizing the threat of Bullingbrook to the kingship, confesses his feelings of alienation in his role as king, as outcast from the mainstream of society as the Jew: "For you have but mistook me all this while. / I live with bread like you, feel want, /. Taste grief, need friends . . ." (3.2.174-76). Both men, as "others," have been denied the crucial bonds of humanity.

virtues, in which Portia abounds, are here seen as the greatest wealth, and they gain in significance when compared to poor Shylock, whose casket of humanity is never opened. He would give but knows not how. Portia, in contrast, gives more than all:

for you,
I would be trebled twenty times myself,
A thousand times more fair, ten thousand times more rich,
That only to stand high in your account,
I might in virtues, beauties, livings, friends,
Exceed account. (3.2.152-57)

This augmentation of love and all its associated wealth constitutes true "natural". usury. Shylock's "worser" usury, in contrast, although necessary to social economics, proves inadequate as the sole basis of human relation. The necessity of giving that Portia, emphasizes would be a good lesson for many of the Christians, who persist in their black and white judgments. Gratiano, for example, foremost in berating Shylock, also debases the value of Portia and her love by referring to her as the Golden Fleece and making an immediate wager based upon the sexual nature of the fertility of her love for Bassanio.

After Shylock becomes firm in his resolve to seek revenge through the "merry bond," his only remaining link of dignity with the Christian society, he begins to grow into the stereotype that others hold of him. Shylock refuses to explain his motivation to ears that have always been closed. Although he presses for his legal bond in the face of denial of his human bonds, Shylock also seeks refuge in a law he thinks inviolable, his only certainty in a society that confusingly redefines his role to suit its convenience. According to Marx, for the usurer "the highest relationship of man is the legal relationship, the relationship to laws that are not valid for him because they are the laws of his own will and essence, but because they are the masters and deviations from them are avenged."[84] Shylock thus views legal enforcement of his bond with Antonio in part as an exercise of power denied him in other arenas and also as a participation in the mainstream of this society, even if it is as plaintiff, antagonist. He forces them to see him as a man, yet he fails at the crucial point to partake of the best part of humanity.

---

[84]Karl Marx, *Selected Writings* ("On the Jewish Question"), edited by David McLellan (Oxford: Oxford Univ. Press, 1977), 60-61.

As Nietzsche explains the history of debt (associated with guilt [*Schuld, Schulden*]), Shylock is hardly a monster in pressing for his due, but instead well within his rights, perhaps even generous: the debtor as a matter of course was pledged to substitute something else if he failed to pay, "his body, his wife, his freedom. ... Above all, however, the creditor could inflict every kind of indignity and torture upon the body of the debtor.[85] Ancient law, moreover, placed legal evaluations on the worth of each limb and organ; the Romans eventually declared that a little more or less exacted from the body was of small consequence to the satisfaction of the creditor.[86]

In pressing for his legal bond, Shylock also attempts to participate in the community of the power structure, which is itself a sort of pleasurable repayment for his injuries. (We must note that Shylock's injuries are ostensibly economic—loss of the money proffered in loan—but that in reality they form a palimpsest of history of abuse of the alien.) Although he is not prone to bloodlust, legal fulfillment of the bond will provide Shylock with "the pleasure of being allowed to vent his power freely upon one who is powerless. . . . This enjoyment will be the greater the lower the creditor stands in the social order. . . . In 'punishing' the debtor, the creditor participates in a right of the masters: at last he, too, may experience for once the exalted sensation of being allowed to despise and mistreat someone as 'beneath him'" (Nietzsche, 65). His motives seem now more logical, especially in light of Jessica's betrayal and the facts of Antonio's abuse of Shylock in the Rialto.

In the trial scene Shylock's otherness is more apparent than ever, as the Christians decry the cold, hard heart that they have forced into its stance. Here the self-fulfilling prophecy of the outcast/villain comes to complete fruition. Since the Christians have misunderstood the original intent of the bond, they now push Shylock even further away, forcing him to rely solely on the justice of the legal bond as his portion of community. Shylock fortifies his

---

[85]Friedrich Nietzsche, *On the Genealogy of Morals*, translated and edited by. Walter Kaufman (New York: Vintage, 1967), 64.

[86]In the words of a law of 451 B.C., "If after the third market day the creditor be not yet paid, he may either put his debtor to death or sell him to any stranger resident beyond the Tiber; but if there be two or more creditors of the same insolvent debtor, and if, after the third market day, his debts to them be yet unpaid, the creditors may cut their several portions off his body. they cut too much or too little, let that be no wrong." See M. J. Landa, *The Jew in Drama* (1926; rpt. Port Washington, N.Y.: Kennikat Press, 1968), 73.

position by pointing to society's economic hypocrisy, especially its confusion of bonds and commodities (4.1.90-100). Shakespeare does not imply, like Marlowe, that *every* man's price is written on his back, but he does indicate the tension caused by a changing emphasis in the function of bonds. Economics insinuates itself into daily ethics and must be reckoned with. This is Shylock's point. In this regard, it is remarkable that Portia's "twice blest" mercy resembles lending upon interest, which blesses—brings profit to—both parties.

Ironically, Shylock overlooks his chance really to participate in this community by forgiving Antonio. Then we might feel that the play is a true comedy, incorporating the economic villain and exorcising all abuses, as in *English-Men for my Money* or *Wily Beguiled.*

But Shakespeare has a different emphasis in mind: the Christians are neither consistent nor unequivocally right in their economic behavior. Portia more than any other character seems on the right track, but her instructions fail to move Shylock and many of her companions. Although the mercy that opposes strict legality here, a legality similar to that which the Duke of *The Comedy of Errors* felt bound to uphold at any cost, is emphasized as more "natural" and socially preferable, it also shows itself imperfect. First, the mercy that the Christians eventually offer Shylock is dubious, since they still negate his individuality by simply trying to make him a copy of themselves; second, as this rather whimsical quality of mercy proves greater than the law, the Christians merely reinforce their position as the locus of social power. Mercy, like everything else in this play, has a binary quality that demands double-seeing. According to Nietzsche, "The justice which began with, 'everything is dischargeable, everything must be discharged,' ends by winking and letting those incapable of discharging their debt go free: it ends, as does every good thing on earth, by overcoming itself" (72-73). Ironically, or perhaps whimsically, the Christians beg for mercy, then insist on legality of the bond once the tables are turned, and then extend a dubious sort of mercy once they achieve their victory.

In this sense the trial, like the original parrying that eventually resulted in the flesh-bond, is a sort of game where wit, if it can succeed, is highly valued and rewarded.[87] Johan Huizinga maintains that all jurisdiction includes an element of play, for each side wants to win: "The lawsuit can be regarded as a game of chance, a contest, or a verbal battle."[88] Shylock, who cannot hazard, who stretches the greatest value from the least expenditure of his words, and who, moreover, is pitted singly against the Christian team, is doomed to failure. His alien religious status simply helps to ensure his defeat, for "The winning *as such* is . . . proof of truth and rightness. The outcome of every contest, be it a trial of strength or a game of chance, is a sacred decision vouchsafed by the gods" (Huizinga, 103). The Christian Venetians are obviously in the right since they win the trial.

What remains for Act V, however, is a still ambiguous undercurrent of criticism of economic behavior new and old. Shylock, while he has in one sense been accepted into the Christian society by his sentence of coerced baptism, will assuredly continue in his profession as usurious moneylender. The stereotypes, moreover, have not disappeared. Gratiano gets in some of his best halter jokes in Act IV, and even in Act V the celebrants persist in calling Shylock "the rich Jew," "the wealthy Jew." This ambiguity extends into Antonio's resumption of his mercantile vocation, for, as Danson observes, Antonio is also economically suspect in that he makes money through the manipulation of money (like Shylock) rather than through labor: "The Venetian moneylender and the Venetian merchant were not entirely separate in the Elizabethan mind" (25-26). At base these two characters are not so very different, except that Antonio is able to give "whole-heartedly," and Shylock can neither give nor receive.[89] No matter what his desires and human needs may be, he remains a type of *Homo economicus* whose first concerns are the fulfillment of chrematistic necessities. Although he attempts to play the game of human bonding, Shylock partakes too much of the economic spirit that "neither trades nor plays; it does not gamble. To dare, to take risks, to bear uncertainty, to endure tension—these are the essence

---

[87] The connection between the two "games" is more than tenuous. Gratiano in fact uses the same phrase, "I have you on the hip" (4.1.334), as Shylock employed in explaining his parrying with Antonio in 1.3.46.

[88] *Homo Ludens*, translated by. George Steiner (New York: Harper and Row, 1970), 99.

[89] See Mark Van Doren, *Shakespeare* (1939; rpt. New York: Anchor, 1953), 81.

of the play-spirit," and in this society, the winning spirit (Huizinga, 72).

Even though the whole world of *The Merchant of Venice* is tainted by a money nexus—indeed, "All may be adjudged contaminated by money, interested in each other mainly as useable or profitable objects"[90]—in a sense the best characters are able to incorporate new economic ethics profitably (*i.e.*, "naturally") into their everyday behavior. Bassanio, for example, while temporarily impecunious, knows that all his wealth runs in his veins, and his inner virtue is eventually rewarded with everything Shakespeare values: beauty, wealth, a community of happy friends, and a promise of fertility. His character seems entirely in tune with the "natural" usury of the sonnets, for increase comes to him effortlessly.[91]

Portia, similarly, represents and embodies total congruency between intrinsic and exchange worth: "Through the character of Portia the conception of money and property in general acquires a new significance, that of being rich both outwardly and inwardly, the two states being interdependent" (Sinsheimer, 90). These two characters, moreover, seem most capable of the sort of double-seeing that this play requires. Bassanio sees into the heart of the leaden casket in hazarding for Portia and recognizes a tinge of kindness in Shylock. Portia is aware of the possible equivocations of justice, mercy, and bonds and exploits them in the guise of her alter ego, Balthazar. The point seems to be that wealth is indigenous to life, not separate from it. Those who most fully recognize its natural quality are best able to profit, both socially and individually.[92]

Shakespeare's position in *The Merchant of Venice* on the proper role of wealth in the bonds of society exhibits a similar ambiguity as other economic plays of this period. While the conclusion brings a reunion of society, celebration of the renewal of love and fertility, and the rewards of material and community

---

[90]Theodore Weiss, *The Breath of Clowns and Kings (*1971; rpt. New York: Atheneum, 1974), 113.

[91]For a suggestion of this concept see Sylvan Barnet, "Prodigality and Time in *The Merchant of Venice*," *PMLA* 87 (1972): 27-28.

[92]See Alexander Leggatt, *Shakespeare's Comedy of Love* (London: Methuen, 1974), 122-23.

wealth that we have come to expect, Shylock remains an alienated economic misfit who cannot be fully assimilated. The Christian victory against the encroaching money ethic—for that is really what Shylock's bond represents to them—seems only stopgap. While Portia and Bassanio may understand the proper expression of love through wealth (and this is why some of Shylock's property is renewed to him), their friends, most notably Gratiano, Lorenzo, Launcelot, and Jessica, have yet much to learn. In their greedy closed-mindedness, these four are nearly worse than Shylock, who at least understands the nature of a bond, in. all senses.

Like his fellow playwrights, Shakespeare knows that the new mercantilism and its associated economic machinery affect the basis of human relationship. Unlike his fellows, though, Shakespeare reconciles its presence not by embracing or ignoring it, but rather by effecting a synthesis of material wealth with everything that is best in the "natural" realm of usury. Such a synthesis is possible, as witnessed in Portia and Bassanio, but Shylock remains somehow suspended between the two realms. This play, in structure, character, and image, posits a world in economic transition where the old values, while still good and to be affirmed, cannot completely encompass the necessities of the world of daily exchange.[93]

IV

Timon of Athens (1607), the last of Shakespeare's most obviously economic plays, reveals an even greater structural confusion resulting from the treatment of its economic theme and moves toward a reckoning with a new financial system of morality obviously here to stay. Although Shakespeare and his editors did not assign a generic title to this play—alone among the tragedies, it is merely *The Life of Timon of Athens*—we can see how it partakes of the characteristics of overlapping genres. Act I ostensibly presents us to the world of comedy. Timon's benevolent household with him installed as king of giving is similar to the situation of Sir

---

[93]In *Twelfth Night* (1600), Shakespeare, through Feste, jokingly accepts usury as a fact of life and nature that helps to bring material increase. In 3.1.49 Feste reaffirms Shylock's doctrine of ewes and rams, when he subtly begs another coin from Cesario so that, put together, they may breed for him. In this play, however, Shakespeare emphasizes giving, especially money, as a positive force of social unification and harmony.

Bounteous Progress in *A Mad World, My Masters*. His initial actions are all pointedly economic and seemingly of the "natural" kind so enjoyed by comedy. He pays the debt of Ventidius, a sizable sum,[94] and then supports him from his own income. Only lines later he donates to Lucilius a sum that allows him to marry for love, basing his gift on the bond of service that Lucilius has faithfully incurred: "For 'tis a bond in men" (1.1.144). For Timon human bounty reiterates and re-enacts nature's free bounty. Thinking himself wealthy in his friends, in the community of concord harmonious as nature's hierarchy, he gives in order to celebrate and acknowledge his social bonds: "We are born to do benefits; and what better or properer can we call our own than the riches of our friends? O, what a precious comfort 'tis to have so many like brothers commanding one another's fortunes!" (1.2.101-05).

Even within this harmonious and "natural" first act, however, hints appear of threats to Timon's order, of motives not quite properly understood, regardless of their outward manifestations. As in *The Merchant of Venice* we must view the characters and their actions with the eyes of double-vision, for they inhabit a world in economic transition and are temporarily suspended in a limbo of values. The Jeweler is first to warn us by emphasizing relative rather than absolute standards of value. Showing Timon his stone, he says, "you well know, / Things of like value differing in the owners / Are prized by their masters" (1.1.169-71). The role of human value in exchange transactions becomes even clearer when the old Athenian, father of Lucilius' fiancee, in effect auctions off his daughter to the highest bidder without regard for her affections. Comedy links love and money, certainly, but usually not in such a crass fashion as this. Apemantus and Flavius both seem to understand the danger of Timon's anachronistic economic action, especially in the Athenian society of opportunists. Their warnings, which Timon refuses to accept, indicate a structural change from comedy to something more resembling tragedy, focusing on a character who suffers because of his economic blindness.

---

[94]On the worth of a talent and Shakespeare's confusion over its value, see Terence Spencer, "Shakespeare Learns the Value of Money: The Dramatist at Work on *Timon of Athens*," *Shakespeare Survey* 6 (1953): 75-78.

The values of the new economic order indicate that while worth is measured almost totally in monetary terms, anything may become currency, a medium of exchange. Timon discovers both of these unhappy truths when he becomes impecunious and is repaid by his friends in a variety of commodities like rejection, false pride, and empty words. Shakespeare capitalizes on the imagistic connection of words and coins, as he did in the portrayal of Shylock, to demonstrate both the workings of the commodity ethic and the lack of sound inner merit that rich show often hides. Early in the play, when Timon squanders his estate in recklessly extravagant gifts and promises of more gifts, his steward is prompted to exclaim, "what he speaks is all in debt: he owes / For ev'ry word" (1.2.198-99), and later, when Timon finally listens to Flavius, he admonishes his master with "O my good lord, the world is but a word; / Were it all yours to give it in a breath, / How quickly were it gone!" (2.2.152-54).

The final blow is represented by the vapid speech of Lucius (3.2.44-58) as his portion of repayment for the "small kindnesses from him, as money, plate, jewels, and such like trifles." These images tend to support Shakespeare's conception of value in a mercantilist society as infinitely various and variable.

Although we are prone to view Timon sympathetically as a man wholeheartedly subscribing to old values in the context of a changed society that mocks these ethics, the character also has shortcomings to temper this sympathy. We may pity the man "shattered and disillusioned to the point of madness by his discovery that the traditional beliefs he has lived by are no longer the beliefs of the world around him" (Pettet 329), but we also realize his own economic faults. In a sense he is an inverse Shylock, for he gives and gives but never learns to accept. Early on, when false friends offer him gifts, he takes them only in order to present even better gifts in return. At the end of the play he vehemently refuses help and good counsel from his best devotees, Apemantus and Flavius. According to Kenneth Burke, Timon gives so excessively in a desperate attempt to make his bounty replace the human bonds which he lacks or feels inadequate to form.[95] While these gifts do represent bonds, sadly enough they do not constitute bonds.

---

[95] *Language as Symbolic Action* (Berkeley: Univ. of California Press, 1966), 122.

Part of Timon's inability to form satisfying human bonds stems from a Lear-like fault. In the guise of bounty, Timon actually establishes himself as an economic judge who rewards good socio-economic behavior and who tests the economic fidelity of his friends (2.2). While Lear eventually learns both to give and to receive, Timon makes no such progress. His giving is faulty in motive and his inability to receive a crucial failing, "an attempt on the part of man to ape divine bounty, ever spontaneously giving without receiving anything in return, . . . presumptuous and . . , inevitably . . . frustrated."[96]

From the beginning to the end of the play he ignores the necessity of reciprocity. His economic abuses, although erring on the side of prodigality rather than frugality, are judged almost as harshly. His excessive bounty, according to one of the Senators, is itself a type of usury or counterfeiting that partakes of the "unnatural" side of economic fertility:

> If I want gold, steal but a beggar's dog
> And give it Timon, why, the dog coins gold.
> If I would sell my horse and buy twenty moe
> Better than he, why, give my horse to Timon,
> Ask nothing, give it him, it foals me straight
> And able horses. (2.5.5-10)

Dogs and horses are not so very different from ewes and rams and evidently just as productive.

By introducing usury into this play, along with the tangible bonds that we have learned invariably accompany moneylending transactions, Shakespeare shows us an equivocation on bonds at least as disturbing as in *The Merchant of Venice.* Burke finds Timon as well to be a play "almost wholly concerned with relations among men (as though all the world were a kind of secular monastery devoted perversely to a universal god of gold)."[97]

As the money ethic gains precedence, the nature of human bonds changes. The Senator who comments on Timon's unnatural propagation of wealth also eventually finds his financial bond

---

[96] J. C. Maxwell, "'Timon of Athens,'" *Scrutiny* 15 (1947-1948): 201.

[97] Burke, 118. See also A. S. Collins, "*Timon of Athens*: A Reconsideration," *Review of English Studies* 22 (1946): 105.

more pressing than the bond of friendship and sues an impecunious Timon for repayment. In this decision of utility the material wins out over the intangible. Similarly, in Act I all of the false lords counterfeit the actions that generally indicate traditional bonds, but they do it only to profit from Timon's gifts and feasts. Alcibiades offers a refreshing counterpoint in that he knows and upholds the bonds of war, fidelity, and honor and lives by their ethics; yet when he argues the case of his friend and fellow soldier before the Senate, he knows enough of their priorities to couch his argument in terms of economic bonds (3.5.76-84).[98] Most of the Athenians treasure riches over virtue; this is the problem of Timon when, pressed by creditors and aware of the betrayal of his friends, he cries out "Cut my heart in sums" (3.4.92) as payment for the bills. Mingling love and money, this image crystallizes Timon's dilemma: he tried to give his heart, but false friends find such a gift ultimately worthless in a money economy.

As the play moves toward tragedy with Timon's realization of his prior blindness and betrayal and with his isolation, it falls short of a satisfying structure because of the economic lessons that remain unlearned. Timon never achieves the proper balance: as Apemantus observes, "The middle of humanity thou never knewest, but the extremity of both ends" (4.3.300-01). Timon still persists in giving without receiving. Having placed too much faith in human bonds, he now denies and curses all bonds, even economic ones. A man can rely only upon their being broken (4.1.3-21). Similarly, he is slow to recognize his bond to Flavius, who has been faithful all along, and when he does accept his service, Timon yet again rewards and repays this human debt with gold, like Lear. Even by the end of the play, Timon still misunderstands the true nature and right use of money. He has learned accurately of his society's dedication to the money ethic and of its faith in the ability of gold to transmute human action; some values, however, cannot be touched by gold. Timon neglects to acknowledge the role of intrinsic values, even with Alcibiades as his teacher. In his society the money morality tends to negate all traditional bonds (4.3.381-92).[99]

---

[98]See O. J. Campbell, *Shakespeare's Satire* (London: Oxford Univ. Press, 1943), 194.

[99]See Winifred M. T. Nowottny, "Acts IV and V of *Timon of Athens*," *Shakespeare Quarterly* 10 (1959): 496.

But there is still a remnant of humanity that finds value in serving its brothers. Timon can only rail against a society that has disappointed him; Alcibiades, in contrast, takes arms against a sea of troubles and emerges victorious. While the money ethic and its companions of usury and financial bonds threaten society, all money is not therefore bad. Alcibiades in fact uses the gold Timon gives him to put down the economic corruption of the Senate, at least temporarily. Timon cannot see the positive power of gold because he confuses the two usuries. As U. M. Ellis-Fermor notes, when Timon lashes out at nature, he misreads the function of "natural" use, which can be productive.[100] Nature is not a thief; it merely operates by a system of reciprocal obligations that Timon does not understand. "Natural" usury and use are desirable. Accepting as well as returning is essential in the hierarchies of both nature and society. Friends, then, are to be "used" in the sense of reciprocal human obligations rather than "put to use" with only the hope of pecuniary gain. Having been slow to recognize the latter, Timon persists in refusing the former.

Timon's persistent wrong-headedness attains its final expression in the first epitaph he proposes, "nothing brings me all things" (5.1.188). [101] Nothing brings him only a self-imposed solitude and an irrational, all-consuming hate. Bounty, used correctly and with discretion, is able to achieve the true sense of community for which he strives. Comparing this last act with Act V of *The Merchant of Venice* instructs us in Shakespeare's theory of proper economics. While wealth may lend itself to abuses, withdrawal is not the right answer. Even Shylock is in a sense incorporated into the society.

Like Shylock, who hangs between censure and sympathy, Timon is an unsatisfying hero. In both structure and character the playwright can only expose the abuses of this new money economy without finding a workable solution. Some traditional values, like those of Alcibiades and the servants of Timon, show themselves strong enough to fend off the corruption of economic ethics, but these values are no longer widespread. Shakespeare acknowledges the presence of a money economy but cannot yet answer the

---

[100]Suggested in *The Jacobean Drama* (London: Methuen, 1936), 265.

[101] According to Aristotle, money was barren and thus could not propagate; this was commonly expressed in the truism "Nothing comes of nothing." Timon plays on the proverb by inverting it.

question of how to cope with its morality. The issue itself breaches the gap in time and setting from ancient Greece to Renaissance England: "If usury then was responsible for this social disintegration and the misery it entailed, one can easily see why . . . Timon [was] so sympathetic to an Elizabethan audience, which saw itself, like [him], in the clutches of gripping creditors."[102] One hope seems to reside in those who can recognize the necessity of human interrelation and interdependence, those who believe in enduring values and have the ability to discern them truly. Flavius, as steward and faithful servant, epitomizes the hope of man in *Timon of Athens*. From the beginning he understands prudent economic management, loves Timon because of his inner values rather than his external shows of wealth, and stands by his master in the direst of circumstances. Like Bassanio, he is eventually rewarded materially for his knowledge of and participation in "natural" economics.

Critics may have trouble with structure and character in this play if they give short shrift to its economic emphasis. Its minimal character development sets the play firmly in the tradition of the moral interlude, which concerned itself with, a similar nexus between the worldly and the spiritual (Collins, 97). The confused generic structure of the play also reflects its economic theme.

While the subject of money in relation to love and friendship usually lies within the province of comedy, Shakespeare found the threats to traditional values growing too menacing to resolve as easily as in *The Comedy of Errors*. The intervening fifteen years witnessed an expanded acceptance of mercantilism and the money ethic. Even though Timon's world initially is the world of comedy, economic threats to this social stability drive the play toward tragedy. The work eventually falls short of true tragedy, however, for Timon never reaches a proper balance in reconciling the two realms of bonds. While *The Merchant of Venice*, written some eleven years earlier, at least made a pro forma attempt at the standard comedic ending, by 1607 even this was no longer possible. Structurally *Timon of Athens* demonstrates the effect of the new mercantilism on society and here decries its moral uncertainties in unresolved tragedy.

---

[102] John W. Draper, "The Theme of 'Timon of Athens,'" *Modern Language Review* 29 (1934): 26-27.

V

While the three major "economic" plays already discussed give a fair summary of the development of Shakespeare's economic attitude, a single situation in *Cymbeline* (1609) indicates the direction this attitude might have taken had the Bard written other economic plays later in his career. In *Cymbeline* as elsewhere, the language of love reflects an economic orientation. Imogen, defending her choice of Posthumus as husband, tells Cymbeline, "he is / A man worth any woman; overbuys me / Almost the sum he pays" (1.1.145-47). Posthumus and Philario express their friendship in terms of a financial bond (1.4.36-38), and when Jachimo challenges Posthumus to prove the virtue of his countrywomen, the argument is one of value. Jachimo pulls Posthumus into a debate that confuses intrinsic and exchange value (1.4.77-85).[103] While Posthumus confidently asserts that Imogen's value (*i.e.,* her inner virtues represented by chastity and tangibly embodied in the "manacle of love" as a token of her worth) is inviolable, Jachimo convincingly shows that virtue may be bought or stolen like any other commodity (ll. 88-93).

The wager that results from this debate—that Jachimo will be able to prove the easy virtue and the depreciated value of Imogen—moves toward an acceptance of the commercial mentality. All values begin to fall under the aegis of exchange, and inner virtue no longer can assert its precedence. In situation, then, *Cymbeline* partially recognizes the primacy of mercantilist ethics. Shakespeare's hierarchy of values, however, will out. Even though Jachimo seems to win easily, Imogen and her unassailable virtues still reinforce the traditional order. Upon first meeting her, even Jachimo is moved to realize that old-style value still lives on:

> All of her that is out of door most rich!
> If she be furnish'd with a mind so rare,
> She is alone th' Arabian bird, and I
> Have lost the wager. (1.6.15-18)

Cloten also subscribes to the new economic ethics and thus is confident that he can buy Imogen for himself. Like Timon, he knows the transmuting agency of gold but revels in it since it lends power and value to little men like himself: "'tis gold / Which

---

[103] Their argument in 1.4 to some extent parallels the debate of Troilus and Hector over the value of Helen.

makes the true man kill'd and saves the thief;/ Nay, sometime hangs both thief and true man. What / Can it not do, and undo?" (2.3.70-73). Imogen, however, refuses to be bought and throughout the play remains faithful to her own sense of inner worth. She knows the difference between love bonds and economic bonds—"Lovers / And men in dangerous bonds pray not alike" (3.2.36-37)—and values most the riches of the heart. When certain that she has lost Posthumus, Imogen desires only death, for in her heart "Thy master is not there, who was indeed / The riches of it" (3.4.70-71).

In the plot of Imogen, Shakespeare exposes an interesting commentary on economic conceptions. When she is alone in the woods and hungry, stumbling upon the cave of Belarius and her brothers, she expects a savage reception. Her comment, "Ho! who's here? / If any thing that's civil, speak; if savage, / Take or lend" (3.6.22-24), indicates that she views economics as the most primitive form of human behavior, not to be participated in by civil society. Ironically, however, these men who have never seen the court scoff at her suggestion of money as recompense for food. To them gold is merely a "dirty god." The prime courtiers, moreover, men like Cloten and Jachimo, live by an economic ethic more savage than one can expect even in the wilds.

For those who break the bonds of love, modern economic bonds seem cold comfort. Once he realizes his error, Posthumus views all of life, in terms of barren finance. He posits God as foremost financier who coins men into the currency of life and then expects repayment for this gift (5.4.18-28). Man's value in this speech derives from "the figure" stamped on the coin, for man is made in God's image. Posthumus feels "light," that is, counterfeit, worthless, emptied of value for his misjudgment of the true gold of Imogen.[104]

Although *Cymbeline* is a romance, in language and situation it incorporates economic considerations as well. While the play moves toward an acceptance of economic relationships as partial determinants of modern behavior, even in man's relation to his creator, it also points out abuses and shortcomings within this new

---

[104]A figure that is extended by the jailer, who sums up all of life in terms of economic bonds (5.4157-70). Other economic analogies in the play include a description of the decapitated Cloten as "a fool, an empty purse, / There was no money in't" (4.2.113-14).

system of exchange. Imogen's virtue, for example, cannot be bought or stolen. Among the best, traditional values remain intact, even when confronted with the corruption of the exchange mentality. Blatant economic activities in Shakespeare usually cause social division, strife between man and wife, father and daughter, master and servant. Those who avoid new finance or incorporate it into their system of "natural" economics defeat the threat of division. Faced with the problems of the new economic system, Shakespeare looked to the past for answers. The threats of commodity ethics were too strong to overcome easily, more so as he progressed in his career. Timon is his greatest statement of indignation and helplessness on new. economic behavior, foreshadowed by the exclusion of Shylock from the hearts of the Christian Venetians. In the situation of the merchandising of Imogen's virtue in *Cymbeline*, Shakespeare accepts the presence of a modified design of bonds which was eventually to include humans as economic objects, commodities to be traded and appraised like any other merchandise. While Shakespeare could not approve of this new order, later playwrights like Middleton, Massinger, and Marston were to embrace it with open arms and exploit it to its fullest potential.

Appendix C

List of London Wages, 1587

To the best and most skillful workmen, journeymen, and hired servants of any the companies hereunder named:

Clothworkers by the year with meat and drink £5.

Fullers by the year with meat and drink £5.

Shearmen by the year with meat and drink £5.

Dyers by the year with meat and drink £6 13s. 4d.

Tailors hosier by the year with meat and drink £4.

Drapers being hosiers by the year with meat and drink £4.

Shoemakers by the year with meat and drink £4.

Pewterers by the year with meat and drink £3 6s. 8d.

Whitebakers by the year with meat and drink £4 13s. 4d.

Brewers by the year with meat and drink £10.

The underbrewer by the year with meat and drink £6.

The foredrayman by the year with meat and drink £6.

The miller by the year with meat and drink £6.

The other drayman by the year with meat and drink £3 6s. 8d.

The tunman by the year with meat and drink £3 6s. 8d.

Alebrewers by the year with meat and drink £6.

Alebrewers by the day with meat and drink 8d.

Saddlers by the year with meat and drink £4.

Turners by the year with meat and drink £4 6s. 8d.

Cutlers by the year with meat and drink £4 6s. 8d.

Blacksmiths by the year with meat and drink £6.

Curriers by the year with meat and drink £6.

Bowyers by the year with meat and drink £4.

Fletchers by the year with meat and drink £4.

Brownbakers by the year with meat and drink £3 6s. 8d.

Farriers by the year with meat and drink £4.

Glovers by the year with meat and drink £3 6s. 8d.

Cappers by the year with meat and drink £4 13s. 4d.

Hatmakers and feltmakers by the year with meat and drink £4 13s. 4d.

Butchers by the year with meat and drink £6.

Cooks by the year with meat and drink £6.

To the workmen, journeymen, or hired servants of any the companies hereunder named:

Goldsmiths by the year with meat and drink £8, by the week 3s. 4d., by the day 7d.; without meat and drink by the week 6s., by the day 12d.

Skinners by the year with meat and drink £4, by the week *3s.* 4d., by the day 8d.; without meat and drink by the week 5s., by the day 13d.

Painter stainers by the year with meat and drink £4, by the week 4s., by the day 9d.; without meat and drink by the year £8, by the week 65. 8d., by the day 13d.

Girdlers by the year with meat and drink £3, by the week 16d., by the day 4d.; without meat and drink by the week 5s. 6d., by the day 10d.

Coopers by the year with meat and drink £4 6s. 8d., by the week 3s. 4d., by the day 8d.; without meat and drink by the year £8 13s. 4d. by the week 6s. 6d., by the day 13d.

Broderers by the year with meat and drink £5, by the week 4s. 6d., by the day 8d.; without meat and drink by the week 6s. 8d., by the day 13d.

Plumbers by the year with meat and drink £3 6s. 8d., by the week 3s. 4d., by the day 8d.; without meat and drink by the week 6s., by the day 14d.

Waxchandlers by the year with meat and drink £4, by the week 2s., by the day 6d.; without meat and drink by the week 4s. 6d., by the day 11d.

Armorers by the year with meat and drink £3 6s. 8d., by the week

3s. 4d., by the day 8d.; without meat and drink by the week 6s., by the day 13d.

Woolwinders by the year with meat and drink £3 6s. 8d., by the week 3s. 4d., by the day 8d.; without meat and drink by the week 6s., by the day 13d. His apprentice having served three years with meat and drink by the week 3s. 4d., by the day 8d.; without meat and drink by the week 5s., by the day 10d.

Tilers with meat and drink by the week 4s. 6d., by the day 9d.; without meat and drink 6s. 6d., by the day 13d. His apprentice with meat and drink by the week 3s. 4d., by the day 13d.; without meat and drink by the week 5s., by the day 11d.

Masons with meat and drink by the week 3s. 4d., by the day 11d.; without meat and drink by the week 5s., by the day 13d.

Joiners by the year with meat and drink £5, by the week 4s. 6d., by the day 9d.; without meat and drink by the week 7s., by the day 14d. His servant by the year with meat and drink £4, by the week 2s., by the day 4d.; without meat and drink by the week 4s., by the day 10d.

Plasterers with meat and drink by the day 9d.; without meat and drink by the day 13d.

Linen weavers by the year with meat and drink £4, by the day 6d.; without meat and drink by the day 10d.

Horners by the year with meat and drink £3, by the week 20d.

Glaziers with meat and drink by the day 9d.; without meat and drink by the day 13d.

Pavers with meat and drink by the day 9d.; without meat and drink by the day 13d.

Longbow stringmakers by the year with meat and drink £4, by the day 8d.; without meat and drink by the day 12d.

Founders by the year with meat and drink £5, by the day 12d.; without meat and drink by the day 16d.

Lorimers by the year with meat and drink £4, 6s. 8d., by the week 20d.

Barbers by the year with meat and drink £3, by the week 20d.

Carmen by the week with meat and drink 2s. 6d.

Watermen by the year with meat and drink 40s., by the week 12d., by the day 4d.; without meat and drink by the week 3s., by the day 7d.

Porters with meat and drink by the day 8d.; without meat and drink by the day 12d.

Carpenters with meat and drink by the week 4s. 6d., by the day 9d.; without meat and drink by the week 6s. 2d., by the day 13d. His apprentice that hath served three years with meat and drink by the week 3s. 4d., by the day 7d.; without meat and drink by the week 5s., by the day 11d.

Sawyers with meat and drink by the week 4s., by the day 8d.; without meat and drink by the week 6s., by the day 12d. To him that saweth the 100 [board feet] with meat and drink by the day 10d.; without meat and drink by the day 20d.

Common laborers with meat and drink by the day 5d.; without meat and drink by the day 9d.

Source: *Tudor Royal Proclamations*, 2:536-39. Reprinted by permission.

Appendix D

***Proclamations Concerning Coins and Money under Mary and Elizabeth,* 1553-1587**

8/20/53	Ordering Reform of Gold and Silver Coin
9/1/53	Renouncing Subsidy
3/4/54	Evaluating French Crown at 6s. 4d.
3/8/54	Evaluating Foreign Coins
5/4/54	Evaluating Portuguese Coins
12/26/54	Reforming Gold and Silver Coin
4/3/56	Warning Against Counterfeit Coins
4/27/56	Offering Reward for Information of Traffic Coin
9/16/56	Prohibiting Irish Pence in England
12/22/56	Prohibiting Rumors of Coin Devaluation
5/1/59	Prohibiting Export of All Gold and Coin
9/27/60	Devaluing Base Coins
10/9/60	Prohibiting Traffic in Coin; Devaluing Foreign Coin
11/2/60	Identifying Pistolet Coins Worth 5s. 10d.
12/23/60	Suppressing Rumors on Currency
2/19/61	Calling in Base Coins, Reforming Coinage
6/12/61	Calling in Last Base Coins by 20 July
11/15/61	Announcing New Small Coins; Outlawing Foreign Coins
1/30/62	Suppressing Rumors of Coinage Devaluation
3/13/62	Draft for Revaluing Coinage ; Suppressing Rumors of Coin Devaluation

12/21/62	Ordering Payment of Obligations to the Queen
11/11/64	Ordering Full Payment of Discounted Privy Seal Loans
6/1/65	Prohibiting Debased Foreign Coins
12/1/65	Prohibiting Counterfeit and Foreign Coins
11/24/71	Announcing Payment of Queen's Debts
9/20/76	Enforcing Statutes for Money Exchange and Rechange
9/27/76	Regulating Rates for Money Exchange and Rechange
9/30/77	Announcing Payment of Queen's Debts
5/19/81	Reviving Statute against Usury
10/12/87	Warning against Foreign Debasement of English Coin

Source*:* Collated from *Tudor Royal Proclamations,* Vol. 2. Not including other economic proclamations regarding import/export, the lottery, regulating wage rates, apparel, vagabonds, and licensing collections.

Appendix E

La mutation de l'appellation:

A partial list of changes in nominal values of English coins and the French crown

ANGEL:
1465—6s.8d.
Aug. 1526—7s. 4d.
Nov. 1526—7s. 6d.
1542—8s.
1549—9s. 8d.
1552—10s.
1610—11s.

CROWN OF THE DOUBLE ROSE:
1526—5s.
@ 1560—3s. 4d.

CROWN OF THE SUN:
1522—4s. 4d.
1526—4s. 6d.

OLD FRENCH CROWN:
1522—4s.
1540—5s.
Aug. 1550—7s.
Dec. 1550—6s. 4d 1562—4s.

GROAT:
1351—4d.
1551—2d.
1560—1 ½ d.

NOBLE:
1344—6s. 8d.
1465—8s. 4d.
1527—111s. 3d.

PENNY: 1560—3 farthings

ROSE NOBLE (RYAL):

1465—10s.
1525—11s. 3d.
1544—12s.
1560—15s.
1562—10s.

SHILLING:

1504—12d.
1551—6d.

SOVEREIGN:

1489—20s.
1526—22s.
1543—20s.
1551—30s.
1561—20s.

TESTON:

1542—12d.
1551—6d.
1560—4 ½d.(portcullis)
2 ¼d. (lion, harp, rose, greyhound, *fleur-de-lis*)

References

Editions of Plays Glossed

Barry, Lodowick. *Ram-Alley*. In *A Select Collection of Old English Plays,* edited by W. Carew Hazlitt. 4th ed. Vol. 5. New York: Benjamin Blom, 1964.

Beaumont, Francis, and John Fletcher. *The Beggars' Bush.* In *The Works of Francis Beaumont and John Fletcher.* Variorum ed. Vol. 2. London: George Bell and Sons, 1905.

----------. *The Scornful Lady.* In *The Works of Beaumont and Fletcher,* edited by Alexander Dyce. Vol. 1. Boston: Phillips, Sampson, 1854.

----------. *Wit without Money.* In *The Works of Beaumont and Fletcher,* edited by Alexander Dyce. Vol. 1. Boston: Phillips, Sampson, 1854.

----------. *The Woman-Hater.* In *The Works of Beaumont and Fletcher,* edited by Alexander Dyce. Vol. 1. Boston: Phillips, Sampson, 1854.

Chapman, George. *The Blind Beggar of Alexandria.* In *The Plays of George Chapman,* edited by Thomas Marc Parrott. Vol. 1. New York: Russell and Russell, 1961.

Chapman, George, Ben Jonson, and John Marston. *Eastward Ho.* In *Elizabethan Plays,* edited by Hazelton Spencer. Lexington, Mass.: D. C. Heath, 1933.

Cook, John. *Greenes Tu quoque, Or, the Cittie Gallant.* In *A Select Collection of Old English Plays,* edited by W. Carew Hazlitt. 4th ed. Vol. 5. New York: Benjamin Blom, 1964.

Dekker, Thomas. *The Honest Whore, Parts 1 and 2.* In *Elizabethan Plays,* edited by Hazelton Spencer. Lexington, Mass.: D. C. Heath, 1933.

----------. *Old Fortunatus.* In *The Dramatic Works of Thomas Dekker,* edited by Fredson Bowers. Vol. 1. Cambridge: Univ. Press, 1953.

Dekker, Thomas, and John Webster. *North-ward Hoe.* In *The Dramatic Works of Thomas Dekker,* edited by Fredson Bowers. Vol. 2. Cambridge: Univ. Press, 1953.

----------. *West-ward Hoe.* In *The Dramatic Works of Thomas Dekker,* edited by Fredson Bowers. Vol. 2. Cambridge: Univ. Press, 1953.

Haughton, William. *English-Men for my Money.* In *A Select Collection of Old English Plays,* edited by W. Carew Hazlitt. 4th ed. Vol. 5. New York: Benjamin Blom, 1964.

Heywood, Thomas. *A Woman Killed with Kindness.* In *Elizabethan Plays,* edited by Hazelton Spencer. Lexington, Mass.: D. C. Heath, 1933.

Jonson, Ben. *Bartholomew Fair.* In *Ben Jonson,* edited by C. H. Herford, Percy Simpson, and Evelyn Simpson. Vol. 6. Oxford: Clarendon, 1938.

----------. *The Case is Altered.* Edited by William Edward Sellin. Yale Studies in English, no. 61. New Haven: Yale Univ. Press, 1917.

----------. *The Devil is an Ass.* In *Ben Jonson,* edited by C. H. Herford, Percy Simpson, and Evelyn Simpson. Vol. 6. Oxford: Clarendon, 1938.

----------. *Every Man Out of His Humour.* In *Ben Jonson,* edited by Brinsley Nicholson. Vol. 1. London: T. Fisher Unwin, n.d.

----------. *The Magnetick Lady.* In *Ben Jonson,* edited by C. H. Herford, Percy Simpson, and Evelyn Simpson. Vol. 6. Oxford: Clarendon, 1938.

----------. *The Staple of News.* Edited by Devra Rowland Kifer. Regents Renaissance Drama Series. Lincoln: Univ. of Nebraska Press, 1975.

----------. *Volpone.* In *Elizabethan Plays,* edited by Hazelton Spencer. Lexington, Mass.: D. C. Heath, 1933.

The London Prodigall. In *The Shakespeare Apocrypha,* edited by C. F. Tucker Brooke. Oxford: Clarendon, 1908.

Marlowe, Christopher. *The Complete Plays of Christopher Marlowe.* Edited by Irving Ribner. New York: Odyssey Press, 1963.

Marston, John. *The Dutch Courtesan.* Edited by Peter Davison. Berkeley and Los Angeles: Univ. of California Press, 1968.

----------. *John Drums Entertainment.* In *The Plays of John Marston,* edited by H. Harvey Wood. Vol. 3. Edinburgh: Oliver and Boyd, 1939.

Massinger, Philip. *The Bond-Man.* In *The Plays and Poems of Philip Massinger,* edited by Philip Edwards and Colin Gibson. Vol. 1. Oxford: Clarendon, 1976.

----------. *The City Madam.* Edited by Cyrus Hoy. Regents Renaissance Drama Series. Lincoln: Univ. of Nebraska Press, 1964.

----------. *A New Way to Pay Old Debts.* In *Elizabethan Plays,* edited by Hazelton Spencer. Lexington, Mass.: D. C. Heath, 1933.

Massinger, Philip, and Nathan Field. *The Fatal Dowry.* Edited by T. A. Dunn. Fountainwell Drama Texts. Berkeley and Los Angeles: Univ. of California Press, 1969.

May, Thomas. *The Heir.* In *Old Plays,* edited by Robert Dodsley. Vol. 8. London: Septimus Prowett, 1825.

Middleton, Thomas. *A Chaste Maid in Cheapside.* Edited by Charles Barber. Fountainwell Drama Texts. Berkeley and Los Angeles: Univ. of California Press. 1969.

---------. *A Mad World, My Masters.* Edited by Standish Henning. Regents Renaissance Drama Series. Lincoln: Univ. of Nebraska Press, 1965.

----------. *Michaelmas Term.* Edited by George R. Price. The Hague: Mouton, 1976.

----------. *A Trick to Catch the Old One.* In *Elizabethan Plays,* edited by Hazelton Spencer. Lexington, Mass.: D. C. Heath, 1933.

----------. *Women Beware Women.* Edited by J. R. Mulryne. Revels Plays. Manchester: Manchester Univ. Press, 1975.

Rowley, William. *A New Wonder, A Woman never Vext.* In A *Select Collection of Old English Plays,* edited by W. Carew Hazlitt. 4th ed. Vol. 6. New York: Benjamin Blom, 1964.

Shakespeare, William. *The Riverside Shakespeare,* edited by G. Blakemore Evans et al. Boston: Houghton Mifflin, 1974.

Wilson, Robert. *The Three Ladies of London.* In A *Select Collection of Old English Plays,* edited by W. Carew Hazlitt. 4th ed. Vol. 3. New York, Benjamin Blom, 1964.

Wily Beguiled.

Secondary Sources

Alter, Robert. "Who is Shylock?" *Commentary* (1993), web.

Boebel, Dagny M. H. "Shylock and Portia: Secret Sharers." *CEA Critic* 53.3 (Spring/Summer 1991): 39-48.

Burckhardt, Sigurd. "*The Merchant of Venice:* The Gentle Bond." *ELH* 29 (1962): 239-62.

Burgon, John William. *The Life and Times of Sir Thomas Gresham, Knt.* 2 vols. New York: Burt Franklin, 1839(?).

Burke, Kenneth. *Language as Symbolic Action.* Berkeley and Los Angeles: Univ. of California Press, 1966.

Calisch, Edward N. *The Jew in English Literature.* 1909. Rpt. Port Washington. N.Y.: Kennikat Press, 1969.

Cambridge Economic History of Europe. Edited by M. M. Postan, E. E. Rich, and Edward Miller. Cambridge: Univ. Press, 1963.

Carey, John. "Donne and Coins." In *English Renaissance Studies.* Oxford: Clarendon, 1980.

Certaine Sermons or Homilies appointed to be read in CHVRCHES. London: John Bill, 1623.

Challis, C. E. *The Tudor Coinage.* New York: Harper and Row, 1978.

Champion, Larry S. *Ben Jonson's "Dotages."* Lexington: Univ. of Kentucky Press, 1967.

Chandos, John, editor. *In God's Name: Examples of Preaching in England from the Act of Supremacy to the Act of Uniformity 1534-1662.* New York: Bobbs-Merrill, 1971.

Cherry, Caroline Lockett. *The Most Unvaluedst Purchase: Women in the Plays of Thomas Middleton.* Salzburg Studies in English Literature, Jacobean Drama Studies, no. 34. Salzburg: Universitat Salzburg, 1973.

Clapham, Sir John. *A Concise Economic History of Britain.* Cambridge: Univ. Press, 1957.

Clark, Sir George. *The Wealth of England from 1496 to 1760.* London: Oxford Univ. Press, 1946.

Clarke, Charles, and Mary Cowden Clarke. *The Shakespeare Key.* New York: Ungar. n.d.

Clarkson, P. S., and C. T. Warren. *The Law of Property in Shakespeare and the Elizabethan Drama.* Baltimore: Johns Hopkins Univ.Press, 1942.

Cohen, Ted. "Metaphor and the Cultivation of Intimacy." In *On Metaphor,* edited by Sheldon Sacks. Chicago: Univ. of Chicago Press, 1979.

Coleman, D. C. *The Economy of England, 1450-1750.* London: Oxford Univ. Press, 1977.

Combs, Homer Carroll, and Zay Rusk Sullens. *A Concordance to the English Poems of John Donne.* Chicago: Packard & Co., 1940.

Cook, Ann Jennalie. *The Privileged Playgoers of Shakespeare's London, 1576-1642.* Princeton: Princeton Univ. Press, 1981.

Cook, B. J. "'This is the very coinage of your brain': Shakespeare and Money Revisited." *British Numismatic Society Journal* (2014): 144-64.

Coursen, H. R. *The Leasing Out of England.* Washington, D.C.: Univ, Press of America, 1982.

Crawford, Charles. *The Marlowe Concordance.* 2 vols. New York: Burt Franklin 1911.

Cunliffe, Richard John. *A New Shakespearean Dictionary.* London: Blackie and Son, 1910.

Deane, Herbert A. *The Political and Social Ideas of St. Augustine.* New York Columbia Univ. Press, 1963.

Deng S. "Rough Economies—The Politics and Poetics of Coinage." In *Coinage and State Formation in Early*

Modern English Literature. Early Modern Cultural Studies. New York: Palgrave Macmillan, 2011.

Dent, R. W. *Shakespeare's Proverbial Language: An Index.* Berkeley and Los Angeles: Univ. of California Press, 1981.

de Roover, Raymond. "The Concept of the Just Price: Theory and Economic Policy." *Journal of Economic History* 18 (1958): 418-34.

Derrida, Jacques. "White Mythology." *New Literary History* 6 (1974): 5-74.

Dictionary of Political Economy. Edited by Sir Robert Harry Inglis Palgrave. 3 vols. 1910. Rpt. Detroit: Gale Research Co., 1976.

A Discourse of the Common Weal of this Realm of England. Edited by Elizabeth Lamond. Cambridge: Univ. Press, 1954.

Documents in English Economic History: England from 1000 to 1760. Edited by B. W. Clapp, H. E. S. Fisher, and A. R. J. Jurica. Vol. 1. London: G. Bell, 1977.

Dolan, Neal. "Shylock in Love: Economic Metaphor in Shakespeare's Sonnets." *Raritan* 22.2 (Fall 2002): 26-51.

Dunbar, Charles F. "The Bank of Venice." *Quarterly Journal of Economics* 6 (1892): 308-35.

Eagleton, Terence. *Shakespeare and Society.* New York: Schocken Books, 1967.

Edwardes, Marian. *A Pocket Lexicon & Concordance to the Temple Shakespeare.* 1909. Rpt. New York: AMS, 1974.

Ehrenberg, Richard. *Capital and Finance in the Age of the Renaissance.* Translated by H. M. Lucas. 1928. Rpt. New York: Augustus Kelley, 1963.

Elukin, Jonathon. "Shylock, the Devil, and the Meaning of Deception in *The Merchant of Venice*." *European Judaism* 51.2 (2018): 44-51.

English Economic History: Select Documents. Edited by A. E. Bland, P. A. Brown, and R. H. Tawney. London: G. Bell, 1914.

Engstrom, J. Eric. *Coins in Shakespeare: A Numismatic Guide.* Hanover: Dartmouth College, 1964.

Everyman. In *Chief Pre-Shakespearean Dramas,* edited by Joseph Quincy Adams. Cambridge, Mass.: Riverside, 1924.

Farnam, Henry W. *Shakespeare's Economics.* New Haven: Yale Univ. Press, 1931.

Feavearyear, Sir Albert. *The Pound Sterling: A History of English Money.* 2d ed., revised. by E. Victor Morgan. Oxford: Clarendon, 1963.

Fifoot, C. H. S. *History and Sources of the Common Law.* 1949. Rpt. New York: Greenwood, 1970.

Fischer, Sandra K. "'Cut my heart in sums': Shakespeare's Economics and *Timon of Athens*," in *Money: Lure, Lore, and Literature*, ed. John L. DiGaetani (London: Greenwood Press, 1994): 187-96.

----------. "'He means to pay': Value and Metaphor in the Lancastrian Tetralogy," *Shakespeare Quarterly* 40, 2 (1989): 149-64.

----------. "'Who steals my purse': Economics and Value in Renaissance Drama," Diss. Univ. of Oregon 1980, Ch. 1, 2.

Fisher, F. J. "Commercial Trends and Policy in Sixteenth-Century England." *Economic History Review* 10 (1940): 95-117.

Fraser, L. M. *Economic Thought and Language.* London: Adam Charles Black, 1947.

Frey, Albert R. *Dictionary of Numismatic Names.* Glossary by Mark M. Salton. New York: Barnes and Noble, 1947.

Gillen, Katherine. *Chaste Value: Economic Crisis, Female Chastity and the Production of Social Difference on Shakespeare's Stage.* Edinburgh: Edinburgh Univ. Press, 2017.

Girard, René. *A Theatre of Envy: William Shakespeare.* Carthage Reprint, 2004.

Gould, J. D. *The Great Debasement: Currency and the Economy in Mid-Tudor England.* Oxford: Clarendon, 1970.

Groseclose, Elgin. *Money and Man: A Survey of Monetary Experience.* 2d ed. New York: Ungar, 1967.

Gross, John. *Shylock: A Legend and its Legacy*. New York: Simon and Schuster, 1994.

Gross, Kenneth. *Shylock is Shakespeare*. Chicago: Univ. of Chicago Press, 2006.

Haines, Charles. "Some Notes on Love and Money in *The Comedy of Errors."* In *Critical Dimensions,* edited by Mario Curreli and Alberto Martino. Cuneo, Italy: SASTE, 1978.

Hamilton, Earl J. "American Treasure and the Rise of Capitalism (1500-1700)." *Economica* 9 (1929): 338-57.

Hansen, Abby Jane Dubman. "Shakespeare and the Lore of Precious Stones." *College Literature 4* (1977): 210-19.

Harbage, Alfred. *Annals of English Drama 975-1700.* 2d ed., revised. by S. Schoenbaum. Philadelphia: Univ.of Pennsylvania Press, 1964.

The Harleian Miscellany. Edited by Thomas Park. London: White and Cochrane, 1812.

Harrison, William. *The Description of England.* Edited by Georges Edelen. Ithaca: Cornell Univ. Press, 1968.

Hawkes, David. *Shakespeare and Economic Theory*. London: Bloomsbury, 2015.

Hazlitt, W. Carew. *English Proverbs and Proverbial Phrases.* London: Reeves and Turner, 1907.

Herbert, George. "Jacula Prudentum." In *The Works of George Herbert,* edited by Robert Aris Willmott. London: Routledge, Warnes, and Routledge, 1859.

Heywood, Thomas. *If you know not me, you know nobody, Parts 1 and 2.* In *The Dramatic Works of Thomas Heywood.* Vol. 1. London: John Pearson, 1874.

Hibbard, G. R. "Love, Marriage and Money in Shakespeare's Theatre and Shakespeare's England." *Elizabethan Theatre* 6 (1975): 134-55.

Hill, Christopher. "Protestantism and the Rise of Capitalism." In *Essays in the Economic and Social History of Tudor and Stuart England,* edited by F. J. Fisher. Cambridge: Univ.Press, 1961.

Hogue, Arthur R. *Origins of the Common Law.* Bloomington: Indiana Univ. Press, 1966.

Homer, Sidney. *A History of Interest Rates.* New Brunswick: Rutgers Univ. Press, 1963.

Hooker, Richard. *Of the Laws of Ecclesiastical Polity.* 2 vols. London: Dent, 1963.

Hubler, Edward. *The Sense of Shakespeare's Sonnets.* Princeton: Princeton Univ. Press, 1952.

Huizinga, Johan. *Homo Ludens.* Translated by George Steiner. New York: Harper and Row, 1970.

Hulme, Hilda M. *Explorations in Shakespeare's Language.* 1962. Rpt. London: Longman, 1977.

Hurstfield, Joel, and Alan G. R. Smith, editors. *Elizabethan People: State and Society.* London: Edward Arnold, 1972.

Jameson, Fredric. *The Prison-House of Language.* Princeton: Princeton Univ. Press, 1972.

Jenks, Edward. "On the Early History of Negotiable Instruments." *Law Quarterly Review 9* (1893): 70-85.

Josset, C. R. *Money in Britain: A History of the Currencies of the British Isles.* London: Frederick Warne, 1962.

Judges, A. V. "A Note on Prices in Shakespeare's Time." In *A Companion to Shakespeare Studies,* edited by Harley Granville-Barker and G. B. Harrison. New York Macmillan, 1934.

Kantorowicz, Ernst H. *The King's Two Bodies: A Study in Medieval Political Theology.* Princeton: Princeton Univ. Press, 1957.

Kent, John. *2000 Years of British Coins and Medals.* London: British Museum Publications, 1978.

Knights, L. C. *Drama and Society in the Age of Jonson.* London: Chatto and Windus, 1937.

Kokeritz, Helge. *Shakespeare's Pronunciation.* New Haven: Yale Univ. Press, 1953.

Landreth, David. *The Face of Mammon: The Matter of Money in English Renaissance Literature.* Oxford: Oxford Univ. Press, 2012.

Lanham, Richard A. *A Handlist of Rhetorical Terms.* Berkeley and Los Angeles: Univ. of California Press, 1968.

Le Comte, Edward. *A Dictionary of Puns in Milton's English Poetry.* New York: Columbia Univ. Press, 1981.

Lepage, Henri. *Tomorrow, Capitalism: The Economics of Economic Freedom.* Translated by Sheilagh C. Ogilvie. LaSalle, Ill.: Open Court Pub. Co., 1982.

Lerner, Laurence. "Literature and Money." *Essays and Studies* 28 (1975): 106-22.

Lucki, Emil. *History of the Renaissance: Economy and Society.* Salt Lake City: Univ. of Utah Press, 1963.

McCulloch, J. R., ed. *Old and Scarce Tracts on Money.* London: P. S. King, 1933.

McLaughlin, T. P. "The Teaching of the Canonists on Usury." *Mediaeval Studies* 1 (1939): 81-147.

Mahood, M. M. *Shakespeare's Wordplay.* 1957. Rpt. London: Methuen, 1979.

Marschak, Jacob. "Economics of Language." *Behavioral Science* 10 (1965): 135-40.

Marx, Karl. *Selected Writings.* Edited by David McLellan. Oxford: Oxford Univ. Press, 1977.

Monroe, Arthur Eli. *Monetary Theory before Adam Smith.* Gloucester, Mass.: Peter Smith, 1965.

Morley, Henry. *Memoirs of Bartholomew Fair.* London: Frederick Warne, n.d.

Muir, Kenneth, "'Timon of Athens' and the Cash-Nexus." *Modern Quarterly Miscellany* 1 (1947): 57-76.

Mull, Donald L. *Henry James's "Sublime Economy": Money as Symbolic Center in the Fiction.* Middletown: Wesleyan Univ.Press, 1973.

Munro, John H. "Money and Coinage of the Age of Erasmus." In *Collected Works of Erasmus.* Vol. 1, *The Correspondence of Erasmus.* Translated by R. A. B. Mynors and D. F. S. Thomson. Annotated by Wallace K. Ferguson. Toronto: Univ. of Toronto Press, 1974.

Nelson, Benjamin. *The Idea of Usury.* 2d ed. Chicago: Univ. of Chicago Press, 1969.

Nider, Johannes. *On the Contracts of Merchants.* Translated by Charles H. Reeves. Edited by Ronald B. Shuman. Norman: Univ. of Oklahoma Press, 1966.

Noonan, John T., Jr. *The Scholastic Analysis of Usury.* Cambridge: Harvard Univ. Press, 1957.

O'Brien, George. *An Essay on Mediceval Economic Teaching.* 1920. Rpt. New York: Augustus Kelley, 1967.

O'Callaghan, Jeremiah. *Usury, Funds, and Banks.* Burlington: n.p., 1834.

O'Hanlon, Redmond L. "Shakespeare's Puns." *Shakespeare Newsletter* 2 (1952): 15.

Onions, C. T. *A Shakespeare Glossary.* 2d ed. Oxford: Clarendon, 1919.

Orchard, Dorothy Johnson, and Geoffrey May. *Moneylending in Great Britain.* New York: Russell Sage, 1933.

Orgel, Stephen. "Imagining Shylock." In *Imagining Shakespeare.* London: Palgrave Macmillan, 2003. 144-62.

Outhwaite, R. B. *Inflation in Tudor and Early Stuart England.* 2d ed. London: Macmillan, 1982.

The Oxford Dictionary of English Proverbs (ODEP). 3d ed., rev. by F. P. Wilson. Oxford: Clarendon, 1970.

The Oxford English Dictionary (OED). Oxford: University Press, 1971.

Partridge, Eric. *Shakespeare's Bawdy.* 2d ed. 1955. Reprint. New York: E. P. Dutton. 1961.

Peacham, Henry. "The Worth of a Penny: or a Caution to keep Money." In *Social England Illustrated,* edited by Andrew Lang. New York: E. P. Dutton, n.d.

Pearlman, E. "Shakespeare, Freud, and the Two Usuries, or, Money's a Meddler." *English Literary Renaissance* 2 (1972): 217-36.

Pettet, E. C. "Timon of Athens: The Disruption of Feudal Morality." *Review of English Studies* 23 (1947): 321-36.

Porteous, John. *Coins in History.* New York: G. P. Putnam's Sons, 1969.

Postan, M. M. "Credit in Medieval Trade." In *Essays in Economic History,* edited by E. M. Carus-Wilson. London: Edward Arnold, 1954.

Postlethwayt, Malachy. *The Universal Dictionary of Trade and Commerce.* 4th ed. 2 vols. 1774. Rpt. New York: Augustus M. Kelley, 1971.

Powell, Chilton Latham. *English Domestic Relations 1487-1653.* 1917. Reprint. London: Frank Cass, 1966.

Ramsey, Peter. *Tudor Economic Problems.* London: Victor Gollancz, 1965.

Richards, R. D. *The Early History of Banking in England.* London: Frank Cass, 1958.

Ricks, Christopher. "Word-Play in *Women Beware Women."* *Review of English Studies* n.s. 12 (1961): 238-50.

Rosenthal, Gilbert S., ed. *Banking and Finance among Jews in Renaissance Italy.* New York: Bloch, 1962.

Ross, Thomas R. *Chaucer's Bawdy.* New York: Dutton, 1972.

Rossi-Landi, Ferruccio. *Linguistics and Economics.* The Hague: Mouton, 1975.

Roth, Cecil. *The Jews in the Renaissance.* Philadelphia: Jewish Publishing Society of America, 1959.

----------. *Venice.* Philadelphia: Jewish Publishing Society of America, 1930.

Rye, William Brenchley, editor. *England as seen by Foreigners.* 1865. Rpt. New York: Benjamin Blom, 1967.

Saussure, Ferdinand de. *Course in General Linguistics.* Translated by Wade Baskin New York: Philosophical Library, 1959.

Schmidt, Alexander. *Shakespeare-Lexicon.* 4th ed. 2 vols. New York: G. E Stechert, 1902.

Schoeck, Richard J. "The Fifth Lateran Council: its partial successes and its larger failures." In *Reform and Authority in the Medieval and Reformation Church.* edited by Guy Fitch

Lytle. Washington, D.C.: Catholic Univ. of America Press, 1981.

Schumpeter, Joseph A. *History of Economic Analysis.* New York: Oxford Univ. Press, 1954.

Shaw, William A., ed. *Select Tracts and Documents Illustrative of English Monetary History 1626-1730.* 1896. Reprint. New York: Augustus M. Kelley, 1967.

Shell, Marc. *The Economy of Literature.* Berkeley and Los Angeles: Univ. of California Press, 1978.

Siegel, Paul N. "Richard III as Businessman." *Shakespeare Jahrbuch* (Weimar) 114 (1978): 101-06.

Silk, Leonard, ed. *Religious Attitudes toward Usury.* New York: Arno Press, 1972.

Skeat, Walter W. *A Glossary of Tudor and Stuart Words.* Edited by A. L. Mayhew. Oxford: Clarendon, 1914.

Southall, Raymond. "*Troilus and Cressida* and the Spirit of Capitalism." In *Shakespeare in a Changing World,* edited by Arnold Kettle. 1964. Rpt. London: Lawrence and Wishart, 1971.

Spencer, Terence. "Shakespeare Learns the Value of Money: The Dramatist at Work on *Timon of Athens.*" *Shakespeare Survey* 6 (1953): 75-78.

Spevack, Martin. *The Harvard Concordance to Shakespeare.* Cambridge, Mass.: Belknap Press, 1973.

Spinoza, Charles. "Shylock and Debt and Contract in *The Merchant of Venice.*" *Law and Literature* (1993): 65-85.

Stoljar, S. J. *A History of Contract at Common Law.* Canberra: Australian National Univ. Press, 1975.

Stone, Lawrence. *The Crisis of the Aristocracy 1558-1641.* Oxford: Clarendon, 1965.

Stonex, Arthur Bivins. "The Usurer in Elizabethan Drama." *PMLA* 31 (1916): 190-210.

Stow[e], John. *Two London Chronicles.* In *Camden Miscellany.* Camden Society, 3d ser., vol. 18. London, 1910.

Stowe, John. *Three Fifteenth-Century Chronicles.* Edited by James Gairdner. Camden Society Reprint, 1880. Rpt. New York: Johnson Reprint Corporation, n.s., vol. 28, 1965.

Stubbes, Phillip. *The Anatomie of Abuses.* London: Richard Jones, 1583. Microfilm.

Suarez, Francisco. *De legibus.* In *Selections from Three Works,* translated by Gwladys L. Williams et al. New York: Oceana, 1964.

Tawney, R. H. *Religion and the Rise of Capitalism.* 1926. Rpt. Gloucester, Mass.: Peter Smith, 1962.

Tawney, R. H., ed. *Studies in Economic History: The Collected Papers of George Unwin.* London: Macmillan, 1927.

Thomas, M. W., ed. *A Survey of English Economic History.* 3d ed. London: Blackie and Son, 1967.

Thomas Aquinas, Saint. *Aquinas Ethicus.* Translated by Joseph Rickaby. 2d ed. 2 vols. London: Burns and Oates, 1896.

----------. *Basic Writings of Saint Thomas Aquinas.* Edited by Anton C. Pegis. 2 vols. 1944. Rpt. New York: Random House, 1945.

Tilley, Morris Palmer. *A Dictionary of the Proverbs in England.* Ann Arbor: Univ. of Michigan Press, 1950.

Tilley, Morris Palmer, and James K. Roy. "Proverbs and Proverbial Allusions in Marlowe." *Modern Language Notes* 50 (1935): 347-55.

Tudor Economic Documents. Ed. R. H. Tawney and Eileen Power. London: Longmans, Green, 1924.

Tudor Royal Proclamations (TRP). Ed. Paul L. Hughes and James F. Larkin. Vol. 2. New Haven, Conn.: Yale Univ. Press, 1969.

Turner, Frederick. *Shakespeare's Twenty-First Century Economics: The Morality of Love and Money.* Oxford: Oxford Univ. Press, 1999.

Unwin, George. "Commerce and Coinage." In *Shakespeare's England.* Vol. 1. 1916. Rpt. Oxford: Clarendon, 1970.

Usher, Abbot Payson. "The Origin of the Bill of Exchange." *Journal of Political Economy* 22 (1914): 566-76.

Vandiver, E. P., Jr. "The Elizabethan Dramatic Parasite." *Studies in Philology* 32 (1935): 411-27.

Walford, Cornelius. *Fairs, Past and Present.* 1883. Reprint. New York: Augustus M. Kelley, 1968.

Warnock, G. J. *Morality and Language.* Totowa, N.J.: Barnes & Noble, 1983.

Weber, Max. *The Protestant Ethic and the Spirit of Capitalism.* Translated by Talcott Parsons. New York: Scribners, 1958.

Welsby, Paul A., ed. *Sermons and Society: An Anglican Anthology.* Baltimore: Penguin, 1970.

Wheeler, John. *A Treatise of Commerce.* 1601. Rpt. Facsimile Text Society. New York: Columbia Univ. Press, 1931.

White, Helen C. *Social Criticism in Popular Religious Literature of the Sixteenth Century.* 1944. Rpt. New York: Octagon, 1965.

Whiting, B. J. *Proverbs in the Earlier English Drama.* Cambridge: Harvard Univ. Press, 1938.

Wilson, Thomas. *A Discourse Upon Usury.* Edited by R. H. Tawney. London: G. Bell and Sons, 1925.

Wright, Celeste Turner. "Some Conventions Regarding the Usurer in Elizabethan Literature." *Studies in Philology* 31 (1934): 176-97.

Wright, Louis B. *Middle-Class Culture in Elizabethan England.* 1935. Rpt. Ithaca: Cornell Univ. Press, 1963.

Wriothesley, Charles. *A Chronicle of England During the Reigns of the Tudors.* Edited by William Douglas Hamilton. 2 vols. 1875, 1877. Rpt. New York: Johnson Reprint Corp., 1965.

Index of Economic Terms by Play Title

Although the glossary itself offers a helpful apparatus for understanding coins and economic terms as they arise individually in study, another avenue of criticism might be to undertake an economic examination of the language of particular plays. Thus the following index lists under individual titles the terms that appear in the glossary as examples. These lists do not include all economic terms in each play, and especially omit the more standard and omnipresent coin terms, like penny, pound, farthing, and so forth, except when they occur in a pun, metaphor, or rhetorical figure, or as a specific measure of value.

Although not all-inclusive, these lists offer a representative matrix of the types of economic concerns in each play, sometimes forming a surprising linguistic configuration. The list for *Cymbeline,* for instance, shows it to be a play greatly concerned with the economics of love and the metaphorical ethic of life as a pecuniary contract. The history plays and tragedies are especially surprising in their number of economic words. Indeed, one could argue that the Henry IV plays and *Lear,* especially, thematically depend upon understanding the changing economic ethic and the link between money and love in the new environment. These foci are illuminated by the econolinguistic matrix.

A&C: Alms, Angle, Boot, Business, Cast, Clip, Doit, Factor, Jump, Make, Plate, Prize, Purchase, Purse, Reckon, Revenue, Riot, Salute, Trade, Use, Waste.

Ado: Account, Agent, Alms, Angel, Angle, Band, Bill, Black and white, Broke, Bullet, Chain, Change, Cheapen, Commodity, Commonwealth, Counterfeit, Ducat, Earnest, Endow, Fit, In question, Lay, Means, Noble, Penny, Pennyworth, Price, Prize, Rack, Render, Scruple, Stamp, Tender, Use, Usurer, Value, Warrant.

Ass: Angel, Current, Denier, Piece, Privy seal note.

AYLI: Bankrout, Bear, Benefit, Booty, Cipher, Compter, Contract, Cope, Credit, Cross, Cut, Dower, Enrich, Entertainment, Estate, Extent, Get, Hire, Jointure, Living, Market, Means, Meed, Mend, Pay, Pence, Ply, Portion, Possess, Practice, Profit, Purchase, Purse, Quittance, Reckoning, Revenue, Satisfaction, Sell, Testament, Touch, Touchstone, Undo, Untreasured, Will, Younger.

BBofA: Cattels, Kentall, Rifle, Tender.

Index of Illustrations

Reviews

"Students and teachers, old-fashioned explicators and new-fashioned historians—all will find here a valuable reference work . . . interesting for its own sake." Jane Donawerth in *Shakespeare Quarterly*

"Invaluable . . . her volume remains an exceptionally valuable collection of material." B. J. Cook, Curator of Early Modern Coins, British Museum

A "foundational study." Katherine Gillen, author of *Chaste Value*

A "most important study on Shakespeare economics." Henry W. Farnam, author of *Shakespeare e economia*

"An indispensable tool . . .an extraordinary range of meaning and connotation . . . ushering in a deluge of economically-oriented studies." David Hawkes, author of *Shakespeare and Economic Theory*

"Extraordinarily helpful. I keep it on my desk, always at hand." Paul A. Jorgensen, author of *Lear's Self-Discovery* and *Our Naked Frailties*

"*Shakespeare's Money Talks* is the kind of reference work I longed for many years ago when I was first captivated by Shakespeare's metaphors. More than just a fascinating glossary, this study shows why proper understanding of Renaissance art and culture requires that we follow the money: not via marketplace exchanges, but rather thought and speech that either governs or is governed by them." Lana Cable, author of *Carnal Rhetoric*

www.ingramcontent.com/pod-product-compliance
Lightning Source LLC
LaVergne TN
LVHW050509100826
845148LV00002B/281

* 9 7 8 1 7 3 7 3 9 5 8 0 5 *